'The concept of moral injury draws at  n
not only wound body and mind but a -
ence, solidarity, and belief in a just wo: ;
in this collection explore moral injury ...osoph-
ical, social, spiritual and religious pe ...urging our view of the
impact of violence far beyond the common trope of trauma. Anyone concerned
to address the human costs of violence will find much to deepen and enrich
their understanding and response to some of the most challenging existential
predicaments we face.'

Professor Laurence J. Kirmayer, MD, FRCPC, FCAHS, FRSC, James
McGill Professor & Director, Division of Social and Transcultural
Psychiatry, McGill University, Canada

'This stimulating compilation of different but complementary perspectives on a
persistent aspect of the human condition sheds light on the full extent of
damage and suffering experienced, individually and collectively, and reveals
deeper understandings of harm and possible repair. The insights and applica-
tions are of interest in fields well beyond those of the contributors.'

Professor John Packer, Neuberger-Jesin Professor of International
Conflict Resolution; Director, Human Rights Research and
Education Centre, University of Ottawa, USA

'This volume testifies eloquently to the urgent need for scholars and practitioners across disciplines to join forces and use all the resources at their disposal—from the medical to the theological—in a common quest to address the
deeply complex and mounting reality of moral injury in the contemporary
world. A timely collection on a pressing topic.'

Dr Alexis Torrance, Department of Theology, University of
Notre Dame, USA

Moral Injury and Beyond

Moral Injury and Beyond: Understanding Human Anguish and Healing Traumatic Wounds uniquely brings together a prominent collection of international contributors from the fields of psychiatry, psychology, philosophy, theology, military chaplaincy and acute crisis care to address the phenomenon of moral injury. Introduced in the 1990s to refer to a type of psychological trauma, experienced especially by soldiers who felt that their actions transgressed the expected moral norms, this innovative volume provides a timely update that progresses and redefines the field of moral injury.

The ten ground-breaking essays expand our understanding of moral injury beyond its original military context, arguing that it can fruitfully be applied to and address predicaments most persons face in their daily lives. Approaching moral injury from different perspectives, the contributors focus on the experiences of combat veterans and other survivors of violent forms of adversity. The chapters address thought-provoking questions and topics, such as how survivors can regain their hope and faith, and how they can, in time, explore ways that will lead them to grow through their suffering. Exploring moral injury with a particular emphasis on spirituality, the Early Church Fathers form the framework within which several chapters examine moral injury, articulating a new perspective on this important subject. The insights advanced are not limited to theoretical innovations but also include practical methods of dealing with the effects of moral injury.

This pioneering collection will be an essential resource for mental health practitioners and trainees working with people suffering from severe trauma. Due to its interdisciplinary nature, it will be useful not only to those academics and professionals engaged with moral injury but will also be a source of inspiration for any perceptive student of the complexities and dilemmas of modern life, especially as it interfaces with issues of mental health and spirituality. It will also be invaluable to academics and students of Jungian psychology, theology, philosophy and history interested in war, migration and the impact of extreme forms of adversity.

Renos K. Papadopoulos, is Professor in the Department of Psychosocial and Psychoanalytic Studies, Director of the Centre for Trauma, Asylum and Refugees at the University of Essex, UK, and Professor at the Antiochian House of Studies, USA. He is a practising clinical psychologist, family psychotherapist and Jungian psychoanalyst as well as a trainer and supervisor.

Moral Injury and Beyond

Understanding Human Anguish and
Healing Traumatic Wounds

Edited by Renos K. Papadopoulos

Routledge
Taylor & Francis Group

LONDON AND NEW YORK

First published 2020
by Routledge
2 Park Square, Milton Park, Abingdon, Oxon OX14 4RN

and by Routledge
52 Vanderbilt Avenue, New York, NY 10017

Routledge is an imprint of the Taylor & Francis Group, an informa business

British Library Cataloguing-in-Publication Data
A catalogue record for this book is available from the British Library

Library of Congress Cataloging-in-Publication Data
A catalog record has been requested for this book

ISBN: 978-1-138-71454-0 (hbk)
ISBN: 978-1-138-71456-4 (pbk)
ISBN: 978-1-315-23057-3 (ebk)

Typeset in Times New Roman
by Swales & Willis, Exeter, Devon, UK

Contents

Preface

This book is based on papers presented at an international symposium on "Forgiveness and Healing in the Face of Moral Injury" that I organised in May 2015 at the University of Essex, UK. The event was sponsored by the John Templeton Foundation in collaboration with the same university, bringing together a diverse group of interdisciplinary academics and practitioners from philosophy, theology, psychiatry, psychology and history, to discuss and link together ideas and findings around the central theme of moral injury.

Accordingly, this book is the product of a most productive collaborative effort. I am very grateful to all the chapter authors for their generosity and exemplary patience in assisting with my editorial comments, as well as to all those individuals and organisations who kindly provided them with the required permissions to include copyrighted material in this publication.

This present volume would not have been possible without Mary Ann Meyers, the John Templeton Foundation's Senior Fellow and the director of the "Humble Approach Initiative", the foundation programme under whose aegis the symposium became a reality. She was an enthusiastic supporter of my initial proposal for that event and, in her characteristic humility, tact and efficiency, she attended to every single detail of its organisation and then, subsequently, of the publication of this book. I am deeply indebted to her for her guidance throughout this project, for her enormous experience, wisdom and magnanimity. Special acknowledgement is due to the late John M. Templeton Jr, MD, a paediatric surgeon, who was the president of the Foundation at the time and who embraced and encouraged both the symposium and the publication of this book. For many years he was intensely involved in the care of children with traumatic injuries at the Children's Hospital of Philadelphia.

I thank my University Department for all their support, especially Debbie Stewart for her assistance with organising the international symposium.

I am also grateful to Susannah Frearson and Heather Evans, the editorial staff at Routledge, for their substantial support, patience and sound advice, as well as to Rosie Stewart and the production team at Swales & Willis for their efficient and competent assistance.

My family, my wife, my children and grandchildren have always been a source of strength for me and I thank them most sincerely for bearing with me during my absences whilst working on this book. Finally, these acknowledgements cannot be complete without expressing my deep gratitude to my special friends in Essex for all their support.

Renos K. Papadopoulos
University of Essex

About the contributors

Renos K. Papadopoulos, PhD, is Professor in the Department of Psychosocial and Psychoanalytic Studies and Director of the Centre for Trauma, Asylum and Refugees, as well as a member of the Human Rights Centre, the Transitional Justice Network and the Armed Conflict and Crisis Hub, all at the University of Essex; also, he is Honorary Clinical Psychologist and Systemic Family Psychotherapist at the Tavistock Clinic. He is a practising Clinical Psychologist, Family Therapist and Jungian Psychoanalyst who has spent most of his professional life training and supervising these three types of specialists. In addition, he is Professor at the Antiochian House of Studies in the USA. As a consultant to the United Nations and other organisations, he has been working with refugees, tortured persons and other survivors of political violence and disasters in many countries. He lectures and offers specialist training internationally and his writings have appeared in 15 languages. Recently, he has received an award from the European Family Therapy Association for his lifetime "outstanding contribution to the field of family therapy and systemic practice", won the University of Essex's Best International Research Impact award, and also has been awarded by two Mexican Foundations for his "exceptional work with vulnerable children and families in Mexico".

D. William Alexander, PhD, is a Visiting Fellow at the Centre for Trauma, Asylum & Refugees at the University of Essex in the United Kingdom. Educated at Fordham University, St Vladimir's Orthodox Theological Seminary, Pittsburgh Theological Seminary (DMin), and the University of Essex (PhD), he specialises at the intersection of spirituality and psychosocial care for survivors of natural disasters and political violence. Having participated himself in combat operations in Afghanistan as a younger man, he has been working therapeutically with combat veterans and their families since 2010.

Fr John Behr is the Fr Georges Florovsky Distinguished Professor of Patristics at St Vladimir's Seminary, where he served as Dean from 2007–17, and the Metropolitan Kallistos Chair of Orthodox Theology at the Vrije Universiteit of Amsterdam. He has published numerous monographs with Oxford

University Press and SVS Press, including an edition and translation of the fragments of Diodore of Tarsus and Theodore of Mopsuestia, setting them in their historical and theological context (OUP, 2011), a full study of St Irenaeus: *St Irenaeus of Lyons: Identifying Christianity* (OUP, 2013), and most recently a new critical edition and translation of Origen's *On First Principles*, together with an extensive introduction, for OUP (2017), and a study of the Gospel of John (OUP, 2019); he has also published various works aimed for a more general audience, such as his more poetic and meditative work entitled *Becoming Human: Theological Anthropology in Word and Image* (SVS Press, 2013). He is currently working on a new edition and translation of *On the Making of the Human Being* by Gregory of Nyssa and a new edition and translation of the works of Irenaeus.

Rita Nakashima Brock is Senior Vice President and Director of the Shay Moral Injury Center at Volunteers of America. An award-winning author, she is co-author of *Soul Repair: Recovering from Moral Injury After War* (2012), *Saving Paradise: How Christianity Traded Love of This World for Crucifixion and Empire* (2008), and *Proverbs of Ashes: Violence, Redemptive Suffering and the Search for What Saves Us* (2001) and author of *Journeys By Heart: A Christology of Erotic Power* (1988). Dr Brock was a professor of religion and women's studies for 18 years before becoming, in 1997, Director of the Bunting Institute at Radcliffe College, a programme for distinguished women scientists, social scientists, scholars, writers, artists and humanitarians. A member of the strategic planning team that negotiated the 1999 merger of Radcliffe with Harvard, she then became Director of the Fellowship Program at the Radcliffe Institute for Advanced Study at Harvard University. From 2001–2002, she was a fellow at the Harvard Divinity School Center for Values in Public Life, and from 2002–2012, she was a visiting scholar at the Starr King School for the Ministry at the Graduate Theological Union in Berkeley, CA. In 2012, she co-founded the Soul Repair Center at Brite Divinity School and directed it until 2017.

Harold G. Koenig, MD, Dr Koenig completed his undergraduate education at Stanford University, his medical school training at the University of California at San Francisco, and his geriatric medicine, psychiatry and biostatistics training at Duke University. He is board certified in general psychiatry, and formerly boarded in family medicine, geriatric medicine and geriatric psychiatry. He is on the faculty at Duke University Medical Center as Professor of Psychiatry and Associate Professor of Medicine, is an Adjunct Professor in the Department of Medicine at King Abdulaziz University, Jeddah, Saudi Arabia, and in the School of Public Health at Ningxia Medical University, Yinchuan, China. Dr Koenig has over 500 scientific peer-reviewed academic publications, nearly 100 book chapters, and more than 50 books. His research has been featured on many national and international TV programmes (including ABC's *World News Tonight, The Today Show, Good*

Morning America, Dr. Oz Show, NBC Nightly News) and hundreds of national and international radio programmes and newspapers/magazines (including *Reader's Digest, Parade Magazine, Newsweek, Time*). Dr Koenig has given testimony before the U.S. Senate (1998) and U.S. House of Representatives (2008) concerning the benefits of religious involvement on public health. He is the recipient of the 2012 Oskar Pfister Award from the American Psychiatric Association.

Romano Màdera is Professor of Moral Philosophy and Philosophical Practices at the University of Milano-Bicocca. He studied philosophy at the University of Milan and sociology at the Milan's School of Sociology. Before his present appointment, he taught at the University of Calabria and at Ca' Foscari University of Venice. He is a practising Jungian analyst. He founded the Open Seminars in Philosophical Practices, which has programmes in several Italian cities, as well as Philo: The Advanced School for Philosophical Practices in Milan and SABOF (*la società degli analisti filosofi*), an association that promotes the use of biographical analysis as a philosophically nuanced method to search for meaning in life experiences that transcend the ego. His books include *Identità e feticismo* (1977); *Dio il Mondo* (1989); *L'alchimia ribelle* (1997); *Carl Gustav Jung: biografia e teoria* (1998); *L'animale visionario* (1999); (with L.V. Tarca) *La filosofia come stile di vita* (2003), which was translated into English as *Philosophy as Life Path. An Introduction to Philosophical Practices* (2007); *Il nudo piacere di vivere* (2006); *La carta del senso* (2012); and, most recently, *Una filosofia per l'anima*, (2013) Its English translation: *Approaching the Navel of the Darkened Soul: Depth Psychology and Philosophical Practices.*

Robert Emmet Meagher is Professor of Humanities, Hampshire College, Amherst, Massachusetts. With degrees from the University of Notre Dame and the University of Chicago, he joined the Hampshire College faculty in 1972. Prior to that, he taught religious studies at Indiana University and the University of Notre Dame. He has also held visiting chairs and professorships at numerous colleges and universities, including Trinity College Dublin and Yale University.

He has offered workshops on the translation and contemporary production of ancient drama here and abroad, and has himself directed productions at such venues as the Samuel Beckett Centre, Dublin and the Nandan Centre for the Performing Arts in Kolkota, India. Across many years he has served in a range of veteran-focused programmes aimed at understanding and healing war's inner wounds and since 2010 has directed a Veterans Administration literature seminar.

His publications include over a dozen books, as well as original plays and numerous translations of ancient Greek drama, most recently: *Herakles Gone Mad: Rethinking Heroism in an Age of Endless War; Killing from the*

Inside Out: Moral Injury and Just War; and (co-edited with LTC Douglas A. Pryer, US Army, retired) *War and Moral Injury: A Reader*.

Aristotle Papanikolaou is Professor of Theology, the Archbishop Demetrios Chair of Orthodox Theology and Culture, and the Co-Director of the Orthodox Christian Studies Center at Fordham University. He is also Senior Fellow at the Emory University Center for the Study of Law and Religion. In 2012, he received the Award for Excellence in Undergraduate Teaching in the Humanities. Among his numerous publications, he is the author of *Being with God: Trinity, Apophaticism, and Divine-Human Communion*, and *The Mystical as Political: Democracy and Non-Radical Orthodoxy*. He is also co-editor of *Political Theologies in Orthodox Christianity, Fundamentalism or Tradition: Christianity after Secularism, Christianity, Democracy and the Shadow of Constantine, Orthodox Constructions of the West, Orthodox Readings of Augustine*, and *Thinking Through Faith: New Perspectives from Orthodox Christian Scholars*.

Nancy Sherman is University Professor and Professor of Philosophy at Georgetown University. A *New York Times* Notable Author, her books include *Afterwar: The Untold War (a NYT editors' pick)*, *Stoic Warriors, Making a Necessity of Virtue*, and *The Fabric of Character*. In the mid-1990s, she served as inaugural Distinguished Chair in Ethics at the U.S. Naval Academy.

Sherman has received fellowships from the Guggenheim Foundation, the Woodrow Wilson Center, the National Endowment for the Humanities, the American Council for Learned Societies, the Mellon Foundation, the American Philosophical Society, the Woodrow Wilson Foundation, and NYU's Center for Ballet and the Arts. In 2005, she visited Guantanamo Bay Detention Center as part of an independent observer team assessing the medical and mental health care of detainees. She is a frequent contributor to the media in the U.S. and abroad. Her work has been featured in the *NY Times, Washington Post, LA Times, The Wall Street Journal, The Independent, Time* and *Newsweek*. She has appeared on many radio/TV programmes, including NPR and BBC.

Sherman holds a BA from Bryn Mawr College, a PhD from Harvard, and an MLitt from the University of Edinburgh. She has research training from the Washington Center for Psychoanalysis. She taught at Yale before teaching at Georgetown.

Rev. Vasileios Thermos, MD, PhD, is a graduate of Medicine (1981) and Theology (1986) at Athens University, where he earned his PhD in 1997. He practices Child and Adolescent Psychiatry in Athens. In 1986 he was ordained and since then he has been engaged in training programmes for clergy in Greece and the USA.

He has been a Visiting Scholar at Harvard Divinity School (1996–97) and a Visiting Research Scholar at the Institute of Medical Humanities of Texas University (2014). Some of his books and articles have been translated into

English, French, Russian, Romanian, Bulgarian, Serbian, Spanish, Italian, German and Finnish. He is the editor of a journal in Greek (*Psyches dromoi*: Ways of the Soul).

A masters thesis on his scholarly work was written by Peter Kazaku at the Theological School of Balamand University, Lebanon, in 2004, and was published in 2013 by Peter Lang publications. Since 2013 he teaches Pastoral Theology and Pastoral Psychology in the University Ecclesiastical Academy of Athens, where he is now an Associate Professor.

In 2017–18 his essay *The Paradox of Mental Health Care and Spirituality: The Culture of Extreme Individualism as a Mediator* was awarded a prize by the Jean-Marc Fischer Foundation in Switzerland.

Introduction

Renos K. Papadopoulos

Human pain and suffering, in their multiple variations, have never been the exclusive domain of one particular discipline. As long as human reflections have been documented, throughout history and even prehistory, persons from all walks of life have been expressing their views, in various forms, on the wide variety of painful predicaments people find themselves in, as part of everyday living. Homer, in both the *Iliad* and *Odyssey*, developed astute observations about many nuances of human anguish, especially when one is exposed to severe forms of adversity. Philosophers, theologians, novelists, sociologists, anthropologists, historians, even economists, politicians and many others have been delving into the subtleties of the troubled and wounded human psyche. Yet, in recent times, with the emergence of discrete specialisations, psychology and, in particular, psychiatry seem to have become the predominant disciplines that claim unique expertise in addressing human turmoil.

The effects of these specialisations have been considerable. Accordingly, now, not only do experiences of human distress tend to be formulated as disorders and, in short, human suffering confused with ill health, but the significant contribution of all other approaches also tends to be overlooked. The hegemonic concept of "trauma" has become emblematic of this skewing domination. How much is "trauma" part of an overall existential upheaval and how much is it a mere expression of a disturbed or even diseased mind?

Psychiatry, as a medical speciality with its rational methods of assessment and treatment, has been providing credible ways of dealing with certain facets and manifestations of human distress, especially those states of anguish that result from the consequences of wars, domestic violence, sexual abuse, forms of involuntary dislocation and even exhausting professional caregiving in extreme situations. For several decades, the paradigm of post-traumatic stress disorder (PTSD) has been dominating the professional as well as the wider societal discourses that have been dealing with these phenomena.

Then, gradually, uneasiness began to arise, as the distorting effects of the excessive dominance of psychiatry became increasingly apparent. People were becoming aware that the complexities and subtleties of these phenomena could not possibly be grasped from an exclusively psychological or psychiatric perspective. It was in the context of this climate that the concept of "moral injury" was proposed, with the explicit intention of expanding the range of viewpoints used to comprehend, at least, one particular class of these excessive forms of human pain and hurt. The argument was simple and convincing: when one is exposed to violence, especially as a perpetrator, it is not only one's mental health that is affected but also one's sense of morality and ethical sensitivities. Accordingly, it was observed that persons exposed to such devastating events were experiencing not only psychiatric difficulties but also negative consequences within their very moral sphere. Therefore, the early theorists of moral injury not only drew from their psychiatric expertise but were also inspired by the Homeric insights into his *Iliad* heroes' painful war experiences.

Once that expansion began, it made perfect sense to question whether the implications of these distressing experiences are limited to only the psychiatric and ethical ones. Surely, a person's entire being tends to become deformed in some way when he or she is exposed to violent forms of extreme inhuman acts, either as a passive recipient or as an active perpetrator. Under these adverse circumstances, it is not only their psychiatric and moral spheres that are impaired but also their human values, their socio-political sensitivities, their spiritual, aesthetic, creative and other facets of their humanity.

The ten chapters of this book address precisely this expansion by focusing predominantly, but not exclusively, on the dimension of spirituality. Using a unique point of departure, each chapter develops insights that extend our understanding of these experiences of soul-wrenching upheavals.

Although the concepts "moral injury" and "wounds of conscience" were initially applied to the experiences of combat veterans, there is plenty of evidence that they are also of relevance to the experiences of other people who have been exposed to a wide variety of forms of adversity. Perpetrating, witnessing or suffering severe forms of violence can shatter one's core beliefs about human nature, society and even God. To put it simply, these experiences make people lose God or find God. This means that the phenomena that this book addresses, as well as the conceptual and professional tools used to comprehend and heal them, are of daily relevance to almost every human being. Therefore, this book is written not only for health professionals and for those interested in spiritual wellbeing but also for a much wider readership, as it addresses the subtleties of fundamental phenomena that every person faces today, with varying degrees of intensity and clarity. More specifically, the book is also of direct interest to other academic disciplines in the humanities and social sciences as well as to professionals and workers in many settings dealing with human anguish.

Our world today is gripped by at least three main groups of catastrophic events: the seemingly unending forms of violence, atrocities and terrorism that are associated with conflict, political instability and war; the incessant adversities (of various types) that create streams of involuntarily dislocated persons seeking safe havens away from their homes; as well as the frightening and multifaceted impact of climate change. Despite their obvious differences, all these phenomena can also be understood as forms of *hubris*, i.e. outcomes of various expressions of human arrogance that, ultimately, have self-damaging effects. The original meaning of *hubris* is a blasphemy against the divine order. Any hubristic action represents not only a violation against the human and wider ecological stability, but it also damages the moral fabric of individuals and groups, impacting on their values and ethical code. Following this understanding, it would not be without justification to claim that all three groups of current catastrophic occurrences produce forms of moral injury. This means that the subject matter of this book is of vital importance in enabling us to grapple with the complexities of many manifestations of human anguish that we all face today.

The chapters in this book do not follow any particular logical sequence. Each one of them represents a unique contribution, rooted in its own intellectual tradition. Although some chapters can be clustered into sub-groupings, each chapter can be read and appreciated in its own right. Nevertheless, all of them, as a collection, articulate a fairly comprehensive and coherent new perspective on moral injury.

The opening chapter sets the epistemological foundations of the book by developing innovative observations about the complexities of the processes that lead to the pathologising and medicalising of human suffering. Proposing that there is an implicit hierarchy of the type of pain that human beings prefer and are also capable of tolerating, it identifies an oscillation between focusing either on morality or on injury when engaging with phenomena of human anguish. The chapter concludes that inappropriate epistemologies lead to erroneous ways of conceptualising these phenomena, excluding positive and renewing effects that can also emerge from being exposed to adversities.

The following two chapters focus on war-related moral injury. Chapter 2 addresses its subject matter from a philosophical perspective whereas Chapter 3 takes a clinical/therapeutic approach. Drawing on another source of classical antiquity, Sherman returns to the war experiences of the Trojan War heroes, this time Sophocles's *Ajax*, in order to develop perceptive observations about guilt and shame in relation to moral responsibility, and then relates them to the remedial function of self-empathy. The emphasis of Brock's chapter is on the therapeutic use of rituals in addressing the ill effects of moral injury in warriors. She discusses the advantages of such rituals over traditional therapeutic approaches, emphasising their function in enabling purification and emotional transition.

Koenig's chapter follows an empirical research methodology to investigate systematically the role religion plays in the mental health of those who survive traumatic experiences from various calamitous adversities, e.g. war, terrorism, rape, natural disasters, etc. Then, based on his reviewed findings that religious involvement and spiritual beliefs do indeed have a positive effect on these survivors, the author proposes the construction of a special manualised treatment for such survivors that also addresses moral injury. Continuing the tradition of using the predicaments of the Homeric heroes of the Trojan War as the point of departure, Father John Behr examines the puzzle of Odysseus's choice to opt for the life of a mortal, with all its painful vulnerabilities, instead of accepting the alluring offer to live the immortal life of a god. Using the writings of Irenaeus of Lyons, one of the earliest Church Fathers, Behr develops a Christian perspective to understand the complexities of suffering and death.

The chapters in this book are not abstract academic treatises. They provide an active and committed engagement with their subject matter and some of them have an obvious polemical edge to them. Robert Emmet Meagher strenuously contests the idea of a "just war" in his historical and ethical analysis of this doctrine. Investigating beliefs about war across time, geographical regions and theoretical perspectives, from ancient Greece and Rome to modern American involvement in armed conflicts, from early Church times to modern Catholic positions, he examines the soul damage engendered in moral injury. Aristotle Papanikolaou creatively connects modern psychiatry and psychotherapy with the writings of another Church Father, Maximus the Confessor, a couple of centuries after Irenaeus, in order to discern the virtue dimension of moral injury.

The last three chapters address moral injury from the viewpoint of specific therapeutic practices. Romano Madera's theoretical orientation is located within the archetypal theories of Carl Gustav Jung, and his chapter revolves around the *leitmotiv* of Dante's concept of the counterpoise. Using examples from his own psychoanalytic practice, he explores moral injury in the context of the relationship between psychology and spirituality. Father Vasileios Thermos discusses moral injury within the interface between Orthodox Christian theology and psychoanalysis, accentuating the dynamics of forgiveness and communion, as well as advocating for the importance of the psychological dimension in pastoral care. Finally, Alexander, drawing on his own clinical experience of caring for traumatised veterans, identifies the advantages of working in multidisciplinary teams (that include not only psychiatrists but also specialists from other perspectives and traditions, e.g. theologians and classicists) in the treatment of what he terms "morally related veteran distress".

I trust this anthology will not only provide innovative and rewarding insights into moral injury but will also stimulate further explorations into this important and topical theme that, unfortunately, is likely to become of increasing concern in the not too distant future.

Chapter I

The traumatising discourse of trauma and moral injury

Distress and renewal

Renos K. Papadopoulos

Trauma and moral injury

This book and this chapter address the complexities of moral injury. "Trauma" is the Greek word for injury and these two terms/words are closely interlinked. It was in the course of exploring the complexities of trauma that the concept of moral injury emerged (Litz, Stein, Delaney, Lebowitz, Nash, Silva & Maguen, 2009; Shay, 2002, 2014; Shay & Munroe, 1999). Therefore, it is important to first examine the relationship between trauma and moral injury in order to delineate the appropriate context of the subject matter of our book, in general, and of this chapter in particular.

As it is known, the primary meaning of trauma has been confined to physical injury. Trauma, in Greek, means wound or injury; more precisely, it refers to the mark that is left when one's skin is pierced. Hence, traumatology predominantly refers to the medical speciality that deals with patients brought to accident and emergency (A&E) hospital departments. The metaphorical meaning of trauma in relation to psychological rather than somatic wounds is as old as the word itself. Even Homer used to use trauma to refer to non-bodily injuries. The New Testament also uses trauma metaphorically.

However, as my etymological research has revealed (Papadopoulos, 2002, 2007; in press b), in Greek, the root of the verb "to pierce" (*titrosko*) is the verb "to rub" (*teiro*), which has two meanings: to rub in and to rub off or rub away. Rubbing in, in effect, results again in piercing, in creating a wound and, therefore, it has an identical effect to that of piercing. Contrastingly, rubbing off or rubbing away has a completely different effect, that of erasing and cleansing, of burnishing and buffing, etc.; that is, resulting in forms of renewal. This meaning is not an abstract etymological observation, it is also corroborated by the actual reality: in addition to (and not instead of) causing injurious and traumatising effects, the powerful experiences that enter one's life in a disruptive way also erase, to varying degrees, many established and accepted ways of being, and previously unquestioned assumptions about life and its priorities, thus creating the possibility of developing refreshed positions and revitalised identities.

Needless to say, the pain of the rubbing-in effect of trauma invariably outweighs all other possible effects to such an extent that the renewing possibilities are often neglected or even ignored completely. Yet, in actual reality, everybody who is exposed to devastating events and circumstances does experience both effects. Everyone who has worked with severely traumatised individuals will have heard such persons saying (directly or indirectly), and in addition to complaining about their pain and suffering (from the wounding effects of trauma), that the entirety of their experience of adversity (their realisation of their limitations, the facing of the unexpected, etc.) made them rethink and reconsider many important aspects of their lives. In struggling to make sense of the overwhelming impact the calamitous and shattering events had on them, they were forced to reconsider many fundamental issues of life in general.

When struck by such truly "awe-some" and "awe-ful" adverse experiences, ordinary people become philosophers, but not of the armchair type. Deeply perturbed and troubled by the unpredictable and catastrophic turn of events, and facing the life-shattering consequences of the experienced adversities, they are shaken to the core of their being, and in deep anguish they struggle to make sense of what has befallen them and to reassess most aspects of their lives. Expressions such as "my life and whole world have turned upside down" express the devastating impact such adversities have on people. Often, without any effective forewarning and regardless of their own personal background (educational, ethnic, cultural, gender, age, race, etc.), they are confronted by painful and unfamiliar questions: e.g. "what is the use of struggling so hard to build up what I thought would be a future for myself and my family, only to then lose everything?"; "how is it possible for people to treat fellow human beings so inhumanly?"; "what should my new priorities for everyday living be now?"; "why do society, the powers that be, or the divine powers permit such appalling destructiveness or injustices?"; "why me?", "why has this happened to me?", etc. All these questions about life, meaning, morality, destiny, the divine, etc. are essentially of a philosophical, theological, existential or ethical nature, and they emerge spontaneously in persons who are exposed to severe forms of adversity which lead to traumatising experiences. These questions affect the totality of one's being and, thus, they may also be called ontological.

It is important to identify, more explicitly, the reasons that lead affected persons not only to refrain from sharing such "philosophical" questions with others, but also not to discern them more clearly in their own minds, despite the fact that such agonising questions (regardless of how ill articulated they may be) do arise in every person who is overwhelmed by such soul-wrenching experiences of severe forms of adversities. I differentiate the five interrelated reasons that follow.

(a) Perceived priority: to eliminate the "trauma pain"

Such experiences are so agonising, that the main focus tends to be restricted to a need that is consider central and of absolute priority: to get rid of the suffering that is inflicted by the exposure to adversity. This need forces itself to the forefront, as the unquestionable priority, and above all other considerations. As I emphasise, rhetorically, in the training programmes I offer, "The trauma story screeches!" The "trauma story" cannot be ignored, and the "trauma pain" demands urgent attention and immediate relief. This priority is experienced not only by the affected persons themselves but also by those who come into contact with them, in whatever capacity, as friends or helpers. Indeed, it is very difficult to concentrate on any other aspects of the totality and complexity of the experiences when this pain is so excruciating; consequently, the pressing need is to find any means to soothe and neutralise this pain. Therefore, it is understandable that any other preoccupations with big, difficult and unanswerable questions, such as the meaning of life, tend to be sidetracked, pushed away and silenced. However, they cannot be eliminated totally, and are always lurking somewhere in the background in every traumatised person.

(b) Hierarchy of tolerable and preferred forms of pain

Neither the caregivers nor the affected persons themselves are used to addressing issues about the meaning of life, morality, the nature of destructiveness, divine (non-)intervention, etc. It is not easy to delve into such fundamental questions because they can be very distressing. The distress they cause can even be more painful than the actual "trauma pain" itself, because these questions are unfamiliar, they are not so easily comprehensible and they address central belief systems, which are invariably taken for granted and are, by and large, invisible.

The general implicit approach society follows in comprehending trauma follows a reasonably clear linear causality that appears to be fairly logical and intelligible. It is widely accepted that severe adversity causes some form of trauma, mostly understood in mental health terms. According to this formulation, adversity is the cause and trauma the effect. Regardless of the degree of severity of the trauma itself, the very conceptualisation of this type of pain appears to be clearly understandable and, hence, bearable.

By contrast, what we could call "existential/ontological pain" – i.e. the pain emanating from the big unanswerable questions – is significantly less bearable because of its very nature, as well as due to the realistic difficulties in grasping it, its nature and effects. The paradox is that, on the one hand, the distressing effects from this type of pain are unmistakably felt, but, on the other hand, their causes and overall comprehension of the entire experience are intangible and more elusive than the causes and comprehension of the "trauma pain", which appears to be understood in terms of a fairly clear-cut cause–effect equation. The whole process of discerning, identifying and addressing existential or philosophical questions is confusing and disorienting; most certainly, it is not part of most persons' repertoire of everyday living.

As it is well known and amply documented, even the "trauma pain" is more difficult to be grasped and addressed than physical pain, precisely because of the same three broad reasons: (i) its causes and overall conceptual formulation are more elusive and bewildering than somatic pain; consequently, (ii) "trauma pain" is less bearable than somatic pain, i.e. it is more troublesome and problematic than the seemingly obvious causes and overall formative process of somatic pain; and (iii) the tangible reality of bodily pain makes it far more familiar than "trauma pain" – the former is an unavoidable part of our repertoire of everyday living, whereas the latter is not.

It is for these reasons that the phenomenon of "somatisation" is so widespread. In short, somatisation refers to the misattribution of psychological stress and trauma to physical symptoms and bodily complaints. Evidently, people find it easier to focus upon, and to complain about bodily pains than to connect with the various forms of the distressfully subtle, indefinable and incomprehensible forms of psychological pain (e.g. De Gucht & Fischler, 2002; De Gucht & Maes, 2006; Gureje, Simon, Ustun & Goldberg, 1997; Kellner, 1990; Kirmayer & Robbins, 1991; Ryder, Yang & Heine, 2002).

Accordingly, it is now possible to identify a hierarchy of tolerable types of pain, with physical pain being the most easily graspable and, therefore, in a sense, the most preferred (so to speak), and "existential pain" being the least comprehensible and, hence, the least tolerable and least preferred pain. In relation to these two, "trauma pain" (psychological pain) lies in between them, i.e. it appears to be more accessible and tolerable than "existential pain", but is more disturbing and less graspable than physical/bodily pain.

Consequently, it is instructive to identify two types of distorting transformations: somatisation of psychological (trauma) pain and psychologisation of existential pain. Whereas somatisation is a well-known and much-researched phenomenon, psychologisation is not.

My argument here is that this hierarchy of tolerable and preferred pain is crucial in not only appreciating the complexities of psychological trauma but also in providing a conceptual framework to comprehend moral injury, as will be discussed below. To sum up, the key criterion of this hierarchy is the combination of the comprehensibility and accessibility of the nature of the distress involved, along with the degree of tolerance for the experienced anguish.

(c) Difficulties in selecting appropriate conceptual frameworks

Related to the above, it should not be forgotten that beyond the individual's own abilities and resources to address big, philosophical questions that are associated with "existential pain", it is very difficult to objectively conceptualise such distressing issues. To begin with, even calling them "questions" is problematic and not entirely accurate. These are not clearly formulated and neatly phrased questions. People do not ask themselves or others "what is the meaning of life?" or "how do I reconcile my previous value system with what has happened to me now?" or "in what ways has this devastating experience impacted on my being?". Instead, they experience some incomprehensible and inarticulate puzzling states of bewilderment, anguish and disorientation.

Regardless of the affected person's individual strength, educational status, psychological sophistication and courage, or the amount and quality of support they may receive from caring others, in such circumstances, the usual means of comprehending life difficulties prove to be inadequate in grasping the complexities of these predicaments, which are experienced as extraordinary. One needs to have the appropriate conceptual tools and frameworks to comprehend such states and, objectively, these are not readily available to the majority of people. I am using the adverb "objectively" here in order to emphasise that these conceptual difficulties are over and above any personal factors, the individual's own history, psychological make-up, etc.; these difficulties are inherent in the very nature of the phenomena themselves.

Lacking the appropriate means to grasp and deal with the complexities of "existential pain", what is instead widely and readily available all around us is a plethora of ready-made sets of philosophical, spiritual and other moral and metaphysical systems which eagerly offer to supply us with definitive answers to all of our life questions and predicaments. These set systems, which come in all shapes and sizes, vary from being serious and well-established frameworks with long-standing and illustrious traditions to ephemeral, makeshift, superficial and opportunistic structures. All these aim at providing formulations that define "the problem" as well as the means of delivering "solutions" towards resolving it. However, for the average modern person, these set systems as well as the definitions, explanations and answers that they provide, appear to be either too abstract or too distant and inapplicable to the immediate realities of the experienced distresses.

This does not mean that every single one of these schemata is completely worthless. Clearly, they exist because they succeed, to a degree, in serving some purpose for some people at some time in their lives. The difficulty is that for the non-discerning person, all of them appear the same and they are either dismissed as irrelevant or adopted without the required scrutiny. However, their existence indicates that people do have a need for connecting with some deeper sense of existential meaning, beyond the evanescent concerns of everydayness.

Regardless of their success or not in being relevant and applicable for individuals or groups, what matters most is that these set systems of meaning do not form part of any practical scheme of organised care for those who suffer from such traumatising disruptions of their ordinary everyday living. As we know, trauma care is often defined exclusively in mental health terms, and such frameworks disregard wider and deeper existential considerations.

(d) Societal structures of systemic organisation of help

Continuing on from the previous reason, it is important to note that the system that is operative in our society to address the plight of traumatised persons is through organised forms of caregiving that are formulated, predominantly, in psychological and even psychiatric terms. This organised system of help is based on a fairly simplistic formula, i.e. what I call "the societal discourse of the expert". In short, this formula dictates the nature and modes of interactions between the specialists/experts and those who require their services. In order to effectively deal with tasks that we consider beyond our capabilities, we appeal to the specialist's expert knowledge, abilities and skills to resolve them. This means that the identification of a specific and clearly delineated "problem" is directly and reciprocally linked with the existence of an identified expert that deals with it. The manner in which we formulate our "problem" dictates the type of specialist we access, and the existence of a particular expert dictates the way we define our "problem". This means that there is a mutual and interactional definition between the two, one defining the other.

Critical questions then arise in relation to the way we experience and conceptualise distress in the context of traumatising experiences: what are the dynamics of the way we formulate our "problem"? How reliably is the articulation of the "problem" expressing our real and actual problematic situation? And, relatedly, how do societal structures and narratives impact on our way of conceptualising the "problem"?

However, once we appreciate that the resulting "problem" from such traumatising experiences includes a dimension of "existential" distress and bewilderment, then what is the appropriate speciality that should deal with it? Obviously, these types of distressing perplexity cannot possibly be grouped under any form of psychiatric pathology. There are no readily available experts and specialist services to help us with existential and ontological questions and predicaments.

Once the formulation of the "problem" is completed, our interactions with the nominated experts are limited to furnishing them only with the relevant information about the nature of our identified "problem", phrased according to the experts' own systems of speciality. Correspondingly, the relevant services are also only geared to providing help with the "problem" that we bring to them, and not in engaging with musings, meditations and deliberations about the meaning of life and other such moral, philosophical or existential considerations.

This discussion suggests that the question should remain open as to whether "mental health" is the most appropriate realm within which our disturbing bewilderment from being exposed to severe forms of adversity, in addition to any "trauma pain" and/or physical pain, can be addressed adequately.

(e) Pathologisation of human suffering

Once traumatising experiences are assigned exclusively to the realm of mental health, devoid of all shades of any existential dimension, then the logical tendency is to make them even more clear and tangible, and to concretise and grasp them in the best possible way. Psychiatry, with its somatic dimension, offers the most concrete paradigm within the mental health spectrum, and it emerges as the most reasonably suited domain within which to locate such confusing phenomena. Having been designated as the specialist for such experiences, hegemonically, psychiatry tends to blot out all perspectives that are not clearly located within its dominion. By assigning such phenomena strictly to the psychiatric speciality, a great deal of perplexity is avoided. Psychiatric problems, unlike the wide range and vagueness of "mental health problems" or "psychological difficulties", refer to specific forms of dysfunctionality, closely allied to the (perceived) concreteness of medical syndromes.

In effect, such an assignment of these phenomena to the field of psychiatry amounts to pathologisation of human pain, suffering and disorientation. Moreover, this type of concretisation of "existential pain" results in the release of everybody involved in the societal structures of organised help for trauma sufferers from the responsibility of addressing any existential, philosophical, theological, moral, ontological and other similar considerations. Such a formulation boldly claims that trauma is not just a psychological phenomenon but, actually, a form of mental *illness*. It should not be forgotten that post-traumatic stress disorder (PTSD) is, in fact, a psychiatric category and not a psychological one nor a vague and general mental health problem. Accordingly, having reduced "existential pain" to "trauma pain", such a construction now medicalises it, thereby demoting it further to a level which is equivalent to physical pain, i.e. "mental pain". This pathologisation reduces all distressingly bewildering states to forms of tangible and easily comprehensible types of illness, akin to physical illness.

Therefore, in addition to the distorting processes of somatisation and psychologisation identified above, we can now discern a further process of concretisation of the disorienting experiences, following exposure to severe forms of adversity. As has already been discussed above, unable to grasp and deal with the existential/ontological pain, through the distorting process of psychologisation, the agonising traumatising experiences are relegated to being conceptualised as "psychological" pain, rendered as "mental health problems". Now we can discern that through the distorting process of psychiatrisation, these phenomena are further downgraded to nosologies of psychiatric disorders and mental illness. Finally, through the distorting process of medicalisation they are further reduced to illnesses of the body.

Whereas "somatisation" is the term that refers to what individuals do when misattributing their own psychological pain to the somatic realm, medicalisation is the process through which societal discourses misattribute any form of traumatising disorientation to the realm of medicine.

These five reasons contribute to rendering almost invisible any manifestations of existential/ontological pain. These reasons indicate why it is difficult, if not impossible, for persons exposed to severe forms of traumatising experience to identify and express any form of existential pain. What these reasons show is that the difficulty is not based entirely on personal factors, or on the presence of any types of psychological defence mechanisms which distort reality in order to avoid the detrimental effects of psychological pain. Instead, these reasons indicate that the downgrading, neglect and, ultimately, invisibility of existential pain is a product of a highly complex combination of many different factors, including conceptual/epistemological and societal parameters.

What this discussion indicates is that it is imperative to have the appropriate epistemological acumen and agility in order to discern these distorting processes. Such awareness would help us appreciate at least three groups of factors that contribute to the creation of these distortions: (i) the role of organisational structures and systemic interactions of services which provide help, (ii) the societal discourses which form the wider framework within which we formulate our own personal understanding of the impact of severe forms of adversity, and, ultimately, (iii) all the epistemological complexities that contribute to the manner in which we conceptualise various types of distress.

Unsettling "onto-ecological settledness"

Etymologically, adversity refers to an outcome that is contrary to the expected turn of events. *Ad-versus*, in Latin, suggests a wrong turning, a bending towards an opposite direction. Ordinarily, our habitual ways of being and interacting with others follow fairly predictable patterns, expecting life to turn the ways that we are accustomed to. This familiarity allows predictability which engenders a sense of settledness. The cluster of familiarity, predictability and settledness enables us to "read life", to have a sense of reasonable assurance in relation to who we are, what we are doing, what the world around us is about, what our life is about, etc. It is this sense of familiarity that is upset when adversity strikes and life takes an unexpected turn.

This cluster of settledness develops shortcuts to many facets of our everyday living which, in turn, free us to focus on specific and important tasks without wasting time and effort in anticipating what we are already well habituated to doing and expecting. Elsewhere, I referred to this process as maintaining a sense of *"onto-ecological settledness"* (Papadopoulos, 2012a, 2015, 2018a; in press a). In short, this term refers to the working arrangement that each person has, at any given time, which relates the totality of one's being with the totality of one's environment.

"Usually, terms that refer to the wholeness of a human being include only certain parts of this totality, e.g. body and mind, personal and social, conscious and unconscious, emotional and intellectual, external and internal" (Papadopoulos, 2015, p. 40), etc. The term "onto-ecological" is intended to address the entirety and completeness of both the person and his or her environment. The term "environment" here includes everything that surrounds us, i.e. all the human dimensions (people, society, belief systems, narratives, etc.) and all the natural dimensions (animate and inanimate).

It needs to be emphasised that this onto-ecological settledness

> is not an ideal state of an individuated, harmonious, and fulfilled personality. Instead, it is the settled arrangement and pattern, which, consisting of the unique mixture of positive and negative elements, creates a certain fluency of life, familiarity, stability, and predictability—regardless of how satisfactory or unsatisfactory this state may be.
>
> (Papadopoulos, 2015, p. 40)

Everybody's "onto-ecological settledness" is dynamic, which means that it is subject to change and adjustments as we and our environment keep changing over time, and in response to specific events that affect us. Ordinarily, these alterations and fluctuations are imperceptible, as long as they remain within certain margins. Such moderate shifts do not upset our sense of continuity and stability. However, when striking external or internal changes take place, then we become aware of them, and realise (in retrospect) that we did have a relatively settled arrangement, which became unsettled.

When certain events and circumstances take place beyond the reasonable margins of what is broadly expected, especially when they occur in a particularly unsettling way, we pause, are startled and become disoriented. Understandably, we experience such events as adverse, because they were unexpected in a negative sense. Once our "onto-ecological settledness" becomes unsettled, then four different but complementary processes are triggered, more or less simultaneously:

(a) The first focuses on dealing with and limiting whatever damage the adversity may have caused;
(b) The second addresses the immediate effects of disorientation, of the unpredictability, of the disruption of the familiar, and of what is confronted as disturbingly unknown;
(c) The third endeavours to make sense of what has happened; and
(d) The fourth, consequently and on the basis of the previous processes, attempts to work out novel ways of comprehending the newly created reality, and our position in it, so that we can invent novel and appropriate tasks and strategies to move forward.

In other words, when confronted by the unexpected and unknown, we are forced to survive its impact, to make sense of it, and to carve out new pathways.

It is important to remember that these four processes, in fact, constitute the basic steps of every form of learning and development in all contexts, and are at the core of all transformational courses of change and growth. However, if we were to conceptualise the impact of adversity and of these processes in exclusively psychiatric terms then, obviously, all our efforts would be concentrated on repairing the damage inflicted, and no attention would be given to any positive transformational possibilities. Once traumatising experiences are understood solely as forms of mental disorder, then any opportunities and potentials for growth become completely invisible. Such conceptualisations lead to perceiving the entire impact on the individual as a form of pathology which, in fact, is what PTSD refers to. It is important to re-emphasise that, despite common misconceptions, PTSD is not referring to ordinary responses to adversity; PTSD is not an inevitable consequence of adversity and of traumatic experiences. Instead, PTSD is an actual psychiatric disorder, which implies considerable forms of dysfunctionality.

This discussion reveals a central paradox: the emergence of two tendencies towards opposite directions, whenever we face severe forms of adversity that lead to traumatising experiences. On the one hand, such experiences activate a process which includes a fundamental and radical expansion of our horizons, stretching our existing and familiar limits, pushing us into new and unexpected ways of viewing ourselves, our world around us, questioning most facets of our being, including morality; whereas on the other hand, the very same experiences tend to significantly narrow the spectrum of our focus, limiting our perception only to "mental pain". The "screeching" of the "trauma story" shrinks our horizons, restricting us to attending to the "trauma pain", which, in order to be made even more concrete, pliable and remediable, is further reduced to being perceived only as a "mental pain" and even as a somatic ailment.

While the first direction fundamentally promotes expansion and potential enrichment, the second direction is profoundly reductionistic. As the five reasons (discussed above) have revealed, the difficulty is that everything conspires to overlooking the first tendency and privileging the second. Yet, whenever we are confronted by adversity, both of these tendencies are activated simultaneously, pulling us in opposite directions in a felt way. Moreover, this pull is both substantial and unavoidable. The tragedy is that only the second tendency is felt and experienced as real and worth attending to.

Accordingly, my argument is that, primarily, it is this very paradoxical and existential conundrum, this confusing impulse towards contradictory perceptions, this felt wrenching towards two polar opposite positions that creates substantial forms of disorientation, which, inevitably, include loss of clarity in relation to moral issues.

The sense of what is right and wrong is an integral part of our settled sense of who we are and how we relate to ourselves and our world around us. Once the familiar arrangement of our "onto-ecological settledness" becomes unsettled, then a considerable disorientation is stirred up shattering our sense of familiarity, predictability and, inevitably, also upsetting our entire system of values. Yet, the multiple implications of the impact of this disorientation are not visible or even sensed and appreciated; the range of the real effects of this disorientation is underestimated because the usual perspectives within which we grasp these changes are limited to only one cluster of effects, i.e. the psychological-psychiatric symptoms. Moreover, as has been shown, these tend to become reduced further to medical-pathological perspectives. Once the resulting disorientation is limited to psychiatric-medical pathology, then no consideration can possibly be given to any other forms of disorientation, e.g. moral issues, and even less to any possibilities for growth or transformation.

Oscillating between morality and injury

The introduction of moral injury as a discrete syndrome in its own right, in the context of addressing traumatising experiences, was intended to rectify the one-sidedness of the medicalisation and pathologisation of trauma and, specifically, the shortcomings of the PTSD psychiatric diagnosis.

Dr Jonathan Shay, the first person who introduced the term (Shay, 2002), emphasised that moral injury "impair[s] the capacity for trust and elevate[s] despair ... [and it] deteriorate[s] character" (2014, p. 182). These types of "impairment" are not typical psychiatric symptoms, as such, and these descriptions are not formulated within a conventional psychiatric vocabulary. "Trust", "despair" and "deterioration of character" refer to a much wider spectrum of effects and phenomena and, by and large, are not typical terms of psychiatric symptomatology. Moreover, the very term "moral injury" designates experiences that are definitely beyond established psychiatric nosologies. Shay clarified emphatically that "pure PTSD, as officially defined, ... is rarely what wrecks veterans' lives, crushes them to suicide, or promotes domestic and/or criminal violence" (2014, p. 184). Such an understanding of the range of impact of these traumatising experiences confirmed his intention to identify a phenomenon that included a wider gamut of negative consequences, whenever one is exposed to certain types of adversity. His contribution was, precisely, the fact that he discerned a phenomenon that was beyond what the existing parameters of PTSD ("as officially defined") could render intelligible.

Therefore, we can note that the development of the field of moral injury, on the one hand, succeeded in expanding the scope of trauma and its implications whereas, on the other hand, especially in the early stages of its introduction, it narrowed significantly the range of affected persons that were studied, concentrating almost exclusively on war veterans, and even more specifically, on members of the U.S. armed forces.

With respect to the specificity of the phenomenon, itself, Shay repeatedly insisted, epigrammatically, that "moral injury is:

- A betrayal of what's right.
- by someone who holds legitimate authority (e.g., in the military—a leader).
- in a high stakes situation.
- All three" (Shay, 2014, p. 183).

The most obvious comment about this definition is that it does not refer to any state of the persons affected, nor to any behavioural disturbances of theirs. Instead, its focus is on the conditions that Shay identifies as triggering moral injury. In other words, it would have been more accurate if Shay had spelled it out more clearly, i.e. that these three points refer to the circumstances that give rise to moral injury, rather than to what moral injury is, in fact, about. However, this obvious inaccuracy is indicative of the type of emphasis that Shay gives to moral injury. Evidently, he must have felt that it was sufficient to have discovered some similarities between the warriors' predicaments in Homer's *Iliad* and *Odyssey* and their equivalent in modern-day U.S. soldiers who are deployed abroad, and also to have discerned a certain moral dimension to this phenomenon. Any further delving into the implications of morality within a broader existential context did not seem to have occupied either him or the other early pioneers of moral injury.

When he does more directly address the effects of moral injury on affected persons, Shay answers his own question – "How does moral injury change someone?" – by stating that

> [i]t deteriorates their character; their ideals, ambitions, and attachments begin to change and shrink ... and sometimes destroy the capacity for trust. When social trust is destroyed, it is replaced by the settled expectancy of harm, exploitation, and humiliation from others.
>
> (Shay, 2014, p. 186)

Here, we observe again Shay's preference for opting for the external manifestations of moral injury, i.e. the destruction of "social trust", rather than the exploration of the nature and implications of such a fundamental moral upheaval within an individual.

The main argument for moral injury has always been that it is different from PTSD. Based on their clinical observations and research findings, the team led by Dr Brett Litz found that these differences were not restricted to the nature of the stressor, the "triggering event", which for PTSD was accepted as "actual or threatened death or serious injury", whereas for moral injury they found that there were "acts that violate deeply held moral values". They also identified that the "predominant painful emotion" in PTSD was "fear, horror, helplessness", whereas for moral injury it was "guilt, shame, anger"; moreover, in relation to clarifying "what necessity is lost", they specified "safety" for PTSD, but "trust" for moral injury (Litz, Stein, Delaney, Lebowitz, Nash, Silva & Maguen, 2009).

Litz and his team proposed a new definition of moral injury, as the situation involving "Perpetrating, failing to prevent, bearing witness to, or learning about acts that transgress deeply held moral beliefs and expectations" and clarified that, essentially, it "requires an act of transgression that severely and abruptly contradicts an individual's personal or shared expectation about the rules or the code of conduct, either during the event or at some point afterwards" (Litz, Stein, Delaney, Lebowitz, Nash, Silva & Maguen, 2009, p. 700). The marked difference between this and Shay's definition is that whereas the latter emphasises external conditions that impose on the individual (i.e. "betrayal"), their understanding gives prominence to the individual's own actions. However, both definitions focus on the conditions (external for Shay, with an added consideration for internal for Litz et al.) that give rise to moral injury, rather than on the detrimental moral impact that these conditions have on the affected person.

This brief discussion shows that the pioneers of moral injury were struggling to balance out the importance of their discovery with the full implications of discerning such a new phenomenon where morality is at its centre. On the one hand, they justified its introduction on the strength that it refers to a distinct new entity (i.e. something different from PTSD) but, on the other hand, they seemed to shy away from delving into the full and radical consequences of a state that is created by nothing less than a wounded morality.

In order to begin to understand the tension between these two types of emphases, we need to keep being reminded that all the early theorists of moral injury were, in fact, psychiatrists, and their work settings were within the system of health care for U.S. veterans. This appears to explain why although they were capable of identifying symptoms such as "impairment", "despair", problems of "trust" as well as deterioration of "character", their actual focus was on clearly identifiable symptoms (with regard to individuals) and dysfunctional organisational patterns (with regard to interpersonal contexts and organisational structures). This is an important point. Regardless of their perceptiveness and creativity in expanding the PTSD syndrome, they had to limit their focus to tangible parameters of the "moral" dimension, as their own working framework was (and still is) based unequivocally within the U.S. mental health system of care provided for veterans experiencing various forms of distress, which PTSD could not account for satisfactorily. The health care system that employs them requires them to produce detectible behaviours and indices that can be recorded in an objective manner and stand up to experts' scrutiny, so that they can form the basis of insurance and other relevant claims and benefits. The difficulty, of course, is that the realm of morality is not easily conducive to such concretisation.

Therefore, we witness yet another paradox, that although moral injury emerged from within the ranks of psychiatry practitioners, as a result of appreciating psychiatry's own limitations to comprehend phenomena beyond its own realm, moral injury still suffers from having been kept captive within the psychiatric domain for a long time, restricted within the confines of psychiatric methodology.

Indeed, the very concept of moral injury is finely balanced on the edge between these two realms: morality and injury. Psychiatry definitely deals with "mental injury" but who then is the specialist for morality? Not only in terms of its "treatment" but also in terms of grasping its very conceptualisation, discerning its very substance, nature and phenomenology? What is a healthy morality and what is an injured morality? Facing this tension, it is not surprising that psychiatrists have opted very definitely towards the injury side of the double-faced moral injury phenomenon, leaving the other side, like the dark side of the moon, as the big unknown, only surmising about it without facing the radical challenge that it poses.

Inevitably, once moral injury was established as a unique phenomenon, it could no longer be contained within the boundaries of psychiatry, and many more theorists, practitioners and thinkers engaged fruitfully with it. Accordingly, theologians, philosophers, psychologists, all types of therapists and psychotherapists, and social commentators contributed substantially in deepening our understanding of its nature, implications and treatment (e.g. Antal & Winings, 2015; Bernstein, 2005; Dombo, Gray & Early, 2013; Drescher & Foy, 2008; Frankfurt & Frazier, 2016; Gilligan, 2014; Harris, Park, Currier, Usset & Voecks, 2015; Jinkerson, 2016; Kinghorn, 2012; Levinson, 2015; Miller, 2009; Nickerson, Schnyder, Bryant, Schick, Mueller & Morina, 2015; Sreenivasan, Smee & Weinberger, 2014; Worthington & Langberg, 2012).

Two definitions are characteristic of this expansion. Still working within the field of returning veterans, Currier, Holland and Malott, arguing for the inclusion of the spiritual dimension in considering moral injury, propose that it should be understood as capturing "the constellation of inappropriate guilt, shame, anger, self-handicapping behaviors, relational and spiritual/existential problems, and social alienation that emerges after witnessing and/or participating in warzone events that challenge one's basic sense of humanity" (Currier, Holland & Malott, 2015, pp. 229–230). The explicit inclusion of "spiritual/existential problems" spells out, in an unambiguous manner, the departure from the clear psychiatric symptomatology.

Also, Hodgson and Carey, following overtly a "bio-psycho-social-spiritual" model, propose even more boldly and unequivocally that "moral injury is essentially an existential-ontological wound that can have lasting psychological, biological, spiritual, behavioural and social consequences and that chaplaincy/pastoral care practitioners are well placed to assist alongside other health care providers to provide rehabilitation that is holistic" (2017, p. 10).

Both definitions testify to the expansion of the understanding of moral injury that has taken place since it was originally proposed, to the need for including explanatory models beyond psychiatry, and to the justification for enlisting non-psychiatric practitioners for its treatment. More specifically, the reference to a "bio-psycho-social-spiritual" model as an example of a holistic approach, confirms the importance of appreciating the impact of moral injury on the totality of a person and not just with regard to a set of psychiatric symptoms. But then why restrict this impact to the bio-psycho-social-spiritual realms? How about financial, educational or environmental and so many other effects? This is precisely the reason that I introduced the term "onto-ecological", to include the totality of a person as s/he is interacting with the totality of his/her environment; this is what is a truly holistic approach.

Moral crisis, morality and *teshuvah*

Returning to the nature of the impact adversity has on us, it is useful to recap that the adversity, as a turn away from the expected, instigates a distressing "onto-ecological unsettledness". This means that it turns most aspects of our existence upside down, causing us to question the way we understand and live our lives and, consequently, shattering our habitual views about what is right and wrong. Reiterating what has been emphasised already, these resulting processes are also the basic ingredients of most forms of learning, and are at the core of most life-transformation processes.

In deepening our exploration of moral injury, clarification is needed concerning the specific nature of the adversity that gives rise to moral injury. For PTSD, the cause is clear – an external event that has a traumatising effect on persons. However, for moral injury, as was discussed above, the cause is often considered to be either an exposure to an external toxic event, e.g. betrayal by superiors, according to Shay, and/or an untoward act that the persons themselves perpetrated, according to Litz et al. Nonetheless, what should not be overlooked is that even in the latter case, a cluster of certain events and circumstances had to exist, creating the conditions for the emergence of the morally injurious act. This clarification is an important epistemological elucidation, and it should not be mistaken as an attempt to relieve the perpetrators of such acts from their moral, legal and any other responsibilities.

Whether the affected person is a soldier committing atrocities, or a family member transgressing family values, or an employee cheating his or her employers, moral injury is an inseparable part of the totality of the turmoil that is created before and after these wrongdoings. The cause of this turmoil is not only the wrongdoings themselves, but also the conditions that gave rise to them in the first place, as well as the specific set of triggers that created an untenable situation to which the perpetrators' transgressions were a response. In other words, given the moral code which the perpetrator was following up until that time, s/he reacted to the trigger situation with those transgressive act/s.

An additional clarification is needed to help us develop a more precise understanding of moral injury. This concerns the distinction between *moral injury* and *moral crisis*. The injury, itself, is only one part of the broader turmoil and unsettledness, which, inevitably, includes a distinct sense of moral confusion and disorientation. Focusing exclusively on the injury part of the wider phenomenon of moral crisis overlooks the complexities that are created in the moral sphere when adversity strikes. The affected persons do not only develop symptoms (psychiatric or otherwise) due to their moral "injuries", but their whole system of values and their clarity as to what is right and what is wrong are also affected. In fact, it should be said that regardless of whether they are morally "injured" or not in responding to morally adverse situations, they will most definitely be morally disoriented.

To clarify further, what creates moral crises is not one isolated act but the combination of (i) all the preceding contributing conditions and factors, (ii) the triggering event/s and circumstances, and (iii) the resulting transgressive acts by the perpetrator. For example, a soldier of weak personality, with a feeble and untested existing moral code, and without substantial support from others (these are the contributing conditions and factors) feels betrayed by his superiors and is overwhelmed by combat stress (these are the triggering events and circumstances) and reacts by committing atrocities against enemy non-combatants (these are the transgressive acts).

Finally, it should be noted that the concept of moral injury focuses exclusively on the damage inflicted on the perpetrator, whereas when we consider the complete set of components of a moral crisis, in addition to the contributing factors, the triggering events and the transgressive acts, the destructive effects on the victims of the perpetrator's actions should not be disregarded.

Following these clarifications and extending the framework that this chapter has developed, it is now possible to examine more clearly the whole phenomenon of moral crisis in response to exposure to various forms of adversity, by turning our attention to morality.

Without going into a detailed analysis of the nature and complexities of morality, it suffices, for the purposes of this chapter, to examine only one relevant characteristic of morality. Etymologically, morality is directly connected with one's actual physical environment. *Mores*, the Latin root of morality, as its Greek equivalent word *ethos*, refers to "an accustomed seat ... the haunts of animals ... [and] ... by extension, ... to the manners and habits" of a person (Papadopoulos, 2013). This means that "etymologically, the character of a person is connected with the actual physical space one habitually occupies" (Papadopoulos, 2013). Thus, the connection between the words "habit" and "habitat" is not accidental. Developing further the etymological meanings, it can be said that *moral* (as well as *ethical*)

> would be an action that fits in with the habitual way that a person acts, that is truthful to the person's character, that fits with the person's place of living and with the manner that one lives as a result of inhabiting a given habitat.
>
> (Papadopoulos, 2013)

This etymological note indicates the direct connection between morality and "onto-ecological settledness". The latter, being the relationship of one's totality of being with the totality of one's environment, suggests that there is an inherent moral dimension in the way we live our lives with others and within the context of a particular habitat. Accordingly, when the "onto-ecological settledness" becomes unsettled, inevitably our sense of morality also becomes unsettled, muddled and disoriented.

The question then arises as to how we define our habitat, our *mores*, the habitual spaces in which we share our living with others, because this would have a direct impact on the type of morality we espouse. This means that if our habitat (with reference to this context) is designated in terms of local and parochial spaces, the resultant morality would be limited to serving the interests of that particular locality, and based on following certain rules of *do's* and *don'ts* suitable for that specific setting, group of people and inter-relationships. Accordingly, the broader the habitat we consider, the more substantial and more widely encompassing morality it would generate. Therefore, if one were to consider our entire planet as one's habitat, then the morality that such a sense of belonging would beget would be a morality that embraces the entire ecology of our earth. Such a sense of morality would not only make one respectful of one's immediate and actual neighbour and of one's local ecological preoccupations, but it would also foster a very broad sense of responsibility and reverence for the entire planet and everything on it – people, animals, plants – and the well-being of all of them.

Adversity upsets our "onto-ecological settledness" because it is a turn away from the expected. The expected is that which one is used to; it is defined according to one's personal wishes, likes and dislikes, personal and local history – in short, based on one's sense of belonging within the confines of one's personal interests and those of one's immediate family and community, in the context of one's locality. Adversity, then, by turning one away from the expected and familiar, in addition to the painful consequences, losses and suffering, also has the possibility of opening up new vistas and broadening one's perspective in relation to not only one's habitual ways of relating (in the context of one's parochial interests) but also to one's entire being, embracing wider onto-ecological perspectives.

The process of Adversity-Activated Development (AAD) (Papadopoulos, 2007, 2012b, 2018b) refers precisely to this renewal, to the development that is specifically activated when one is exposed to adversity. The well-known saying that exists in most languages and cultures, that whatever does not kill you strengthens you, testifies to the reality that, in addition to all the negative effects, adversity also spurs re-examination of the accepted and familiar, opening up the possibility for renewal. As Shakespeare wisely expressed it,

> Sweet are the uses of adversity
> Which, like the toad, ugly and venomous,
> Wears yet a precious jewel in his head.
>
> (*As You Like It*, II, 1)

The term that the Early Church Fathers used to refer to the total transformation of a person is *metanoia*, which is usually translated as repentance but, literally, it means the change of one's *noos*. *Noos*, for them, was not only one's mind (the *noetic* part of a person) but also one's heart, i.e. the totality of what makes a person human. The Old Testament term for *metanoia* is *teshuvah*, which has a very specific meaning, referring to the person's turning to God's call. *Shuv* refers to turning, which is at the core of adversity. Accordingly, it can be said, poetically, that adversity and trauma are God's call, the unexpected turn of events that prompts us to turn to Him, i.e. an invitation to expand our own personal and selfish concerns and to embrace the well-being of the totality of the entire universe. Indeed, according to Saint Silouan the Athonite, a truly transformed person embraces and prays for the whole world, and not only for oneself or for one's close relatives and local interests (Sakharov, 2002, 1991; Zacharou, 2015).

To end, what emerges from the discussion in this chapter is the need to re-examine the traditional epistemologies of trauma and moral injury. As it has been shown, these widely accepted discourses focus exclusively on the traumatising effects, on the damage and distress inflicted, at the expense of the wider spectrum of responses to exposure to adversity, which also include existential and ontological dimensions. These dimensions inherently include a serious re-examination of one's morality that can lead to a substantial renewal.

It is an irony that discourses that aim at remedying trauma, due to inappropriate epistemological scrutiny, tend to become traumatised themselves, i.e. focusing pathologically on trauma, at the exclusion of the renewing potentialities that are also activated in these situations (Papadopoulos & Gionakis, 2018). Inevitably, such traumatised discourses keep traumatising our conceptualisations of any phenomena related to trauma and moral injury, by fostering distorting transformations such as psychologisation, pathologisation, etc., which were examined here. Conversely, epistemologically astute discourses enable us to appreciate the disorienting impact of the existential conundrums engendered in moral injury, thus transforming the destructiveness of the adversity turn into a renewed and expanded morality.

References

Antal, C. J., & Winings, K. (2015). Moral injury, soul repair, and creating a place for grace. *Religious Education, 110*(4), 382–394.

Bernstein, J. M. (2005). Suffering injustice: Misrecognition as moral injury in critical theory. *International Journal of Philosophical Studies, 13*(3), 303–324.

Currier, J. M., Holland, J. M., & Malott, J. (2015). Moral injury, meaning making, and mental health in returning veterans. *Journal of Clinical Psychology, 71*(3), 229–240. doi:10.1002/jclp.22134.

De Gucht, V., & Fischler, B. (2002). Somatization: A critical review of conceptual and methodological issues. *Psychosomatics, 43*(1), 1–9.

De Gucht, V., & Maes, S. (2006). Explaining medically unexplained symptoms: Toward a multidimensional, theory-based approach to somatization. *Journal of Psychosomatic Research, 60*(4), 349–352.

Dombo, E. A., Gray, C., & Early, B. P. (2013). The trauma of moral injury: Beyond the battlefield. *Journal of Religion & Spirituality in Social Work: Social Thought, 32*(3), 197–210.

Drescher, K. D., & Foy, D. W. (2008). When they come home: Posttraumatic stress, moral injury, and spiritual consequences for veterans. *Reflective Practice: Formation and Supervision in Ministry, 28*, 85–102.

Frankfurt, S., & Frazier, P. (2016). A review of research on moral injury in combat veterans. *Military Psychology, 28*(5), 318–330.

Gilligan, C. (2014). Moral injury and the ethic of care: Reframing the conversation about differences. *Journal of Social Philosophy, 45*(1), 89–106.

Gureje, O., Simon, G. E., Ustun, T. B., & Goldberg, D. P. (1997). Somatization in cross-cultural perspective: A World Health Organization study in primary care. *American Journal of Psychiatry, 154*(7), 989–995.

Harris, J. I., Park, C. L., Currier, J. M., Usset, T. J., & Voecks, C. D. (2015). Moral injury and psycho-spiritual development: Considering the developmental context. *Spirituality in Clinical Practice, 2*(4), 256.

Hodgson, T. J., & Carey, L. B. (2017). Moral injury and definitional clarity: Betrayal, spirituality and the role of chaplains. *Journal of Religion and Health, 56*(4), 1212–1228.

Jinkerson, J. D. (2016). Defining and assessing moral injury: A syndrome perspective. *Traumatology, 22*(2), 122.

Kellner, R. (1990). Somatization: Theories and research. *Journal of Nervous and Mental Disease, 178,* 150–160.

Kinghorn, W. (2012). Combat trauma and moral fragmentation: A theological account of moral injury. *Journal of the Society of Christian Ethics, 32*(2), 57–74.

Kirmayer, L. J., & Robbins, J. M. (1991). Introduction: Concepts of somatization. In L. J. Kirmayer & J. M. Robbins (Eds.), *Current Concepts of Somatization* (pp. 1–19). Washington: American Psychiatric Press.

Levinson, M. (2015). Moral injury and the ethics of educational injustice. *Harvard Educational Review, 85*(2), 203–228.

Litz, B. T., Stein, N., Delaney, E., Lebowitz, L., Nash, W. P., Silva, C., & Maguen, S. (2009). Moral injury and moral repair in war veterans: A preliminary model and intervention strategy. *Clinical Psychology Review, 29,* 695–706. doi:10.1016/j.cpr.2009.07.003.

Miller, S. C. (2009). Moral injury and relational harm: Analyzing rape in Darfur. *Journal of Social Philosophy, 40*(4), 504–523.

Nickerson, A., Schnyder, U., Bryant, R. A., Schick, M., Mueller, J., & Morina, N. (2015). Moral injury in traumatized refugees. *Psychotherapy and Psychosomatics, 84*(2), 122–123.

Papadopoulos, R. K. (2002). Refugees, home and trauma. In R. K. Papadopoulos (Ed.), *Therapeutic Care for Refugees. No Place Like Home* (pp. 9–39). London: Karnac, Tavistock Clinic Series.

Papadopoulos, R. K. (2007). Refugees, trauma and adversity-activated development. *European Journal of Psychotherapy and Counselling, 9*(3), 301–312.

Papadopoulos, R. K. (2012a). Jung e l' approccio allo straniero. Alcune considerazioni storiche e applicative. (Jung and the approach towards the stranger. Some historical and applied considerations). *Rivista di Psicologia Analitica, 33*(85), 15–36.

Papadopoulos, R. K. (2012b). Keep thy mind in hell and despair not. Reflections on psychosocial work with survivors of political violence. In M. Welker (Ed.), *The Spirit of Creation and New Creation: Science and Theology in Western and Orthodox Realms* (pp. 143–160). Grand Rapids, MI: Eerdmans.

Papadopoulos, R. K. (2013). Ethnopsychologische Annäherungen an Überlebende von Katastrophen. Prolegomena zu einer jungianischen Perspektive (Ethnopsychological approaches to survivors of disasters. Prolegomena to a Jungian perspective). *Analytische Psychologie. Zeitschrift für Psychotherapie und Psychanalyse, 172*(44), 134–171.

Papadopoulos, R. K. (2015). Failure and success in sorms of involuntary dislocation: Trauma, resilience, and adversity-activated development. In U. Wirtz et al. (Ed.), *The Crucible of Failure* (pp. 25–49). New Orleans, LA: Spring Publications.

Papadopoulos, R. K. (2018a). Home: Paradoxes, complexities, and vital dynamism. In S. Bahun & B. Petrić (Eds.), *Thinking Home: Interdisciplinary Dialogues* (pp. 53–69). London: Bloomsbury.

Papadopoulos, R. K. (2018b). Trauma and Umwelt. An archetypal framework for humanitarian interventions. In A. Maercker, E. Heim & L. J. Kirmayer (Eds.), *Cultural Clinical Psychology and PTSD* (pp. 91–107). Göttingen: Hogrefe.

Papadopoulos, R. K. (in press a). Families migrating together. In D. Bhurga (Ed.), *Oxford Textbook of Migrant Psychiatry*. Oxford: Oxford University Press.

Papadopoulos, R. K. (in press b). *Involuntary Dislocation. Home, Trauma, Resilience, and Adversity-Activated Development*. London and New York: Routledge.

Papadopoulos, R. K., & Gionakis, N. (2018). The neglected complexities of refugee fathers. *Psychotherapy and Politics International*, 16, 1. doi:10.1002/ppi.1438.

Ryder, A. G., Yang, J., & Heine, S. J. (2002). Somatization vs. psychologization of emotional distress: A paradigmatic example for cultural psychopathology. *Online Readings in Psychology and Culture, 10*(2), 3.

Sakharov, N. V. (2002). *I Love, Therefore I Am: The Theological Legacy of Archimandrite Sophrony*. Yonkers, NY: St Vladimir's Seminary Press.

Sakharov, S. (1991). *Saint Silouan the Athonite*. Tolleshunt Knights: Stavropegic Monastery of St John the Baptist.

Shay, J. (2002). *Odysseus in America: Combat Trauma and the Trials of Homecoming*. New York: Scribner.

Shay, J. (2014). Moral injury. *Psychoanalytic Psychology, 31*(2), 182–191.

Shay, J., & Munroe, J. (1999). Group and milieu therapy for veterans with complex posttraumatic stress disorder. In P. A. Saigh & J. D. Bremner (Eds.), *Posttraumatic Stress Disorder: A Comprehensive Text* (pp. 391–413). Boston, MA: Allyn & Bacon.

Sreenivasan, S., Smee, D. E., & Weinberger, L. E. (2014). Moral injury: A meaning-based model for Iraq/Afghanistan combat veterans. *The International Forum for Logotherapy, 37*(1), 26–31.

Worthington E. L., Jr, & Langberg, D. (2012). Religious considerations and self-forgiveness in treating complex trauma and moral injury in present and former soldiers. *Journal of Psychology and Theology, 40*(4), 274–288.

Zacharou, A. Z. (2015). *Man the Target of God*. Tolleshunt Knights: Stavropegic Monastery of St John the Baptist.

Chapter 2

Moral injury and self-empathy

Lessons from Sophocles' *Ajax*

Nancy Sherman

The notion of "moral injury" resonates with many military service members and veterans. For some, the term feels safe, non-stigmatizing and non-clinical, inviting of reflection about the moral burdens carried in war and the awful moral conflicts that can come with donning the uniform. More specifically, the term points to the moral dimensions of psychological anguish too often eclipsed in more traditional and narrower diagnoses of post-traumatic stress as a fear-conditioned response to life threat. My own work in a series of books has been to reflect on this resonance through in-depth interviews with service members, whether in thinking about issues to do with the appeal of ancient Stoicism for warriors (Sherman, 2005), or responses to moral luck in the fog of war (Sherman, 2010), or what philosophers call "reactive attitudes," that is, emotions constitutive of how individuals hold themselves and others to account (Sherman, 2015).

In this chapter, I want to revisit the notion of military-related moral injury, with an eye to moral healing or repair through compassionate self-empathy. Specifically, I want to consider moral trauma through the double lens of contemporary soldiers and lessons from ancient Greek warriors, the latter as portrayed by an ancient Greek general, who was more famously a tragedian—namely, Sophocles. The plan is this: I begin with clarification about my conception of moral injury and repair. Then I turn to two contemporary cases that deal with shame and guilt, and compassionate self-empathy. I introduce Sophocles' *Ajax* to shed important light on the cases.

Moral injury

First, we need to clarify terms. I use the term "*moral injury*" to identify an experience in which a person suffers severe moral conflict, trauma, or anguish to do with real or apparent moral transgressions and or falling short of personal, professional, and moral ideals. I focus here on moral injury in the context of military service (though, moral injury needn't be restricted to military contexts), whether in a war zone or not. The injuring or damaging can be "by self" from the point of view of agent, "to self" from the point of view of victim, or "to another" from the point of view of a close-up bystander of what is done by or to others. It is important to note that the occasions for such moral injury needn't be physical acts involving killing, maiming, collateral harm, torturing, or other atrocities and grotesqueries associated with war. That view of moral injury in military service as arising only from deadly or highly assaultive and physically visceral experiences is simply too limiting. The contexts are far more wide-ranging, and include interpersonal transactions (physical *and* verbal) to do with real or perceived deep betrayals, profound breaches of good will, and violations of dignitary respect (as in acts of exploitation, discrimination, scapegoating, and so on). That said, my emphasis is not on a list of representative external conditions that are necessary or sufficient causes for moral injury. Rather, my interest is in the nature of the anguish itself, as a reactive attitude or emotion.

In talking about reactive attitudes, I draw on the seminal essay of P. F. Strawson "Freedom and Resentment," (1962) and the fertile philosophical literature that essay spawned.[1] Following in that tradition, I argue that moral injury is felt and often publically expressed by a host of negative reactive attitudes that constitute a sense of holding self and others morally to account in terms of certain implicit or explicit norms and ideals. Those emotions include: *guilt, shame, resentment, moral disappointment, moral indignation*, and a *sense of moral betrayal*. Additional, more globalized negative feelings expressive of moral injury might be *moral despair, moral anxiety*, or *moral disillusionment*, though these emotions do not record that same sense of moral reproach or blame that the first set do. Moral healing is a process of *moral recovery* or *moral repair* that involves, again, in a constitutive way, positive emotions of holding persons to account. These positive reactive attitudes include such emotions as trust, hope in persons, forgiveness, and a sense of compassionate empathy that positions one to move beyond the raw sense of hurt and blame.[2]

It is clear that I am thinking about moral injury and repair as a philosopher and not a clinician.[3] Though I have psychoanalytic research training, I do not see patients and do not view my work as clinical. Moreover, as I have suggested, clinical diagnoses can be unduly restrictive, especially those to do with the *DSM* (*Diagnostic and Statistics Manual*) that, it can be argued, were designed by the American Psychiatric Association as a diagnostic guide for mainly insurance-filing purposes. The original post-traumatic stress disorder (PTSD) diagnosis (*DSM-III* 1980), while a remarkable breakthrough in the diagnosis and treatment of neurasthenia and war (as well as rape-related) psychological trauma, nonetheless bears the marks of its behaviorist era in its view of trauma as a fear-conditioned response to life threat, characterized primarily by symptoms of re-experiencing, avoidance, and arousal/hypervigilance. Recovery typically involves a desensitization of the fear response, often through a combination of exposure techniques and cognitive behavioral therapy. While I do not dispute the prevalence of PTSD in military-related trauma or the effectiveness of various forms of exposure or cognitive behavioral therapy,[4] I do question viewing the fear response as the ubiquitous traumatic response to war, whether one is agent, victim, or bystander.[5] War, by any sane reckoning, is filled with moral ambiguity and epistemic indefiniteness, with causes that are often only dubiously just but not manifestly unjust, and moral fog that rolls in all too thick, especially in today's population-centric wars where enemy uniforms are largely absent and combatants and noncombatants shift in and out of role in a 24-hour period. An uptick in challenges in discerning the particulars can mean a diminution in agency and give an open hand to tragic moral luck. All this is a contributor to the moral and psychological stress that modern warfare wreaks on the psyche. But add to this the moral injuries that can come from interpersonal violations—betrayals from command or buddies, from moral exploitations of various kinds, sexual assault, predation, and harassment that aren't specific to the military or war, but are often exacerbated by the tension of deployments at home or abroad and the hierarchy of male command in a deeply misogynistic military.[6] The seeds for moral injury in military service abound.

The wounds of shame and the healing of self-empathy[7]

Consider the following case:

An army major, whom I shall here call Major Briant, deployed to Iraq twice, commanding infantry and artillery units (at the time, at the rank of captain) near Baghdad and Fallujah.[8] He signed up for the army at 17, and at 40, despite having implemented versions of COIN (counterinsurgency operations) in those last deployments—serving as mayor of a local advisory council of elders, painting schools and laying sewers, outfitting scores of children with shoes (who having never worn them before had no clue that shoes, or their feet, had a right and a left), and risking life to bring food and medical care to families in need—he still thinks what he should do in armed conflict, and what he is good at and trained to do as a soldier, is engage and destroy an enemy.

And yet that was not what his war in Iraq was about. Once Baghdad fell in 2003, he found himself deep in softer and more cultural methods of warfare, often inadequately supported, and unclear of the cause or mission. He often felt betrayed by his command, and as a result, he, in turn, was forced to betray those who counted on him. Stateside, he was diagnosed with severe, near suicidal PTSD. As he puts it, "You have to understand. My PTSD had everything to do with moral injury. It was not from killing, or seeing bodies severed, or blown up. It was from betrayal, from moral betrayal."

One incident stands out. In his first deployment in 2003, a civilian family driving home from a luncheon near Baghdad crossed a cordon and got caught in the crossfire of a U.S. attack on a high-value target. Briant's unit didn't carry out the attack, but he was near the scene at the time. The mother and son were evacuated from the car, though died shortly thereafter. The father was instantly killed, his body parts strewn over the road. Briant and a buddy gathered up the fragments and rolled them up in a rug that they then loaded onto an ambulance. "It was collateral damage that happens and that is probably justified in war," Briant says philosophically. "The car just turned a corner at the wrong place at the wrong time." But in his mind what followed was not at all justified or unavoidable, and it is that aftermath that unravels him.

Shortly after the accident, Briant got orders from his battalion headquarters to find the surviving family members and begin to make amends. He found the home and a young daughter and elderly uncle, who had stepped in as guardian. Over chai the family made it clear that what they wanted most was the return of the bodies for a prompt burial. Briant set to work, but his efforts were stymied at every turn. His battalion was partnered with the Coalition Provisional Agency (CPA), Paul Bremer's American occupation administration set up to govern Iraq after the fall of Baghdad, and incompetence, by many accounts, ran deep.[9] Hoping to cut through the bureaucracy, Briant drove to the morgue himself and located the bodies. But the CPA wouldn't release them without official paper work authorized and signed by the Iraqi Ministry of Health. So began the wait for over a month for the bodies.

In the meantime, Briant's commander called to inform him that the CPA had issued solace money for the family. With cautious excitement, Briant drove to battalion headquarters to pick up the money; finally, he'd have something positive to show the uncle and daughter. He was speechless when he opened the envelope and counted the bills. It was a piddling US$750. He let his commander know how he felt: "Sir, they lost a father, a mother, and a son. And a car that is probably as important to them as the other losses." He handed the money back to the commander in disgust: "You go pay them with this!" The commander, cocooned for much of the war inside Sadam's former palace in the Green Zone, was unmoved. Briant had an unequivocal order to deliver the money.

And so he did. In silence, he handed the uncle the envelope and watched as he counted the bills, and then flung them to the ground. "I deserve whatever this man does," Briant recalls thinking. "If he slaps me in my face, I will take it. I will just take it." But the uncle just stood up, turned his back to Briant, and walked out of the room, the money still strewn on the floor. With the young girl's eyes glued on him, Briant put on his helmet, snapped his chinstrap, and left the house, covered in shame.

But the ordeal, and the shame, wouldn't end. The bodies were finally returned to the family, unembalmed and rotted beyond recognition by the scorching desert heat. The family had one last request of Briant. They needed death certificates to finalize the burial. And so Briant returned to the Ministry of Health and was given the certificates. On each was stamped in bold red letters: "ENEMY." "Can't you give me something that doesn't have 'enemy' stamped on it?" Briant beseeched. "No," the official curtly replied. "They are enemies. They are considered enemies."

The incompetence of Briant's superiors verges on the comedic, but the profound moral injury that Briant suffered verges on the tragic.[10] Disarmed of much of his usual arsenal as a warrior, more than ever, he needed to be able to trust his own basic goodness and have some assurance that he could compassionately help these noncombatants caught in war. Although minimizing collateral damage is part of the code of just conduct of a soldier, for Briant, the duty was more basic; it was an intimate duty to a family he had come to know and care for. He felt thoroughly impotent in the role. He felt profoundly betrayed by his command and coalition and humiliated that their massive incompetence forced him to betray innocents who had suffered so grievously. When he says the injury was worse and more lasting than what he suffered from seeing the detritus of war for three years, what he means, in part, is that the betrayal by command put him in a position of feeling trapped and helpless, much more powerless and captive than he had ever felt in facing enemy fire. He was stripped defenseless, with nowhere to go. That shame haunted him until one day when back home on base at Fort Riley, Kansas, he simply couldn't put his combat boots on. Suicidal feelings and ideas took over. It was at that point that a new, far more benign commander than his previous one got him help. Empathy and self-empathy were a critical part of the healing.

The idea of self-empathy may strike some as odd. As an epistemic notion, empathy is typically directed at another and is a vehicle for understanding how to see the world from her particular corner. As an affective mode, it is a way of being able to share someone else's emotion and so have congruent feeling. But what work does empathy do when directed at self? Even if we are never *fully* in sync with our own minds and emotions, for most of us, there isn't the same kind of gap within us as there is between us. The idea of empathizing with oneself, some might say, is redundant. I argue in this chapter that this is not so. Even if we are already in sync with many aspects of ourselves, there are still corners we don't peek into because their contents are too alien, so possibilities for change are thereby closed off. Self-empathy (or what I am interested in, therapeutic self-empathy) can play a role in peering into those corners and opening doors. It can be an important part of recovering a sense of lost goodness. It can be a way of calling out to oneself that one is hurt and in need of attention and response.[11]

Put this way, self-empathy can be construed as a kind of positive reactive attitude, alongside trust and certain forms of hope in persons—in ourselves and in others. These emotions, each in their own way, and whether directed at the self or others, expose vulnerability and call out to others about one's needs, dependence, aspirations, normative expectations, and so on—*and* they seek a response. With trust, we call upon another to tend to our interests when we cannot. With hope, we call upon another to aspire to heights that we may not expect her to reach without our setting the challenge. And with self-empathy, too, we call upon ourselves to re-evaluate our past actions, and to show mercy and understanding where we could not before. Sometimes we "grow" responsiveness in those we engage through our emotional calls. This is often true in the case of trust, where if we are a bit wise with regard to whom we trust for what and when, our very act of trusting may elicit and reinforce another's trustworthiness.[12] Something similar may happen in the case of therapeutic self-empathy. We uncover our hurt to ourselves, and in that acknowledgment can sometimes elicit resources for responding to and ameliorating the suffering. In the case of punishing guilt, in empathetically reviewing the very evaluations that are at the core of our self-reproach, we may find room to hold ourselves to account in a more compassionate and equitable way. Rather than focusing on the fact that we have fallen short of some standard to which we hold ourselves, as we do when we take up the perspective of the accuser, we learn to empathize with our imperfect selves: we take up the perspective of the accused, of one who genuinely attempted to meet the endorsed standard, but failed through no fault of her own.

We shall come to the various dimensions of self-empathy and their healing powers. But first I retell another story of shame, this one an ancient tale. And then I turn to a contemporary story of guilt that opens the door for self-empathy.

Ajax's shame

I first met Major Briant at a reading of Sophocles' *Ajax*, performed by the Theater of War before a mostly military audience.[13] The play is another story of shame, with disastrous outcomes. Ajax is stripped of his *timê*, his honor and status, when the Greek chiefs vote to award Achilles' armor—a prize given to the best fighter—to Odysseus rather than him, despite his legendary status. As Homer chronicles in the *Iliad*, Ajax was "the bulwark of the Achaeans" in their fight against Troy, "giant" in size, "powerful and well-built," "the giant god of battle," unrivaled as a fighter (Homer, 1990, III, lines 270–290, VII, lines 242–332).[14] In a famed duel with Hector, he is easily the victor. His own warrior mettle is storied, god-like, but so too is his father's. He is the son of Telamon, who battled the Trojans alongside

Heracles and who, for his bravery, was awarded the Trojan king's daughter, Hesione, as a war bride.

In the play, Ajax's shock and shame of losing a prize comparable to his father's becomes part of a more generalized, psychological breakdown. He has lost all face before those who matter: "I will return from Troy having earned nothing. How could he [my father, Telamon] stand to even look at me?" (Sophocles, 2007, lines 464–465). In a pique of blazing rage, he sets out to take revenge on Odysseus and his troops, and to prove once and for all his unmatched skill as a swordsman. But the goddess Athena blinds him and he flails his sword in the dark, mistaking barnyard animals for his rival: He "hacked at this chief and that chief," recounts Athena. And after tiring of the slaughter, he took the rest of the beasts captive and tortured them. Ajax "comes to" in a bloodbath of butchered carcasses and mutilated livestock. He mocks the sight of himself: "Look at the valiant man! The brave heart! The one who unflinchingly faced the enemy! You see the great deeds I have done to harmless beasts? Oh, the ridicule runs riot against me!" (Sophocles, 2007, lines 364–367).

There is ironic distance,[15] but it fails to insulate. Ajax's self-evaluation couldn't be more unforgiving. He seems to look on at himself as someone in the past. But his past is not *past*. It consumes him in the present. In an unparalleled moment in Greek tragedy, this great Greek general falls on his sword on stage. In this particular staging of the play, before a community that has come to know suicide all too intimately, the scene brought a hush like few moments I have known in theater. Ajax was in the room, in Major Briant and in many others, who felt they had lost their identity as warriors, and then their good name.

The experience of shame—as Ajax's and Briant's stories, ancient and contemporary, show—is about being seen and about having nowhere to hide.[16] Greek etymology is a reminder. *Aidôs* is related to *aidoia*, genitals. To be ashamed is to be caught without your fig leaf.[17] The audience can be real or imagined. When Aristotle says, "eyes are upon you," he should not be read literally (Aristotle, 1984, *Nicomachean Ethics*, II.6 1384a35–1384b1). That is how shame *feels*.

"I was never going to be the one-stop intel analyst for the whole army"

Consider another case, this one more to do with guilt than shame, and involving a student of mine. I turn to this case, for the guilt led, in critical ways, to healing through self-empathy. Billy O'Rourke served in Iraq between July 2001 and December 2005.[18] At 21 he was a young sergeant and a team leader of a group of intelligence analysts attached to an army cavalry squadron of 410 men in Tal Afar, a desert town not far from Mosul, about 40 miles from the Syrian border. As cavalry, his unit served as the "eyes and ears" of the battalion, collecting and sorting intelligence critical for a dynamic picture of the current battlefield. The unit was a "bridge" between those inside and outside the wire, with O'Rourke himself spending much of his time outside, talking to troops and locals, and drawing and re-drawing a visual, first-hand picture of the vicinity and its dangers. He knew how tall buildings were on different streets, where snipers could lurk, where you did and didn't want to be. He became the point guy to whom noncommissioned officers and officers alike turned to get their information. As he put it, with modesty but candor, his superiors "had confidence in his competence."

About three months before his deployment was up, he was ordered to take a few days of "R and R" (rest and relaxation) in Qatar before returning to the States for a longer two-week leave. O'Rourke was reluctant to abandon the unit so close to the end of their deployment, but an order was an order and leave-time was mandatory anyway. He was stressed of late, "bouncing inside and outside the wire," as he put it, and at some level, he knew that a break was probably a good idea.

En route to Qatar, he learned that his unit was about to run a cordon and search operation in the southeast corner of the town Tal Afar which had become a major smuggling hub, with weapons pouring in from the unsecured borders with Syria. It was now time to flush out the weapon caches and insurgents with a strong show of troop forces and a door-to-door raid. What O'Rourke didn't know was that as part of the preparation, one of the platoons, headed by a close friend, had been ordered to scout out a potential egress route at the backside of the city where a wall of troops could be mounted to block insurgents from fleeing the raid into the desert. It was during this preparatory drive-through that an improvised explosive device (IED) struck his friend's vehicle, killing him and two others. O'Rourke learned about the incident a few days after he arrived in Qatar. It hit him hard:

> What bothered me was that it was in an area that I knew very well. It was in a part of the city that you really had to see in order to visualize. And I had this lurking suspicion that my soldiers, who had never actually, personally been there, didn't really have a grasp on all the information that I felt I did. In some way, I almost felt responsible for not being there to provide them with the information that may have potentially resulted in a different outcome. So it is rough. It is a difficult thing for me to process. ... So here I was sitting by a pool, and I hear this. It was—I don't even know how to describe it. It was—devastating.

Had O'Rourke been there, he is sure he would have recommended against his buddy taking that road. He knew that back area of the city was especially dangerous and that no unit vehicles had traveled down that road for good reason. He would have urged more reconnaissance on the routes and potential alternatives. "Whether or not I would have been successful in getting that to become the battle plan, I don't know." But given that he was relied on for this kind of information, he had a good chance of making the case. In his mind, he let down his command as well as his friend. What happened, as he puts it, "reflected poorly" on him. He "faults" himself for not being there, and though he is "frustrated" that his unit members "didn't have the same clout" as he did and couldn't "pick up the slack" in his absence, he doesn't fault them for failing to make the call.

Significantly, it is just this sense of feeling that he is the only guy that can do the job and that it is a job that requires constant vigilance, without gaps and breaks, that both hounds him and ultimately opens the way for self-exculpation. The fact that he didn't *choose* to take the leave—that he was acting on an order—only gets him so far. The real exculpation comes some three to four months after the incident, when his deployment is over and he reflects on the incident in connection with whether he should re-enlist and return to Iraq after what would amount to a longer period away. He now sees, somehow, that the demand he put on himself to be quasi-omniscient, to keep constant vigil of the changing battlefield, as he puts it several times, without "gaps in his knowledge," is unsustainable. He reconstructs the thinking:

> Well, God, I thought to myself, if I am not here in a two-week period of time and things go to hell in a hand basket … what is the situation going to be like when I get back, having been away longer? I am going to be less equipped to handle any further situations, because now I have a real gap in my knowledge. So all of this was coalescing at the same time, and it took me a while to sort of realize that I couldn't be the person that was there all the time. I could only be in one spot at a time. I could reenlist and I could stay in the job. But ultimately I am never going to cover the whole country. I was never going to be the one-stop intel analyst for the whole Army. Maybe my role was actually very small.

Looking on from the outside, we might say, "Well, of course." However well O'Rourke served in his role and however critical he was to the safety of his unit, he wasn't there that day, wasn't at fault for not being there that day, and wasn't at fault for not briefing in advance his unit about a mission that he didn't even know was going to take place. Yet for O'Rourke, it was an epiphany to see that holding himself responsible was grandiose. It required too idealized a sense of his role responsibilities and duties, and too idealized a set of expectations and injunctions about how he was supposed to function. And yet the unreasonableness of the demands he held himself to only dawned on him with time, when he realized their absurd implications—that he was expecting of himself something close to full omniscience and omnipresence, a constant vigil on the battlefield that could produce an accurate, automatically refreshed picture without gaps, breaks, and breaches. He chuckles as he thinks about the absurdity of it all and of the *reductio* that it took to get him to realize it. But, it is a tentative laugh. He still knows the pull of those expectations, and what it is like to be in their grip. He may no longer endorse the evaluations so intimately related to the feelings, but when he says, "I kind of fault myself," "I almost felt responsible for not being there," he can still put himself in the mindset of what it was like to endorse those evaluations and feel their tugs. He is now at a point where he has moved on. But he got there only through an honest moral struggle about what it means to be vigilant as an intel guy. There were limits to his knowledge and frailties that he had to accept, however much they compromised his agency. Like many soldiers I have spoken to, O'Rourke doesn't easily volunteer the word "guilt." His words are "fault" and "responsibility." But, it is clear that he is talking about self-blame.

I tell this story to illustrate the function of guilt, here, as a way of working out the boundaries of moral responsibility. There is genuine *intellectual* figuring out. The emotion of guilt is not just recalcitrant (Brady, 2009, p. 429). O'Rourke is not sure what he believes, and he is not going to let himself off the hook until he is sure. The rub, of course, is that having "to be sure" quickly spirals into intellectualization and rationalization, an inventing of reasons. In short, it becomes primitive thinking that mixes rational processing with the illogicality of wishful/magical thinking and presumptions of omniscience. There are elements of this in O'Rourke's thinking.[19] Without any inkling of the planned raid, O'Rourke had no reason to inform his commanders of potential dangers before he left for R and R. Yet, he repeatedly put himself back in the reporting chain as if he knew, or should have known, what would become relevant only later. Similarly, there was little reason for him to have pointed out that particular street to his buddy, though projecting forward he helps himself to what is now the salience of that piece of knowledge and faults himself for failing to share it earlier. He faults himself for an epistemic stance he couldn't easily have had then.

But my point is what O'Rourke was going through wasn't *just* that. He was also thinking, as he put it: Was he like the homeowner who never quite got around to putting a fence around the backyard pool and then one day discovers a child has wandered into the pool and drowned? Or was he more like the cop who might have had helpful information but was legitimately off-duty at the moment and nowhere near the scene of danger? In the end, he seemed to think he was more like the cop than the homeowner, but accepting that required a lengthy, psychological process of surmounting his self-reproach. It required accepting his limits and the bad luck of being up against them then. It required self-empathy.

More on self-empathy

One way to think about self-empathy is as a conceptually or causally derivative notion. We look at ourselves as if from outside, from a spectatorial point of view. Adam Smith develops the stance:

> Whatever judgment we can form concerning [our own conduct], accordingly, must always bear some secret reference, either to what are, or to what, upon a certain condition, would be, or to what, we imagine, ought to be the judgment of others.
>
> (Smith, 2000, p. 161, III.I.1)

So an individual may come to self-empathy by internalizing a second personal instance of it, as when she learns a measure of self-empathy through the empathy of a therapist toward her. In this case, she may internalize another's stance. But she may also internalize her own stance that she takes toward others. So a rape victim in a support group may come to feel self-empathy only after first feeling empathy toward others in the group who were similarly victimized. "Oh my, God, that's what happened to me," she might come to say to herself.[20] The recognition of experiences similar to her own and the ensuing empathy toward others may enable her to now look at herself through new eyes. Second-person empathy, both the receiving and giving of it, may thus prepare one for first-person empathy. One gains an outside perspective on oneself that is qualitatively different from the punishing and shaming stance that has held one hostage until now. Veteran support groups may similarly enable self-empathy through the validating experience of empathizing and being empathized with.

In thinking about self-empathy, it is useful to turn to Aristotle's remarks about self-love (or self-friendship) in *Nicomachean* IX.8. He is aware that the idea of self-love may be a bit strained, both because it requires that we stand as subject *and* object towards ourselves,[21] but more importantly because it connotes a problematic sort of selfishness. However, there is room for a good kind of self-love, he insists, that is the capacity of a self to listen to practical reason with equanimity. He associates this kind of self-love with nobility and the sacrifice characteristic of virtue and practical wisdom, and contrasts it with the baser kind of self-love that involves taking material advantage for oneself (Aristotle, 1984, *Nicomachean Ethics*, IX.8).

However, in the soldiers' stories that are my focus, there is no shortage of nobility and sacrifice. If anything, that aspiration for virtue is too hard-driving, giving way to too much self-punishment when luck runs out. Even so, Aristotle's idea of finding the right way to befriend oneself is useful here.

The best kind of friendship—that of character friendship, he tells us—is an arena for character critique and moral growth (Aristotle, 1984, *Nicomachean Ethics*, IX.12 1172a)[22] which, like all friendship, requires positive feelings (*philêsis*) toward one's object and feelings of goodwill (*eunoia*).[23]

Self-empathy, as I am imagining it, involves a similar kind of self-friendship and requires a minimal measure of good will or compassion. I am also imagining it in the service of moral growth and in the cases I have limned of moral repair, of being called forth when one has held oneself accountable in a way that begins to seem unfair or at least, requires further reconsideration and reassessment of the nature of that accountability. And so the self-empathy I have in mind emerges as part of a moral process and is *earned* as a counterweight to overbearing self-judgment. This helps deflect various popular images of self-empathy as essentially self-kindness or self-compassion, a going-gentle-on-oneself, or, relatedly, the kind of self-esteem that is a contrived boost to undo self-deprecation, or a narcissistic self-absorption where gaze turns too much to self and not enough to others.[24] This is not the kind of self-empathy I have in mind. I am envisioning self-empathy as an emotional attitude that predisposes one to a fairer self-assessment, especially in the cases I have focused on, where luck and accident and power ceded to others squeeze out one's moral efficacy or cast doubt on one's goodness.

As a kind of felt reactive attitude, self-empathy operates by drawing us in, in the way that *emotions*, and not less charged mental states do, reining in our attention on what is morally salient and significant to our moral agency and well-being.[25] One way of thinking about Billy O'Rourke's experience is that he entreated himself to look back at the specific evaluations in his self-condemnation and the need for reopening the case. He went back to the very scenes that caused so much pain and assessed them from a new perspective that time and distance allow. In the to-and-fro dialogue of expressed reactive attitudes, overwrought guilt calls on the self to consider the reasonableness of showing oneself some compassion and empathy in the same way that resentment asks those who have transgressed us to now give us reasons for reassurance or trust.[26] The call in each case has the standing to expect a reply.

To sum up, in thinking about self-empathy I have focused on moral injuries that may *seem* only apparent because the wrongs are only apparent. But the injuries are no less real. And the soldiers' suffering is no less real. Soldiers routinely impose moral responsibility on themselves in the face of factors that make light of their own agency, whether flukish accident, the tyranny of bureaucracy and public indifference, gappy intelligence, or all too lethal weaponry. All this begs for healing, in part, through the consolations of self-empathy that allow one to touch the past in a way that doesn't devastate, and to see a future filled with some sense of trust and hope in self and others.[27]

Notes

1 To name a few: (Macnamara, 2011, 2012, 2013a, 2013b, 2015; Watson, 2004).
2 I discuss this fuller range of healing emotions in more detail in *Afterwar* (Sherman, 2015).
3 For a good clinical study of military moral injury, in the context of therapy protocols for military trauma, see Litz, Lebowitz, Gray, and Nash (2016).
4 For discussion, see Litz, Lebowitz, Gray, and Nash (2016).
5 *DSM-V* importantly adds new criteria to the symptom list that includes persistent and exaggerated negative beliefs, or negative mood states. But shame and guilt experiences are combined in a single criterion, and the notion that each is a distinct kind of reactive attitude to holding persons accountable is eclipsed by the idea of a persistent mood state (American Psychiatric Association, 2013).
6 For further discussion of gender-related moral injury, see chs. 5, 6, and 7 of *Afterwar* (Sherman, 2015).
7 For the following discussion through to the end of this chapter, I draw on extracts (c. 5000w) from pp. 78–97 and 101–103 from ch.4 of *Afterwar: Healing the Moral Wounds of Our Soldiers* by Sherman, Nancy (2015) by permission of Oxford University Press, USA.
8 I first interviewed this soldier (whose name I have changed for the purpose of this chapter), in September 2010 and several times later that year and thereafter.
9 For an excellent account, see Chandrasekaran (2006).
10 There may be comedic elements in the incredible incompetence that characterized much work of the Coalition Provisional Agency: "You couldn't invent more comedic war narratives," Rajiv Chandrasekaran (2006) said in a seminar at the Wilson Center, September 2011, reflecting on his own research and writing about that period of the war in Iraq.
11 Here, I am influenced by the work of Kukla and Lance (2009) and Macnamara (2012) on Strawsonian models of reactive attitudes. See Strawson (1993).
12 See Jones (2012).
13 For more on the Theater of War, and the larger umbrella theater group under the direction of Bryan Doerries, see: www.philoctetesproject.org/l; see also Patrick Healy, "The Anguish of War for Today's Soldiers, Explored by Sophocles," *New York Times*, November 22, 2009, at: www.nytimes.com/2009/11/12/theater/12greeks.html?pagewanted=all.
14 For a wonderful account of lessons to be learned from a retelling of the Ajax story, see Woodruff (2011).
15 On narrative and ironic distance, see Goldie (2007, 2011, p. 87).
16 For a penetrating study of the ancients on shame, see Williams (1993).
17 Susan Brison has raised the question with me as to whether shame must have this sense of being exposed, in addition to the sense, I discuss later, of falling short of an ideal. She suggests that these may be two very different features of shame, and the latter is a more central part of the concept.
18 I interviewed this soldier in 2010. I have changed his name for the purpose of this chapter.
19 Similarly, a therapist who works with soldiers recently told me of a patient who repeatedly went over the site of where he lost a buddy, homing in over and over on the spot on Google Maps, working out how he could have prevented the death if he had only taken this route rather than that.
20 I thank Susan Brison for this point.
21 After all, there is only one chapter on this odd kind of friendship in a discussion that goes on for 26 chapters (at least in the *Nicomachean Ethics*).

22 See also Sherman (1997), ch. 5.
23 See Aristotle (1984), *Nicomachean Ethics*, VIII.2 for the criteria of friendship.
24 See Neff (2003).
25 See Sherman (1997, p. 68) on the idea that emotions are ways of tracking, in defeasible ways, the morally relevant news. See also Hurley and Macnamara (2010).
26 See Walker (2006, pp. 42, 73; Williams, 1995). Just as blame "asks" a transgressor for "acknowledgment" of one's standing, so too does self-blame ask one's condemner for acknowledgment of the hurt and reconsideration of the charges. On the call and response nature of reactive attitudes, see Macnamara (2012).
27 I wish to thank Francisco Gallegos for early help in researching this chapter and Kris Bradley for help with references. Also, I thank Christina Biedermann, Susan Brison, and Jessica Stern for helpful comments on various drafts. I thank Trip Glazer and Katherine Ward for research assistance at later stages in the life of this chapter.

References

American Psychiatric Association. (2013). *Posttraumatic Stress Disorder Diagnostic and Statistical Manual of Mental Disorders* (5th ed.). Arlington, VA: American Psychiatric Publishing.

Aristotle. (1984). *The Complete Works of Aristotle: The Revised Oxford Translation.* Bollingen series (71: 2). Princeton, NJ: Princeton University Press.

Brady, M. S. (2009). The Irrationality of Recalcitrant Emotions. *Philosophical Studies: An International Journal for Philosophy in the Analytic Tradition, 145*(3), 413–430.

Chandrasekaran, R. (2006). *Imperial Life in the Emerald City: Inside Iraq's Green Zone.* New York: Alfred A. Knopf.

Goldie, P. (2007). Dramatic Irony, Narrative, and the External Perspective. *Philosophy: The Journal of the Royal Institute of Philosophy, 60*(Supp), 69–84.

Goldie, P. (2011). Self-Forgiveness and the Narrative Sense of Self. In C. Fricke (Ed.), *The Ethics of Forgiveness: A Collection of Essays* (pp. 81–96). New York: Routledge.

Homer. (1990). *The Iliad* (R. Fagles, Trans.). New York: Penguin.

Hurley, E., & Macnamara, C. (2010). Beyond Belief: Toward a Theory of Reactive Attitudes. *Philosophical Papers, 39*, 373–399.

Jones, K. (2012). Trustworthiness. *Ethics, 123*(1), 61–85.

Kukla, R., & Lance, M. N. (2009). *'Yo!' and 'Lo!': The Pragmatic Topography of the Space of Reasons.* Cambridge, MA: Harvard University Press.

Litz, B., Lebowitz, Leslie, Gray, Matt. J., & Nash, William. (2016). *Adaptive Disclosure: A New Treatment for Military Trauma, Loss, and Moral Injury.* New York and London: Guilford Press.

Macnamara, C. (2011). Holding Others Responsible. *Philosophical Studies, 152,* 81–102.

Macnamara, C. (2012). "Screw You" & "Thank You". *Philosophical Studies, 130*(2), 893–914.

Macnamara, C. (2013a). Reactive Attitudes as Communicative Entities. *Philosophy & Phenomenological Research, XC*(3), 546–569.

Macnamara, C. (2013b). Taking Demands Out of Blame. In D. J. Coates & N. A. Tognazzini (Eds.), *Blame: Its Nature and Norms* (pp. 141–161). Oxford: Oxford University Press.

Macnamara, C. (2015). Blame, Communication, and Morally Responsible Agency. In R. Clarke, M. McKenna & A. M. Smith (Eds.), *The Nature of Moral Responsibility: New Essays* (pp. 211–236). New York: Oxford University Press.

Neff, K. (2003). Self-Compassion: An Alternative Conceptualization of a Healthy Attitude Toward Oneself. *Self & Identity, 2*(2), 85.

Sherman, N. (1997). *Making a Necessity of Virtue: Aristotle and Kant on Virtue.* New York: Cambridge University Press.

Sherman, N. (2005). *Stoic Warriors: The Ancient Philosophy Behind the Military Mind.* New York: Oxford University Press.

Sherman, N. (2010). *The Untold War: Inside the Hearts, Minds, and Souls of Our Soldiers.* New York: W.W. Norton.

Sherman, N. (2015). *Afterwar: Healing the Moral Injuries of Our Soldiers.* New York: Oxford University Press.

Smith, A. (2000). *The Theory of Moral Sentiments.* New York: Prometheus.

Sophocles. (2007). Ajax. (P. Meineck & P. Woodruff, Trans.)In *Four Tragedies* (pp. 1–62). Indianapolis: Hackett.

Strawson, P. F. (1962). Freedom and Resentment. *Proceedings of the British Academy, 48*, 1–25.

Strawson, P. F. (1993). Freedom and Resentment. In J. Fischer & M. Ravizza (Eds.), *Perspectives on Moral Responsibility* (pp. 45–66). Ithaca: Cornell University Press.

Walker, M. U. (2006). *Moral Repair: Reconstructing Moral Relations after Wrongdoing.* New York: Cambridge University Press.

Watson, G. (2004). *Agency and Answerability.* New York: Oxford.

Williams, B. (1993). *Shame and Necessity.* Berkeley: University of California Press.

Williams, B. (1995). *Making Sense of Humanity.* Cambridge: Cambridge University Press.

Woodruff, P. (2011). *The Ajax Dilemma: Justice, Fairness, and Rewards.* New York: Oxford University Press.

Chapter 3

Moral conscience, moral injury, and rituals for recovery

Rita Nakashima Brock

Two of Us
Thought I was lucky.
Eleven months over there—
no Article 15s,
still stand 6'3", have ten fingers
ten toes. Only my throat tightens
when thunder sounds.
Is it incoming or outgoing?
Years later my brother says,
his brother never came home.
      —James Hugo Rifenbark

Moral conscience emerges slowly in human beings, as anyone acquainted with a 2-year-old can attest. It develops as a function of empathy and cognitive awareness of social relationships. As one of the most complex aspects of human character, it may also be what many religions call soul, a self-aware capacity of relating to the world that is crucial to well-being and human flourishing. It begins with a newborn's dependency and ability to mimic, absorb, and respond to human behaviors through mirror neurons. Years before self-understanding, conscience, and moral reasoning are fully formed, children feel, perceive, and perform moral behavior in their closest relationships of love and care until they can act morally through intuition and habit. The "Golden Rule" of reciprocity—do unto others as you would have them do unto you—is found in some form in virtually every cultural meaning system, not just because harmful behavior may be returned by another and escalate conflict, but because, in the immediacy of mirroring harm, one's own inner state is affected and that state impacts one's relationships (Knowles, 2013).

Empathy requires both the capacity to sense the emotions of others and to be aware of a self–other distinction that enables perspective-taking (Decety and Ickes, 2011). When others are distressed, perspective-taking enables us to consider how best to help and to evaluate the impact of the choices we make. Through memory and imagination, empathy can be expanded from our personal relationships to a generalized sense of compassion, even for strangers and people we will never meet.

Conscience, through empathy, evaluates how we relate to others and our environment in ways that conform to our meaning system and deepest moral values. Through the use of personal agency, we maintain our sense of good conscience and being worthy of respect and love when we use our power and faculties to sustain well-being, alleviate suffering, and maintain relationships of love and care. Hence, moral conscience is not just inner subjective intent, i.e. the desire and choice do the right thing, but a complex, interactive, and fallible system of action, intention, and evaluation that constitutes good character. When we fail conscience, as, inevitably, we do, we need ways to stabilize our inner emotional state so that memory and imagination are not trapped in self-punishment and suffering. To restore relationships, we must reconnect to those we have failed.

Recent research on moral injury in U.S. military veterans raises three core questions about moral conscience and good character that are addressed here: When core moral values can be so changed that people can desire to cause harm to others, what is required to effect such change? And, if such a change results in inner distress and trauma and destroys good character, is it further changeable? How can this further change be effected to support well-being and empathy?

Human willingness to inflict harm must be learned in relationships that sanction it by enacting and authorizing the behavior and giving it purpose. Otherwise, harm without purpose is simply cruelty, regarded as social pathology and experienced as evil (Noddings, 1991). For example, a surgical theater supports the purposeful infliction of bodily injury for the sake of removing disease, repairing injury, and saving life, whereas deliberately cutting someone without social sanction is criminal assault.

Changing moral systems

Military training re-shapes desire in relation to killing other human beings, but the capacity to kill is accompanied by a moral meaning system that sanctions it under prescribed circumstances for a higher purpose, such as defense of country, territory, or tribe. The U.S. military effects this change with at least 1000 hours of intense, holistic training to instill stoic military values (Sherman, 2007; Litz, Lebowitz, Gray, and Nash, 2016: ch. 3). The young age range of enlistees constitutes the formative years of transition that begin modern adulthood, a time that completes the firming of thinking capacities and emotional maturity. The training is sustained within an authoritarian social system, with guidelines for how to kill, training under conditions that authorize it, the formation of close relationships to others similarly trained, and multiple surveillance systems to monitor compliance.

Recruits train in the liminal state of basic training, which ritualizes every activity as comprehensively as monastic initiation (Brock and Thistlethwaite, 1996: 80–97). Throughout, the ideals of military service are delivered in stories of heroism that valorize aspirations to serve one's country, love one's comrades, and defend freedom. Strangers at first, their camaraderie connects their individual aspirations and pride in service to bonds so intense that people are willing to die to save their comrades, even when they may not personally like them. Many will experience deep friendships that supersede any others in their young lives.

Within hours of leaving home, young men and women have all marks of personal identity rapidly stripped, even their names, and their individual mistakes incur public reprimand and punishments for their entire group. The place and duration of sleep are tightly scheduled to break down resistance and improve physical and mental performance under stress. Walking, standing, speaking, and running must be re-learned as collective skills. Intense pressure from shouting instructors—all memorized performances— simulates the fierce stresses of battle (Davis, 2013). Constantly repeated drilling in consort with others focuses and toughens mental capacities and shapes and strengthens bodies and minds. At graduation, a collection of diverse individuals will have become tightly bonded competent units in a professional military that is among the most powerful in history.

All members of the military are required to know the rules of engagement; endure the crushing noise, blood, smells, and smoke of battle; ignore stress and distractions that make them vulnerable to harm; and obey the orders of superiors and hurry toward danger (Litz, Lebowitz, Gray, and Nash, 2016: ch. 3). Aversions to killing must also be overridden to make them competent at killing. As trainees become intimately acquainted with their various weapons, their relationship to killing is re-aligned so that it is done reflexively, on command (Grossman, 1996). But they are also able to refrain from killing when the emotional impulse to do so is fierce. For example, they must capture enemy combatants who surrender, rather than kill them, and medical corpsmen and chaplains must serve all combatants on all sides, even to the extent of saving the life of a wounded enemy who may have killed their comrades. These acts to save are understood as honorable demonstrations of moral courage in battle.

Without this comprehensive stoic moral system, the fears and stresses of military training would be torture, and few would survive war (Shay, 2014). Despite a desire to follow military codes of conduct, however, service members discover that war does not follow the rules. It inevitably involves harm to noncombatants and, by intent, forms of mass destruction, such as bombs and missiles, which undermine moral distinctions and thwart aspirations to do the right thing. Truman Smith, a B-17 co-pilot

who flew thirty-five harrowing bombing missions over Germany in the first
half of 1944, observes in his memoir *The Wrong Stuff*,

> Good guys don't win wars; victory goes to the bad guys. The Japs, as
> they were called ... and the Nazis ... were finally defeated by the good
> guys because we were better at being bad than they were.
>
> (Smith, 2011)

He did not set foot in Germany until 1953, when he saw the devastation to
the land, people, and cities. He returned home to Ponca City, Oklahoma,
after marrying a German woman with whom he made a successful life for
half a century.

The simplistic phrase "brain-washing" fails to capture the emotional
complexity of the palimpsest that characterizes human socialization to
military life, its interplay with conscience, and the destruction to good
character from trauma. The very pliability of youth that military training
relies upon offers clues to how empathy and the sense of being a good
person worthy of love might return. The success of military training in
stoic fortitude paradoxically illuminates the vulnerability and pliability of
moral meaning systems and pathways to recovery.

Moral injury

Moral injury is the cost to conscience when human beings inflict harm and
clear distinctions between good and evil become unsustainable. Military
training can overwrite the moral values taught by families, but the removal
of barriers to killing other human beings—even when such acts are lawful
and necessary—can inflict great anguish, especially if belief in the mission
collapses and camaraderie disappears (Maguen et al., 2011; Woods, 2014).

Psychiatrist Jonathan Shay, who worked with U.S. veterans of the war in
Vietnam, first defined moral injury in 1994 as the violation of what is right
by someone in legitimate authority in a high-stakes situation, which is
accompanied by a physiological response of feeling attacked or completely
swallowed up and emotions such as distrust and fierce outrage (Shay,
2014). Among such betrayals, sexual assault can be experienced by men
and women alike as akin to incest, as a violation of trust and profound
betrayal of unit cohesion.

In 2009, Veterans Affairs clinicians expanded moral injury beyond
"someone in legitimate authority" to include anyone, including the self.
They described it as:

> Perpetrating, failing to prevent, bearing witness to, or learning about
> acts that transgress deeply held moral beliefs and expectations. This
> may entail participating in or witnessing inhumane or cruel actions,

failing to prevent the immoral acts of others, as well as engaging in subtle acts or experiencing reactions that, upon reflection, transgress a moral code. … bearing witness to the aftermath of violence and human carnage [can] be potentially morally injurious. Moral injury requires an act of transgression that severely and abruptly contradicts an individual's personal or shared expectation about the rules or the code of conduct, either during the event or at some point afterwards … The event can be an act of wrongdoing, failing to prevent serious unethical behavior, or witnessing or learning about such an event. The individual also must be (or become) aware of the discrepancy between his or her morals and the experience (i.e., moral violation), causing dissonance and inner conflict.

(Litz et al., 2009: 700)

This definition widens moral injury to those in noncombat roles, such as mortuary affairs, chaplaincy, engineering, intelligence, psychiatry, journalism, and medical work, who can also be haunted by a sense of betrayal, things they failed to do, acts they supported, taboos they violated, harm they witnessed or heard about, or, in the aftermath of violence, handling human carnage (Synder, 2014). In addition, while sometimes referred to as "secondary" trauma, experiences of another's trauma can invade the inner states and inhabit the imaginations of others such as caregivers and families as something like emotional contagion.

In both definitions, moral injury can precipitate, aggravate, or occur concurrently with PTSD, but it is likely a greater—and still largely unaddressed—factor in poor veteran mental health (Litz et al., 2009; Shay, 2014). The tendency to confuse the fear-based trauma of PTSD with moral injury may even deepen the suffering of moral injury. For example, a treatment for PTSD, exposure therapy, uses re-experiencing a traumatic experience until fear is mitigated (Nash et al., 2013). Such remembering may aggravate, rather than diminish, feelings of outrage, remorse, or shame.

Moral injury is not simply doing something one believes is wrong and feeling terrible, which, in the face of human finitude, is a common experience of most human beings. War requires that combatants must be trained to desire and enact what they once were taught to eschew as wrong—their character is distorted (Shay, 2014). This socially sanctioned, axiological shift means, according to Iraq veteran, Brian Powers, that people do not simply violate "an interior value," but rather that the values they were previously taught must be changed. Thus, "their deepest internal understanding of what is 'good' and 'right'" is "profoundly violated." Moral injury, according to Powers, is the lasting consequence of the key element of this transformation, the axiological pivot that reshapes desire.

Viewed as pursuit of distorted and poisoned moral goods, moral injury can be framed as the realization that one's moral orientation, to which one commits his or her willing, is aligned toward a "good" that is ultimately false.

(Powers, 2017: 327)

Michael Yandell was a 17-year-old high school graduate in 2001 who enlisted in the U.S. Army after the terrorist attacks of September 11. Like many of his generation, he wanted to defend his country and grew up in a family with a history of military service. He qualified to be an ordinance disposal specialist and left for Iraq in 2003. He observes:

I was 19 when I left for war. I did not know I was leaving a world that made sense—a world where people respected one another's lives and dignity, a world where violence and murder were understood to be wrong and punished by laws—and entering a world where all bets were off. I was a willing participant in this war.

(Yandell, 2015)

In Iraq, he was exposed to sarin gas from a corroded canister buried in the ground, made in the United States, filled in Europe, and sold to Saddam Hussein in the 1980s. Caches of chemical weapons from that era, mostly mustard gas, injured over 600 troops who were ordered to keep the discoveries secret and who were not given adequate medical treatment (Chivers, 2014).

Yandell began to doubt the purpose of the war, even as he continued to respect and honor his comrades. Suffering in a hospital from delayed sarin effects, he attempted to kill himself and was discharged as "unfit for service." In reflecting on his experience after a decade of thinking and processing, he concluded:

I categorically reject the unleashing of "good" and "evil" as fundamental ways of understanding human beings, the notion that we can place ourselves on a moral high ground and, having done so, completely disregard any moral obligation to avoid violence and death-dealing. I reject the notion that the value of life can be laid flat to be reclaimed later ... I expected to be able to return to the solid foundations of the world I had left, with its understandings of moral truth. But when I arrived home, I could not. Everything was laid flat. I returned, like so many others, to sleepless nights and to the thoughts and memories of war. There is no moral shelter when all is laid flat.

(Yandell, 2015)

Yandell had to struggle with two dimensions of moral injury: first, his own willing participation in war and desire to be a "good guy" and second, his sense of betrayal for having been used for what he concluded was a false cause. In coming to oppose all war, he observes that having war as a definitive experience of his life and also profoundly hating war creates an experience of being uncomfortable in his own skin.

Moral emotions arising from self-condemnation, such as guilt or shame, are often treated by mental health professionals as neurotic forms of distorted thinking and self-handicapping. And professional psychiatry has resisted ideas that adult experiences can devastate good character. According to Shay,

> the American Psychiatric Association (APA) has rejected every diagnostic concept that even hints at the possibility that bad experience in adulthood can damage good character. … It has rejected "Enduring Personality Change after Catastrophic Experience," which is a current diagnosis in the WHO International Classification of Diseases, and "Post Traumatic Embitterment Disorder,"… the work of Professor Michael Linden's group at the Free University of Berlin and Charité in Berlin.
>
> (Shay, 2014)

Many veterans, however, view their moral injury not as a disorder or distorted thinking, but as an understandable response to having engaged in acts of harm and in killing, and a permanent change in themselves. Iraq veteran, Tyler Boudreau notes:

> Moral injury is about the damage done to our moral fiber when transgressions occur by our hands, through our orders, or with our connivance. When we accept these transgressions, however pragmatically (for survival, for instance), we sacrifice a piece of our moral integrity. That's what moral injury is all about. … Killing hurts the killer, too, even in self-defense or in the line of duty and … no justification, legal, political, religious, or otherwise, can heal those wounds.
>
> (Boudreau, 2011: 748–749)

The unwillingness of many veterans to justify, rationalize, or redefine killing can be a way they maintain moral conscience and moral clarity. The stoic virtue of honesty and integrity leads many to understand negative moral emotions as a warranted consequence of violating core values. Iraq veteran Camilo Mejia asks, "what moral person ever feels good about killing another human being?" For him, receiving forgiveness is not possible because he had no prior relationship with, knowledge about, or means to make amends to the man he killed. He seeks instead to accept what he did as an important truth about his life that informs it but is not the whole of it. He moves into the future with a desire to be a good father to his daughter and to live a life that is of service and value to others (Brock and Lettini, 2012).

Moral injury is the trauma of moral conscience, when harm cannot be amended and empathy yields only pain and self-condemnation. Moral emotions, such as guilt, shame, remorse, and outrage at others, result in broken trust, poor health, social isolation, and, in extreme cases, suicide or violence. Moral injury means the existing core moral foundations or faith of a person or group are unable to justify, make sense of, and integrate traumatic experiences into a reliable personal identity that enables relationships and human flourishing. Like a missing limb, it is not a reversible injury, so survival is a process of learning to live with an experience that cannot be forgotten. But how the experience is remembered is crucial.

While it has no diagnostic threshold or formal diagnosis and treatment protocol, moral injury identifies the power of moral conscience to inflict great suffering. This chapter focuses on military veterans, but moral injury is a human experience that can occur in many professions and contexts of extremity. Oppressive or coercive contexts, especially, often pose no-win choices and deny the possibility of making a "good" choice. Under such conditions, the desire to do the right thing can sour into hate, anger, or shame, and distort self-perception in terms of the trauma without remainder. Moral conscience, thus, can become isolating, punishing, and lethal.

Rituals for recovery

Moral injury is as old as war itself (Shay, 1994). Some ancient cultures required a lengthy sequestered ritual process for armies returning home or processed them in a subgroup within their midst as an Order of Penitents, supported by the community (Verkamp, 2005). Purification rituals for causing harm or experiencing carnage still exist in many traditional practices that have survived modernism, such as the Navajo Enemy Way.

Chester Nez, one of the original Navajo code talkers in World War II who fought in the Pacific theater, reports how the Enemy Way ceremonial, used for exposure to irregular forms of death, saved his life. After six months home, he admitted to his family that he wanted to kill himself because of the many ghosts that haunted him day and night. His parents sponsored the nine days of rituals, and members of the community who attended were obligated to stay for the entire duration of sequestered activity. The *hataalii*, or singer, organized and led the entire ceremonial by memory, a production, according to Nez, akin to staging, conducting, and singing the entire Wagnerian Ring Cycle of operas. Nez was returned to the daily practices of what Navajo traditions call "living in Beauty"; he married, had children, and, once the Code was declassified in 1964, told the story of his war experiences for the first time (Nez and Avila, 2011).

Current programs to transition people out of the U.S. military are woefully inadequate (Office of the Joint Chiefs of Staff Chairman's Office of Reintegration, 2014; Thompson, 2012). When unit cohesion is gone and military service ends, veterans who have lost the camaraderie and world that once defined them are left on their own to function in civilian relationships, which can seem shallow, hollow, or opportunistic after the intensity of military bonds. Consumerism and personal success can seem like a paltry life purpose compared to service to country. Many will have to acquire adult life skills far later than their peers, while at the same time, they will be emotionally more mature than civilians of the same age.

Moral injury exposes the limitations of transition programs for veterans. Yearning for the most intense experiences of love they have known means carrying the searing condemnations of moral conscience. They may be blind-sided by complex forms of grief and loss when they expected to feel relieved and happy to leave. While modern clinical treatment can alleviate some forms of acute suffering, such as PTSD, and help to stabilize people in crisis states, therapy is too confined and constricted a context to overcome the isolation from love and empathy that characterizes moral injury.

Military training uses shame to train recruits, so it should not be surprising that many veterans feel ashamed of failing to adapt to civilian life. They will struggle to hide vulnerability because admitting weakness, inner anguish, and failure feels shameful. Strong until they break, their rates of suffering—homelessness, unemployment, substance misuse, incarceration, divorce, and suicide—significantly exceed civilian rates (Hosek, 2009; Lehren, 2013; Pew Research Social and Demographic Trends, 2011; Ramchand, 2011). Even when they would benefit from clinical help, however, many resist seeking help, partly because of their stoic values and also because of social stigma attached to needing therapy. When individuals are left to their own volition to recover, we place the entire burden of reintegration and recovery on the veterans and their families who already carry too much.

Religious rituals for purification and emotional transition have become a valuable arena for veterans struggling with moral injury. In the military, chaplains are frequently sought out for counseling and help instead of clinicians, partly because conversations with them are kept confidential and do not have to impact a person's service record. Clergy also do not carry the stigma of therapy. Hence, it may be easier for veterans to trust religious strategies for their suffering (Moon, 2017). Like military training, rituals integrate the body's autonomic functions, emotions, and perception and focus attention and thinking in liminal space and time. Rituals also offer a different value system from clinical treatment, which handles moral injury as a psychological condition that inhibits social adjustment. This approach usually brackets the theological questions of a shattered meaning system and loss of good character that makes adjustment to civilian society impossible. Without social support for the reconstruction of a moral identity within a meaningful system, the underlying isolation of moral injury will remain unaddressed.

Some religious value systems, however, can aggravate moral injury. Clinician and Presbyterian minister, Kent Drescher, who works with veterans, observes that the more punitive and harsh a person's view of ultimate power, the more likely he or she is to fail to recover from moral injury (Drescher, Foy, Kelly, Leshner, and Schutz, 2011). When one believes one is unforgiveable, a God who requires punishment for redemption may deepen one's despair. The axiological pivot embedded in moral injury is not reversible, so it must be processed and integrated through trusted relationships that support the rebuilding of meaning and moral identity. As moral injury processing proceeds, self-understanding, memory, and evaluations of the past will evolve and change in their telling. The imposition of answers or formulaic pieties can impede that evolution and change (Brock, 2015).

Effective rituals can teach veterans ways to monitor inner states and process feelings which stoic virtue has suppressed. Offering ritual training to everyone leaving military service, with skills for self-care and spiritual resiliency as key components, could prevent a descent into a life-threatening emotional crisis and mitigate the power of moral injury to control and dominate the future. Such ritual processes can begin recovery and impart the tools, inner strength, and patience to be deeply moved by one's own story and to accept it.

Some veterans have sought out Native American traditional ceremonies or Eastern spiritual practices as ways to alleviate their moral injury. Chris Webb, a U.S. Army veteran and doctoral student in anthropology, is studying the use of Native American rituals as an alternative to conventional Western treatment options. He was treated by Veterans Affairs for "combat trauma and the difficulties of making sense of what I had participated in during my time in Afghanistan." He found treatment for PTSD helpful for understanding "how my body had responded to the experience of being wounded and nearly losing my life in an ambush." But he continued to struggle.

> I recognized that there were parts of my soul that were suffering in ways that are not adequately described by the PTSD diagnosis and that do not respond to PTSD therapy.... Exhausted with pharmacological treatments, my research led me to explore the forms of ritualistic healing that are increasingly available to people suffering with combat trauma. In the western United States, a handful of VA hospitals offer sweat lodge ceremonies, conducted by American Indian

spiritual leaders. Having gone to the lodge, I found it both exhausting and exhilarating … it treats the suffering human as a holistic being, connected to the environment and other people. It speaks to the parts of myself that are not addressed by conventional PTSD therapy and, the morning after my first ceremony, I awoke feeling lighter and filled with an overwhelming compulsion to return.

(Webb, 2017)

This transpersonal nature of ritual—its ability to structure access to transcendence that both embraces and relativizes the individual—can break isolation, invite reconnection, and reintroduce positive community values. Rituals accomplish these outcomes by employing narrative and poetry, visual art, sound, fragrances, altered states of consciousness, and ideas. These elements guide changes in emotions, and, with powerful experiences such as loss and grief, they offer a container for release that moves through catharsis and delivers a conclusion that connects participants through a shared experience. They also focus attention on the purpose of the ritual as important and meaningful, and thus, implant and reinforce belief, behavior, feeling, intuition, and meaning (Alcorta and Sosis, 2005; Graybiel, 2008).

Increasingly, Buddhist meditation practices and various forms of Hindu yoga are attracting veterans. They have a long history and relationship to warriors. Many ancient accounts of moral transformations, such as the third century BCE Emperor Ashoka Maurya, share similar components of a conquering warrior who, faced with profound moral questions of meaning, was changed. According to edicts from Ashoka's reign, his adoption of Buddhism included instituting "a moral polity of active social concern, religious tolerance, ecological awareness, respect for parents, generosity, the observance of ethical precepts, and the renunciation of war" (Strong, 1983: 4).

The ancient ritual practices from these millennia-old traditions stabilize people emotionally, restore their thinking capacities, and enable the processing of traumatic experiences. They can be combined with temporary therapeutic interventions for a particular problem, but are otherwise used to maintain overall health. Once learned, they can be sustained over the lifespan.

Because religious rituals use common elements of human physiology, psychology, and behavior, some ritual practices can be helpful to people who do not know or understand the religious meaning system of a ritual.

Teachers of Buddhism often assert that simply engaging in meditation has efficacy to alleviate suffering; ideas, such as the transmigration of souls or a monistic cosmology that is indifferent to gods, are optional. As a ritual system designed to alleviate suffering by stabilizing and calming inner states and focusing awareness on the present, it has been refined and adapted for centuries by lineages of practitioners across many cultures and eras, carried forward by living transmission through teachers. Evidence-based research on Buddhist mindfulness bears out its effectiveness. In fact, it has become so common in therapeutic uses that "Buddhist" has mostly ceased to modify the term mindfulness (Vujanovic, Niles, Potter, Pietrefesa, and Schmertz, 2011).

Brendan Ozawa-de Silva has applied multiple Buddhist rituals to moral injury while teaching meditation in a prison (Ozawa-de Silva, 2015). Combining mindfulness with a Tibetan *blo sbyong* form of analytic meditation, called cognitively-based compassion training (CBCT), he also added aspects of a practice called Naikan from Japanese Shin Buddhism (Ozawa-de Silva, 2006). CBCT directs attention to a particular emotional problem and invites investigation, using multiple angles on cause and effect and the equalizing and exchanging of self and other. Naikan involves "contemplating three questions with regard to a significant person in one's life, such as one's mother: What did I receive from this person? What did I give back to this person? What trouble did I cause this person?" The questions, applied chronologically, from ages 1 to 5, 6 to 10, and so forth, are engaged in processing the life course. Writing answers takes place from 10 to 16 hours daily for one week, totaling 70 to 142 hours. The writer sits behind a screen in a room with the teacher, and they confer about what is being learned at set intervals throughout the day.

These practices guide people in examining how trauma impacts them in ways that draw on their memories and capacities for empathy. Ozawa-de Silva found that they enable a person to develop "new insight into [trauma] that will change one's perspectives in an ongoing way, thereby resulting in changes in emotion and behavior." One of his meditation students was a murderer he calls C. who refused to do the analytic practice:

> From a very young age, she suffered sexual abuse for over a decade at the hands of her mother's drug dealer. When her mother couldn't pay for her drugs, she offered her daughter to the man … she was abused for years while her mother got high in the next room. By the time she was 19, her own abuse had ended, but when visiting her home from college, she saw her baby brother run out of the house with his clothes dishevelled and bloodstained … Upon entering the house, she saw what she feared: her mother and the dealer. She led her brother calmly to the car, then went back inside to where her mother kept a gun in the house, and shot them both—"like Rambo" she said—wounding the dealer, but killing her mother.
>
> (Ozawa-de Silva, 2015: 2)

After refusing Naikan for two weeks, C. agreed to try it, but because she was in prison, she could only do a half hour each day. She agreed to write for 200 days and found herself writing an hour a day.

She later reported that the chief gift Naikan had given her was memory recall. Before, she had only been able to remember sadness, abuse and disappointment in her childhood. Yet by going through the process—over 200 hours—of remembering what her mother had given her, she began to recover memories of happiness and well-being. Her childhood had not all been abuse and pain. There were many moments of joy there as well ... C. began to see her mother not just as her mother, but as a young woman struggling to raise a child on her own ... As she saw the larger context and remembered all the kindness her mother had shown her over the years, her image of her mother and therefore her image of her own past changed.

(Ozawa-de Silva, 2015: 4)

In Naikan, the guide or teacher provides a liminal frame that frees the participant to write without having to create and maintain the structure. The teacher is like a coach who can offer encouragement to persist through difficult moments, to elicit insights, and to mark stages of moving through the process. The ritual works by shining inner illumination on faint or invisible layers of memory that trauma has concealed, like the many lost layers of a palimpsest that can only be seen with exposure to ultraviolet light, still present below the dark ink visible on its surface. Exposing years of hidden memory offered C. a more complete and complex reading of her life upon which she could compose a new layer from the perspective of a hard-earned compassion.

What Ozawa-de Silva captures is how recovery from moral injury is not the forgetting of trauma, but a way to place it in perspective with the support of a "benevolent moral authority" (Litz et al., 2009). A benevolent moral authority, like the Naikan teacher behind the screen, accompanies a journey through moral injury by offering empathetic, careful listening, asking compassionate questions to deepen memory, and letting the answers emerge from the remembering process. Eventually, equilibrium comes with the acceptance of trauma as a true experience, but not the whole, defining focus of a life.

Unlike a therapeutic framework, no mental illness stigma attaches to rituals, and this is also true of the arts. Instead of seeking therapy, some veterans write about their experiences in memoirs, poetry, and fiction, or express them in music, visual art, dance, and theater. All these activities externalize inner trauma, which can enable perspective-taking on one's own suffering and offer openings to self-understanding, resilience, and acceptance.

Memories of the past cannot be erased or overcome but they can be placed in perspective, and as meaningful relationships form, the present can be experienced with equanimity, appreciation, and love; and the future becomes a horizon of possibility for adventure and hope. This flexible connection to and freedom from memory and suffering is the key to what we might call self-forgiveness, a capacity for empathy for self and an expansion of it to wider and wider worlds. Such self-forgiveness might sound something like what C. experienced:

> Learning to view and interpret my past horrific childhood experiences in a different way makes me confront and acknowledge these experiences for what and how they were, yet not be controlled and overwhelmed by them. My experiences have given me a passion and desire to share my story and to be of help to those who suffer or have suffered in similar ways as I.
>
> For me, forgiveness has been the most profound act of self-compassion that I have experienced thus far. ... The cup of poison that I drank from for years is now officially emptied and retired. What a refreshing, liberating relief!
>
> I truly do believe that gratitude is the moral memory of mankind.
>
> (Ozawa-de Silva, 2015: 4)

Bibliography

Alcorta, C. S. and Sosis, R. (2005). "Ritual, Emotion, and Sacred Symbols: The Evolution of Religion as an Adaptive Complex." *Human Nature* 16, no. 4, 323–359.

Boudreau, T. (2011). "The Morally Injured." *Massachusetts Review* 52, no. 3/4, 746–754.

Brock, R. N. (2015). "Post Traumatic Stress, Moral Injury, and Soul Repair: The Implications of Western Christian Theology." *Issues in Science and Theology: Do Emotions Shape the World?* D. Evers, M. Fuller, A. Runehov, and K. Sæther, eds. Edinburgh: Springer Press, vol. 3: 27–40.

Brock, R. N. and Lettini, G. (2012). *Soul Repair: Recovering from Moral Injury after War.* Boston: Beacon.

Brock, R. N. and Thistlethwaite, S. (1996). *Casting Stones: Prostitution and Liberation in Asia and the United States.* Minneapolis: Fortress: 80–97.

Chivers, C. J. (2014). "The Secret Casualties of Iraq's Abandoned Chemical Weapons." *New York Times,* A1.

Davis, J. (2013). "Why Are Military Boot Camps So Intense?" *Slate online.* Available at: www.slate.com/blogs/quora/2013/03/05/why_is_boot_camp_so_intense.html

Decety, J. and Ickes, W. eds. (2011). *The Social Neuroscience of Empathy.* Cambridge, MA: MIT Press.

Drescher, K. D., Foy, D. W., Kelly, C., Leshner, A., and Schutz, K. (2011). "An Exploration of the Viability and Usefulness of the Construct of Moral Injury in War Veterans." *Traumatology* 17, no. 1, 8–13.

Graybiel, A. M. (2008). "Habits, Rituals, and the Evaluative Brain." *Neuroscience* 31, 359–387.

Grossman, D. (1996). *On Killing: The Psychological Cost of Learning to Kill in War and Society.* Boston: Back Bay Books.

Hosek, J. ed. (2009). Veteran Homelessness: A Supplemental Report to the Annual Homeless Assessment Report to Congress. Washington, DC: US Department of Housing and Urban Development and the US Department of Veterans' Affairs.

Knowles, C. (2013). Notes toward a Neuropsychology of Moral Injury. *Reflective Practice: Formation and Supervision in Ministry*. Vol. 33. Available at: http://jour nals.sfu.ca/rpfs/index.php/rpfs/article/view/265/264. Accessed January 25, 2017.

Lehren, A. (2013). "Why National Guard and Reservist Suicide Numbers May Be Misleading." *New York Times*. Available at: http://atwar.blogs.nytimes.com/2013/05/16/why-national-guard-and-reservist-suicide-numbers-may-be-misleading/?_r=0. Accessed January 25, 2017.

Litz, B. T., Lebowitz, L, Gray, M. J., and Nash, W. P. (2016). *Adaptive Disclosure: A New Treatment Protocol for Military Trauma, Loss and Moral Injury*. New York: Guilford.

Litz, B.T., Stein, N., Delaney, E., Lebowitz, L, Nash, W. P., Silva, C., and Maguen, S. (2009). "Moral Injury and Moral Repair in War Veterans: A Preliminary Model and Intervention Strategy." *Clinical Psychology Review* 29, 695–706.

Maguen, S., Luxton, D. D., Skopp, N. A., Gahm, G. A., Reger, M. A., Metzler, T. J., and Marmar, C. A. (2011). "Killing in Combat, Mental Health Symptoms, and Suicidal Ideation in Iraq War Veterans." *Journal of Anxiety Disorders* 25, no. 4, 563–567.

Moon, Z. (2017). Standing with Veterans at Standing Rock. Chaplaining Between Divided Worlds. [Blog] *Bearings Online*. Available at: http://collegevilleinstitute. org/bearings/standing-veterans-standing-rock/. Accessed January 30, 2017.

Nash, W.P., Marino Carper, T. L., Mills, M. A., Au, T., Goldsmith, A., and Litz, B. T. (2013). "Psychometric Evaluation of the Moral Injury Events Scale." *Military Medicine* 178, no. 6, 646–652.

Nez, C., with Avila, J. S. (2011). *Code Talker: The First and Only Memoir by One of the Original Navajo Code Talkers of WW II*. New York: Penguin.

Noddings, N. (1989). *Women and Evil*. Berkeley, CA: University of California.

Office of the Joint Chiefs of Staff Chairman's Office of Reintegration. (2014). After the Sea of Goodwill. Washington, DC, October 2014. Available at: www.jcs.mil/Portals/36/Documents/CORe/After_the_Sea_of_Goodwill.pdf. Accessed January 25, 2016.

Ozawa-de Silva, B., et al. (2012). "Compassion and Ethics: Scientific and Practical Approaches to the Cultivation of Compassion as a Foundation for Ethical Subjectivity and Well-Being." *Journal of Healthcare, Science and the Humanities* II, 1. Available at: https://tibet.emory.edu/documents/Ozawa-deSilva-Compassionand Ethics-FinalPrintVersion-JHSH2012.pdf. Accessed January 30, 2017.

Ozawa-de Silva, B. (2015). Possible Implications for Addressing Moral Injury through the Use of Lojong-Based Contemplative Practice. International Society for Psychological and Social Approaches to Psychosis. Boston. Paper presented Dec. 13.

Ozawa-de Silva, B. (2016). "Contemplative Science and Secular Ethics." *Religions* 7, no. 8. doi:10.3390/rel7080098. Available at: http:///Users/ritabrock/Downloads/religions-07-00098.pdf. Accessed January 30, 2017.

Ozawa-de Silva, C. (2006). *Psychotherapy and Religion in Japan: The Japanese Introspection Practice of Naikan*. New York: Routledge.

Pew Research Social and Demographic Trends. (2011). War and Sacrifice in the Post-9/11 Era: The Military-Civilian Gap. Available at: www.pewsocialtrends.org/2011/10/05/war-and-sacrifice-in-the-post-911-era/. Accessed January 27, 2017.

Powers, B. (2017). Moral Injury and Original Sin: The Applicability of Augustinian Moral Psychology in Light of Combat Trauma. *Theology Today* 73(4), 325–337.

Ramchand, R. (2011). *The War Within: Preventing Suicide Within the Military.* Washington, DC: Rand Corporation. Available at: www.rand.org/content/dam/rand/pubs/monographs/2011/RAND_MG953.pdf. Accessed January 27, 2017.

Rifenbark, J. H. (2017). The Two of Us. *Proud to Be: Writing by American Warriors.* Kansas City: Missouri Humanities Council & Southeast Missouri State University Press, vol. 5. Printed with permissions.

Shay, J. (1994). *Achilles in Vietnam: Combat Trauma and the Undoing of Character.* New York: Scribner.

Shay, J. (2014). "Moral Injury." *Psychoanalytic Psychology* 31, no. 2, 182–191.

Sherman, N. (2007). *Stoic Warriors: The Ancient Philosophy behind the Military Mind.* New York: Oxford University Press.

Smith, T. (2011). *The Wrong Stuff.* Oklahoma City: University of Oklahoma.

Strong, J. S. (1983). *Legend of King Asoka: A Study and Translation of the Asokavadana.* Princeton: Princeton University Press.

Synder, J. (2014). "'Blood, Guts, and Gore Galore': Bodies, Moral Pollution, and Combat Trauma." *Symbolic Interaction.* September. doi: 10.1002/SYMB.116.

Thompson, M. (2012). "They Don't Seem to Get Better." *Time online.* Available at: http://nation.time.com/2012/02/23/they-dont-seem-to-get-better/. Accessed January 15, 2017.

Verkamp, G. (2005). *Moral Treatment of Returning Warriors in Early Medieval and Modern Times.* Scranton: University of Scranton.

Vujanovic, A. A., Niles, B., Potter, A. C., Pietrefesa, M., and Schmertz, S. K. (2011). "Mindfulness in the Treatment of Posttraumatic Stress Disorder Among Military Veterans." *Professional Psychology: Research and Practice* 42, no. 1, 24–31. Available at: www.researchgate.net/profile/Barbara_Niles/publication/232558974_Mindfulness_in_the_Treatment_of_Posttraumatic_Stress_Disorder_Among_Military_Veterans/links/564262b008ae997866c499ad.pdf. Accessed January 25, 2017.

Webb, C. (2017). Email correspondence from Webb to author. "Healing from War" forthcoming in *Sapiens.* Available from C. Webb at cmw88@duke.edu.

Woods, D. (2014). "The Grunts: Damned If They Kill, Damned If They Don't." *Huffington Post.* Available at: http://projects.huffingtonpost.com/moral-injury/the-grunts. Accessed January 15, 2017.

Yandell, M. (2015). "The War Within: A Veteran's Moral Injury." *The Christian Century.* Available at: www.youtube.com/watch?v=Ex_2pS6Ekkk. Accessed January 27, 2017.

Chapter 4

The role of religious faith in severe trauma

Harold G. Koenig

Introduction

Every trauma is different, whether related to human-caused or natural events. Every individual is different, due to inherited strengths and vulnerabilities and varying experiences, and all of these will affect their perceptions of events. Consequently, there is a wide range of emotional responses to a given traumatic event. These responses will differ depending on the length of time that has elapsed since the event. The time period during and following the trauma has been divided up into four phases: (1) the impact phase (immediate, while the event is taking place); (2) the early aftermath phase (after the risk of harm has passed and shock has set in); (3) the short-term aftermath phase (realization of what has happened and its consequences); and (4) the long-term aftermath phase (recovery period that may last for the rest of the person's life) (Adachi et al., 2002; Perry & Lindell, 2003). Severe trauma adversely affects a person's worldview, and while seeds are planted during the early phases, it is during the recovery phase that these events have their greatest toll on the notion that the world is a safe and predictable place.

Religious belief and practice can help buffer the psychological consequences of severe trauma. First, though, what are those psychological consequences? In an analysis of 52 studies of natural disasters (i.e., a moderate level of trauma), researchers found that the most common long-term psychological sequelae among survivors were anxiety (40%), physical complaints (36%), alcohol use (36%), phobia (fear of a specific object or situation) (32%), and depression (26%) (Rubonis & Bickman, 1991). With regard to the consequences of surviving acts of terror, a survey of 1,008 adults conducted one to two months after September 11th found that 8% met the criteria for post-traumatic stress disorder (PTSD) and 10% for a depressive disorder in the Manhattan area overall; among those who lived near the World Trade Center, 20% met the criteria for PTSD (Galea et al., 2002). Concerning war and combat, a study of 3,671 soldiers in the U.S. infantry conducted three to four months after returning from combat in 2003 found that 15.6–17.1% of those returning from Iraq and 11.2% of those returning from Afghanistan met the criteria for major depression, generalized anxiety, or PTSD (Hoge et al., 2004). Those at greatest risk after natural disasters appear to be persons in middle-age (ages 31 to 65) because of multiple responsibilities and roles (Norris et al., 2002). Emergency medical service (EMS) workers are also at high-risk for psychological trauma, with 16% of firefighters experiencing PTSD at some time in their lives (McFarlane, 1988). A person's religious faith can help deal with every one of these psychological consequences – depression, anxiety, PTSD, substance misuse, and physical health problems (or prevent them).

Most of us view the world as stable, safe, and predictable. We plan and act in ways that are expected to have certain consequences. If we do good things, then we expect good to result. If we do bad things, then most of us (with some exceptions) understand that these actions could have negative consequences. When sudden, bad events happen that we are not responsible for, that are out of our control, and that are out of the range of normal human experience, then these events challenge our view of the world as a safe and predictable place (and the concept that our actions influence outcomes). Dynamics of this nature are important to remember when considering factors that may protect against emotional/moral injury or facilitate healing. As noted above, one of the factors that helps to protect and heal the emotional trauma and moral injury from distressing life events is religion; and it is time to address this directly.

Religious belief, practices such as prayer, and involvement in religious community help people to pick up the pieces of a shattered world and enable them to reconstruct one that is once again stable, safe, and predictable, in which he or she believes it is possible to have control over things that happen (or no longer needs to have control). Finding meaning in traumatic events is crucial in order to reconstruct a life where survival is possible and desirable (Gibbs, 1989). The Christian scriptures say that "all things work together for good to them that love God, to them who are the called according to his purpose" (Romans 8:28, KJV). In the Jewish scriptures there is a verse that says "For I HaShem thy God hold thy right hand, who say unto thee: 'Fear not, I help thee'" (Isaiah 41:13, Jewish Publication Society Bible). These are powerful promises to the Christian or Jewish believer, and there are many more promises of this kind contained in the core scriptures of every major religious tradition (see Qur'an 42:26, 30–32; Pali Tipitaka, Dhammapada 190–191; Bhagavad Gita 4:7). Helping people to cope with difficult times is a function that religion has served throughout the ages.

Religion helps to explain and give meaning to events, and having an explanation for a traumatic event (whether or not it is the right explanation) helps people to cope better. Such explanations provide reassurance that the event is not completely random, senseless, and uncontrollable, and that actions are possible to avoid it in the future. For example, consider the tropical cyclone Martin that in 1997 devastated much of the Cook

Islands in the South Pacific (Taylor, 1998, 1999). The 23,000 islanders that make up this community were on the whole deeply religious. In the aftermath, conflict arose between local clergy and trauma therapists who came to the islands to help. The clergy (and even local politicians) explained that the cyclone was punishment for the population's departure from the paths of righteousness, attributing the disaster to the community's failure to attend church regularly, to their working on Sundays, and to excessive focus on the island's pearl industry. Therapists were aghast at these explanations, believing that this approach was not helpful to those grieving over their dead and attempting to cope with losses, and worried that this response might further impair the sense of security and self-esteem of survivors. Whether the religious community's approach, one that offered a clear explanation for the event and distinct rituals for dealing with it, was better or worse than what therapists had to offer was not examined. However, observers did note that Cook Island residents showed remarkable resilience in the face of this event. Anecdotal descriptions of second-hand reports are one thing, whereas systematic research is quite another.

Systematic research

Literally hundreds of qualitative and quantitative studies conducted with people undergoing almost every imaginable traumatic event have found that religion is often where people turn to find solace and hope. I review a few of these studies here and refer the reader elsewhere for a more comprehensive review (Koenig, 2006).

War

In a study of 115 women in northern Israel during the 2006 war with Lebanon, researchers found that "psalm recitation" was associated with significantly lower anxiety among the 33 women who chose to remain in this region despite Hezbollah Katyusha attacks (Sosis & Handwerker, 2011). Similarly, in a qualitative study of 17 Iranian war veterans who had been poisoned by mustard gas during the Iran–Iraq conflict in the 1980s, investigators found that the primary way of coping was through religious beliefs and practices (Hassankhani et al., 2010).

Terrorism

A survey of the U.S. population during the week after the 9/11 terrorist attacks found that the most common way that Americans coped with anxiety and fear was by "turning to religion" (90%), which was second only to "talking with others" (Schuster et al., 2001). Bible sales rose by 27% and 60% of Americans attended a religious or memorial service during the weekend afterward (Biema, 2001). In fact, Gallup Polls indicated that 71% of the U.S. population said that religion was having an increasing influence on their life, a figure which exceeded all previous figures since 1957 when the question was first asked (Newport, 2013). However, three months later – when anxiety levels decreased – religious interest and activity fell back to baseline.

Rape

Studying a nationally representative sample of 3,543 women veterans who used Veterans Administration (VA) ambulatory care, researchers found that religious involvement was associated with both better mental health and less depression among those who had experienced sexual assault (23%) during their time in the military (Chang et al., 2001). Similarly, in a longitudinal study of 2,427 male veterans, frequent religious attendance and greater subjective religiosity predicted better mental health and less depression among those reporting sexual assault (4%) (Chang et al., 2003). More recently, researchers interviewed 103 female rape survivors living in Long Beach, California (Ahrens et al., 2010). Religious coping was common among the 100 participants who believed in God. The most common practice was turning to religion to find meaning, solace, and support; this was followed by attending religious services and providing help to other church members. Those who used these positive forms of religious coping experienced higher levels of psychological well-being and lower levels of depression, assessed using standard scales of these constructs.

Hurricanes

Hurricane Hugo hit the south-eastern U.S. in 1989 causing 61 fatalities in the Caribbean and South Carolina, left nearly 100,000 people homeless, and resulted in US$10 billion in damage. The most frequent coping strategies were talking about their experiences (95%), humor (82%), turning to religion (74%), and helping others get through it (47%) (Weinrich et al., 1990). More recently, researchers examined the relationship between religious coping and mental health among survivors of Hurricane Katrina, finding that positive religious coping was associated with less PTSD, less depression, better quality of life, and less alcohol use (Hensleea et al., 2015). Similar findings have been reported by other researchers who reported that positive forms of religious coping led to greater post-traumatic growth in 386 low-income mothers who survived Katrina (Chan & Rhodes, 2013).

Tornadoes

In a study of 42 survivors of tornadoes that hit northern Florida in the 1980s, researchers reported that many indicated their religious beliefs and practices helped them to cope with and make sense of the destruction of their homes and businesses. These activities involved reading the Bible, reminding themselves to be grateful for what they had and for being alive, prayer, and going to church (North et al., 1989). More recent studies of tornado and wild fire survivors have reported similar findings demonstrating that turning to religion for comfort when trauma strikes is as common today as it was 30 years ago (Afifi et al., 2014; P. A. Miller et al., 2012).

Earthquakes

On January 26, 2001, the Gujarat earthquake in northwest India killed 20,000 people, injured another 167,000, and destroyed nearly 400,000 homes. Survivors who believed that discharging their duties (karma) would lead them to peace and harmony with nature adapted more quickly and experienced greater healing (Priya, 2002). Likewise, following the New Zealand earthquake that nearly demolished Christchurch in 2011, religious faith increased among those directly affected by the earthquake, despite a previous decline in religious faith among those elsewhere in the country, providing evidence that secular people turn to religion at times of natural disaster (Sibley & Bulbulia, 2012). Among those affected by the earthquake who indicated a loss of religious faith, however, there was a significant decline in health status.

Floods

After the 1993 Midwest floods when the Missouri and Mississippi Rivers overflowed their banks destroying hundreds of farms and houses, researchers examined how 209 church members coped (Smith et al., 2000). Many reported that religious stories, sermons, the fellowship of church members, and strength from God helped them to cope with the devastation brought on by the flood. Many found solace in being able to save their church building. For example, a rabbit – whom they named Noah – found refuge from the flood waters by escaping behind the sandbags that surrounded the church. They said the rabbit helped remind them that God was present and would get them through this difficult period.

Religion and mental health

There is a large and growing volume of research suggesting that those who are more religious, whether undergoing traumatic stress or not, experience better mental health and greater resilience. In a period of only 10 years, from 2001–2010, the research base on religion/spirituality (R/S) and health nearly tripled from 1,200 studies to over 3,300 (80% examining mental health) (Koenig et al., 2012). For example, among 326 studies that examined relationships between R/S and well-being, life satisfaction, or happiness, 256 (79%) found positive associations (<1% reported lower well-being). Of 40 studies that examined relationships between R/S and hope, three-quarters (73%) reported positive associations. Of 45 studies that examined relationships between R/S and meaning or purpose, 42 (93%) reported significant positive links.

Besides generating positive emotions, R/S also appears to neutralize negative ones – especially in stressed populations. One meta-analysis of research on religiosity and depression found that the effects were about 50% larger in stressed groups (Smith et al., 2003). Overall, of 444 studies examining quantitative relationships between R/S and depression, 272 (61%) reported less depression or faster recovery from depression (6% reporting the opposite). Of 141 studies examining relationships between R/S and attitudes toward suicide, suicidal thoughts, suicide attempts, or completed suicide, 106 (75%) reported inverse relationships (3% reporting the opposite). Recent research suggests that religious involvement may help to reverse the pathological changes in the brain associated with being at high risk for depressive disorder (Miller et al., 2014), and contemporary research from the Nurses' Health Study suggests dramatically lower rates of suicide and depression rates among women who are more involved in faith community activities (Koenig, 2016; Li et al., 2016a; VanderWeele et al., 2016), as well as lower all-cause mortality, and lower mortality from cardiovascular disease and cancer specifically (Li et al., 2016b), and the biological mechanisms involved (Hill et al., 2016; Koenig et al., 2016).

The findings are even more striking for substance abuse, which often follows traumatic stress. Of 278 studies that examined relationships between R/S and alcohol use, abuse, and dependence, inverse relationships were reported in 240 (86%) (vs. 1% reporting positive relationships) (Koenig et al., 2012). Of 185 studies examining relationships between drug use/abuse and R/S involvement, 155 (84%) reported inverse relationships (vs. 1% reporting positive relationships). Thus, there is growing research suggesting a connection between religious involvement and better mental and physical health.

Religion and PTSD

With regard to PTSD, much research has examined links with R/S involvement, suggesting *both* greater resilience and greater vulnerability in the face of severe trauma among those who are more R/S. In a study of 1,385 veterans from the Vietnam War (95%), Korean War or World War II treated in VA outpatient or inpatient PTSD programs, researchers examined relationships between traumatic stress, PTSD, change in religious faith as a result of wartime experiences, and use of VA mental health services (Fontana & Rosenheck, 2004). Results indicated that a weakened religious faith (sometimes called spiritual injury) was one of the most powerful predictors of VA mental health service use, even after controlling for severity of PTSD symptoms and social support. In fact, use of mental health services was driven more by unrecognized spiritual injury than by clinical symptoms or by social factors. Investigators concluded that pastoral counseling should become a central part of the treatment program for PTSD patients.

Spiritual struggles are common in those with PTSD (Fontana & Rosenheck, 2004; Witvliet et al., 2004; Currier et al., 2014), and PTSD symptoms have been significantly and positively associated with alienation from God, religious rifts, religious fear, and religious guilt (Currier et al., 2014). In contrast, post-traumatic growth (PTG) is significantly and positively associated with spiritual practices (Ogden et al., 2011). Recent studies reinforce these earlier findings. One survey of 3,157 U.S. veterans found that spirituality/religion was the second strongest predictor of overall PTG, stronger than any other psychological or social measure (Tsai et al., 2015). A second prospective study of 532 veterans with severe PTSD found that those with spiritual resources had better outcomes during an inpatient treatment program (Currier et al., 2015). In contrast, spiritual struggles in that study were associated with worse PTSD outcomes, as others have likewise reported (Witvliet et al., 2004; Ogden et al., 2011; Currier et al., 2014).

Given these many earlier and new findings (L. Miller et al., 2012; Ford & Hill, 2012; Kleiman & Liu, 2014; Miller et al., 2014), investigators have begun to consider developing religious/spiritual interventions to treat those with emotional disorders, particularly depression (Koenig, 2012), substance abuse (Humphreys et al., 2014), and traumatic stress (Koenig et al., 2017).

Interventions for traumatic stress

If many people suffering from traumatic life experiences find comfort in religious beliefs and religious involvement is related to less depression, lower anxiety, and better mental health then why not develop interventions that utilize individuals' religious beliefs in treatment? Cognitive-behavioral approaches are the most common types of psychotherapy now used to treat emotional disorders and traumatic stress in particular. This therapy can be adapted so that it utilizes a person's religious resources to boost the therapeutic effects. We have recently developed a form of religiously integrated cognitive behavioral therapy (RCBT) to treat depression in those with chronic medical illness (Pearce et al., 2015), and have demonstrated its effectiveness in comparison to conventional CBT, especially in highly religious individuals (Koenig et al., 2015). Religiously integrated CBT could be easily modified to treat persons suffering from depression, anxiety, or PTSD resulting from natural disasters, war, terrorism, rape, or other severe traumatic conditions, and we are now working on such a treatment (Koenig et al., 2017).

Spiritually oriented cognitive processing therapy (SOCPT)

SOCPT is a version of cognitive processing therapy (CPT), the most common evidence-based psychological treatment for PTSD (Difede et al., 2014). More than 2,300 Veterans Administration (VA) clinicians have been trained in CPT and 1,500 in prolonged exposure (PE) therapy (Karlin et al., 2010; Eftekhari et al., 2013). In fact, the VA has mandated that veterans with PTSD receive either CPT or PE (McHugh and Barlow, 2010). Unfortunately, these treatments seldom address the issue of "moral injury" (particularly the spiritual aspects) that frequently accompany PTSD. It should not be surprising, then, that despite the VA mandate, less than 10% of veterans with PTSD have completed a course in either CPT or PE (Seal et al., 2010; Shiner et al., 2012; Mott et al., 2014).

One reason for failure to complete therapy may be that neither CPT nor PE specifically addresses the spiritual struggles that often accompany PTSD or intentionally utilizes a person's religious faith to address both the spiritual and the psychological aspects of moral injury. Those with moral injury view themselves as immoral, irredeemable, and un-repairable, or struggle with their faith and believe they live in an immoral world, which may interfere with PTSD treatment unless addressed (Currier et al., 2015). Would it not seem logical that a spiritual/religious treatment that targets moral injury would be more effective than secular approaches that tend to ignore religious values and ethical principles? This may be especially true for those who are religious (Worthington & Langberg, 2012). The long-standing conflict between experts in religion and mental health, however, has created a divide between these professionals who address mental health issues using different approaches (Freud, 1927). If there is any doubt about such a division, consider the findings of a systematic review of the religious content of the *Diagnostic and Statistical Manual of Mental Disorders* that found nearly one-quarter of all cases of mental illness used religious descriptions to illustrate them (Larson et al., 1993). Clergy, who represent a major first-line treatment for mental health problems in the community (Weaver, 1995), may be reluctant to refer members of their congregation to mental health professionals or support the treatment offered, especially if it involves psychotherapy that seeks to alter beliefs and attitudes (which CBT and CPT attempt to do).

SOCPT, however, addresses the problem of moral injury by taking both a psychological and religious/spiritual approach. This form of therapy considers religious/spiritual beliefs and practices as *resources* to combat the moral injury that may be present in those with traumatic stress. Because moral injury may stand directly in the pathway between the traumatic stressful event and the development of PTSD, we have proposed that by utilizing spiritual resources to address moral injury SOCPT will help to relieve PTSD symptoms and the comorbidity associated with it (depression, anxiety, substance abuse, relationship problems, work-related problems, and disability).

How exactly does SOCPT address issues of moral injury? SOCPT is a manual-based 12-session treatment delivered over six weeks that corrects erroneous interpretations of trauma by focusing on cognitive restructuring using clients' religious resources (i.e., religious beliefs, practices, scriptures, values, and motivations) to challenge maladaptive thinking patterns. Religious concepts of mercy, grace, repentance, forgiveness, spiritual surrender, prayer/contemplation, divine justice, hope, and divine affirmations are discussed in order to reverse negative emotional responses such as shame, guilt, anger, and humiliation – painful emotions that often prevent exposure to memories of the trauma and promote avoidance. These techniques are supplemented by powerful rituals involving religious confession, making amends, giving and receiving forgiveness, religious song, and emersion within a supportive faith community. Role models are also presented from the person's religious scriptures. Many great religious figures suffered severe trauma, were almost killed, or were forced to engage in war and combat to survive – including Job, Abraham, Moses, Joshua, David (author of the Psalms, most of which involved David's coping with traumatic experiences from being pursued by Saul), the Prophet Mohammad (as he fought for the establishment of monotheism in a polytheistic Arabic culture), and Lord Krishna (who in the Bhagavad Gita had to encourage and support Arjuna to fight for moral and ethical causes that were threatening to destroy his people). These are role models with whom traumatized individuals can easily identify.

There will be six versions of SOCPT adapted to the specific spiritual and religious beliefs of the client. On the one hand, there will be a more general spiritual version that broadly addresses spiritual issues among those who are spiritual but not religious. On the other hand, there will be five religious versions for Christians, Jews, Muslims, Hindus, and Buddhists, developed in consultation with experts in these traditions – following the model that we have developed for religiously integrated cognitive behavioral therapy.

Next steps

Our goal is to ultimately compare the effectiveness of SOCPT to standard secular CPT in a randomized clinical trial in order to establish the evidence base for this treatment. Given the cost of such a clinical trial, and the pilot data that are necessary to successfully compete for funding support, we have begun a series of surveys of veterans (Durham VA, San Antonio VA, Los Angeles VA) and active duty service members (Fort Gordon and Fort Bragg) with PTSD to: (1) identify the prevalence of moral injury symptoms; (2) develop an objective, reliable multi-dimensional measure of moral injury symptoms; (3) examine the role that spiritual resources play as a moderator between moral injury and PTSD symptoms/comorbidity (see Figure 4.1); and (4) determine whether a spiritual oriented

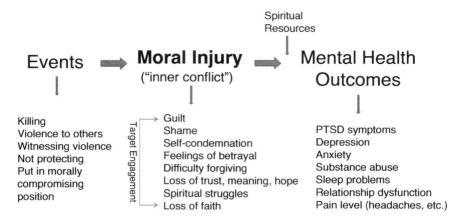

Figure 4.1 Hypothesized relationships between traumatic life events, moral injury, spiritual resources, and mental health outcomes.

intervention for engaging moral injury would be acceptable to those with PTSD symptoms. These studies, without funding support, are now in the field to gather the necessary pilot data prior to applying for support to conduct a relatively small randomized clinical trial preliminary to a much larger multi-site study.

Conclusions and further resources

Many people who undergo traumatic life experiences turn to religion for comfort and hope. The above review suggests that religious beliefs and practices may be effective in this regard. The time is ripe for the development of interventions that utilize the religious and spiritual beliefs of traumatized persons to facilitate their healing. We are now in the process of developing a spiritually oriented form of cognitive processing therapy to target moral injury in those who have experienced severe trauma, and are doing pilot studies in veterans and active duty service members prior to conducting a randomized clinical trial that we hope will provide the evidence base for such a treatment. Our website at Duke University describes research training programs, manuals and therapist/client workbooks for conducting religiously integrated therapies, and the latest research publications coming out of these projects (CSTH, 2016). Resources on both conducting research (Koenig, 2011) and integrating spirituality into practice (Koenig, 2013) are also available here, as well as for staying updated on the latest research being published in this area (Crossroads, 2008–2016).

References

Adachi, K., Bertman, S., Corr, C., Cory, J., Doka, K., Gilbert, K., Gjertsen, E., Glassock, G., Hall, C., Hansson, R., Jaramillo, I., Kallenberg, K., Lattanzi-Licht, M., Lickiss, N., Oechsle, P., Oltjenbruns, K. A., Papadatou, D., Parkes, C. M., Schuurman, D., & Worden, W. (2002). Assumptions and principles about psychosocial aspects of disasters. *Death Studies*, 26(6): 449–462.

Afifi, W. A., Afifi, T. D., & Merrill, A. (2014). Uncertainty and control in the context of a category-five tornado. *Research in Nursing and Health*, 37(5): 358–366.

Ahrens, C. E., Abeling, S., Ahmad, S., & Hinman, J. (2010). Spirituality and well-being: The relationship between religious coping and recovery from sexual assault. *Journal of Interpersonal Violence*, 25(7): 1242–1263.

Biema, D. (2001). Faith after the fall. *Time Magazine*, 158(16) October 8. http://content.time.com/time/magazine/article/0,9171,1000951,00.html

Chan, C. S., & Rhodes, J. E. (2013). Religious coping, posttraumatic stress, psychological distress, and posttraumatic growth among female survivors four years after Hurricane Katrina. *Journal of Traumatic Stress*, 26: 257–265.

Chang, B. H., Skinner, K. M., & Boehmer, U. (2001). Religion and mental health among women veterans with sexual assault experience. *International Journal of Psychiatry in Medicine*, 31(1): 77–95.

Chang, B. H., Skinner, K. M., Zhou, C., & Kazis, L. E. (2003). The relationship between sexual assault, religiosity and mental health among male veterans. *International Journal of Psychiatry in Medicine*, 33(3): 223–239.

Crossroads. (2008–2017). *A Monthly e-Newsletter of the Center for Spirituality, Theology and Health*. Durham, NC: Duke University Medical Center. See website: www.spiritualityandhealth.duke.edu/index.php/publications/crossroads. Accessed 8/26/2016.

CSTH. (2016). *Center for Spirituality, Theology and Health, Duke University Medical Center*. Durham, NC: Duke University Medical Center. www.spiritualityandhealth.duke.edu/. Accessed 8/26/2016.

Currier, J. M., Drescher, K. D., & Harris, J. I. (2014). Spiritual functioning among veterans seeking residential treatment for PTSD: A matched control group study. *Spirituality in Clinical Practice*, 1(1): 3–15.

Currier, J. M., Holland, J. M., & Drescher, K. D. (2015). Spirituality factors in the prediction of outcomes of PTSD treatment for U.S. military veterans. *Journal of Traumatic Stress*, 28(1): 57–64.

Difede, J., Olden, M., & Cukor, J. (2014). Evidence-based treatment of post-traumatic stress disorder. *Annual Review of Medicine*, 65: 319–332.

Eftekhari, A., Ruzek, J. I., Crowley, J. J., Rosen, C. S., Greenbaum, M. A., & Karlin, B. E. (2013). Effectiveness of national implementation of prolonged exposure therapy in veterans affairs care. *JAMA Psychiatry (Archives of General Psychiatry)*, 70: 949–955.

Fontana, A., & Rosenheck, R. (2004). Trauma, change in strength of religious faith, and mental health service use among veterans treated for PTSD. *Journal of Nervous & Mental Disease*, 192: 579–584.

Ford, J. A., & Hill, T. D. (2012). Religiosity and adolescent substance use: Evidence from the national survey on drug use and health. *Substance Use and Misuse*, 47(7): 787–798.

Freud, S. (1927). Future of an illusion. In *Standard Edition of the Complete Psychological Works of Sigmund Freud*, J. Strachey, editor and translator London: Hogarth Press. 1962, p. 43.

Galea, S., Ahern, J., Resnick, H., Kilpatrick, D., Bucuvalas, M., Gold, J., & Vlahov, D. (2002). Psychological sequelae of the September 11 terrorist attacks in New York City. *New England Journal of Medicine*, 346(13): 982–987.

Gibbs, M. S. (1989). Factors in the victim that mediate between disaster and psychopathology: A review. *Journal of Traumatic Stress*, 2(4): 489–514.

Hassankhani, H., Taleghani, F., Mills, J., Birks, M., Francis, K., & Ahmadi, F. (2010). Being hopeful and continuing to move ahead: Religious coping in Iranian chemical warfare poisoned veterans, a qualitative study. *Journal of Religion and Health*, 49(3): 311–321.

Hensleea, A. M., Coffey, S. F., Schumacher, J. A., Tracy, M., Norris, F., & Galea, S. (2015). Religious coping and psychological and behavioral adjustment after Hurricane Katrina. *Journal of Psychology*, 149(6): 630–642.

Hill, T. D., Ellison, C. G., Burdette, A. M., Taylor, J., & Friedman, K. L. (2016). Dimensions of religious involvement and leukocyte telomere length. *Social Science and Medicine*, 163: 168–175. doi: 10.1016/j.socscimed.2016.04.032.

Hoge, C. W., Castro, C. A., Messer, S. C., McGurk, D., Cotting, D. I., & Koffman, R. L. (2004). Combat duty in Iraq and Afghanistan, mental health problems, and barriers to care. *New England Journal of Medicine*, 351(1): 13–224.

Humphreys, K., Blodgett, J. C., & Wagner, T. H. (2014). Estimating the efficacy of alcoholics anonymous without self-selection bias: An instrumental variables re-analysis of randomized clinical trials. *Alcoholism: Clinical and Experimental Research*, 38(11): 2688–2694.

Karlin, B. E., Ruzek, J. I., Chard, K. M., Eftekhari, A., Monson, C. M., Hembree, E. A., & Foa, E. B. (2010). Dissemination of evidence-based psychological treatments for posttraumatic stress disorder in the Veterans Health Administration. *Journal of Traumatic Stress*, 23: 663–673.

Kleiman, E. M., & Liu, R. T. (2014). Prospective prediction of suicide in a nationally representative sample: Religious service attendance as a protective factor. *British Journal of Psychiatry*, 204: 262–266.

Koenig, H. G. (2006). *In the Wake of Disaster: Religious Responses to Terrorism and Catastrophe*. Philadelphia, PA: Templeton Foundation Press.

Koenig, H. G. (2011). *Spirituality and Health Research: Methods, Measurement, Statistics, and Resources*. Conshohocken, PA: Templeton Foundation Press.

Koenig, H. G. (2012). Religious vs. conventional psychotherapy for major depression in patients with chronic medical illness: Rationale, methods, and preliminary results. *Depression Research and Treatment, Article ID 460419*, doi:10.1155/2012/460419.

Koenig, H. G.. (2013). *Spirituality in Patient Care*, 3rd ed. Conshohocken, PA: Templeton Foundation Press.

Koenig, H. G. (2016). Association of religious involvement and suicide (editorial). *JAMA Psychiatry (Archives of General Psychiatry)*, 73(8): 775–776.

Koenig, H. G., Boucher, N. A., Oliver, R. J. P., Youssef, N., Mooney, S. R., Currier, J. M., & Pearce, M. P. (2017). Rationale for spiritually oriented cognitive processing therapy for moral injury in active duty military and veterans with posttraumatic stress disorder. *Journal of Nervous and Mental Disease*, 205(2): 147–153.

Koenig, H. G., King, D. E., & Carson, V. B. (2012). *Handbook of Religion and Health*, 2nd ed. New York: Oxford University Press.

Koenig, H. G., Nelson, B., Shaw, S. F., Saxena, S., & Cohen, H. J. (2016). Religious involvement and telomere length in women family caregivers. *Journal of Nervous & Mental Disease*, 204(1): 36–42.

Koenig, H. G., Pearce, M. J., Nelson, B., Shaw, S. F., Robins, C. J., Daher, N., Cohen, H. J., Berk, L. S., Belinger, D., Pargament, K. I., Rosmarin, D. H., Vasegh, S., Kristeller, J., Juthani, N., Nies, D., & King, M. B. (2015). Religious vs. conventional cognitive-behavioral therapy for major depression in persons with chronic medical illness. *Journal of Nervous and Mental Disease*, 203(4): 243–251.

Larson, D. B., Thielman, S. B., Greenwold, M. A., Lyons, J. S., Post, S. G., Sherrill, K. A., Wood, G. G., & Larson, S. S. (1993). Religious content in the DSM-III-R glossary of technical terms. *American Journal of Psychiatry*, 150: 1884–1885.

Li, S., Okereke, O. I., Chang, S. C., Kawachi, I., & VanderWeele, T. J. (2016a). Religious service attendance and lower depression among women – A prospective cohort study. *Annals of Behavioral Medicine*, July 16, E-pub ahead of press.

Li, S., Stampfer, M. J., Williams, D. R., & VanderWeele, T. J. (2016b). Association of religious service attendance with mortality among women. *JAMA Internal Medicine*, 176(6): 777–785.

McFarlane, A. C. (1988). The phenomenology of posttraumatic stress disorders following a natural disaster. *Journal of Nervous & Mental Disease*, 176(1): 22–29.

McHugh, R. K., & Barlow, D. H. (2010). The dissemination and implementation of evidence-based psychological treatments: A review of current efforts. *American Psychologist*, 65: 73–84.

Miller, L., Bansal, R., Wickramaratne, P., Hao, X., Tenke, C. E., Weissman, M. M., & Peterson, B. S. (2014). Neuroanatomical correlates of religiosity and spirituality: A study in adults at high and low familial risk for depression. *JAMA Psychiatry (Archives of General Psychiatry)*, 71(2): 128–135.

Miller, L., Wickramaratne, P., Gameroff, M. J., Sage, M., Tenke, C. E., & Weissman, M. M. (2012). Religiosity and major depression in adults at high risk: A ten-year prospective study. *American Journal of Psychiatry*, 169(1): 89–94.

Miller, P. A., Roberts, N. A., Zamora, A. D., Weber, D. J., Burleson, M. H., Robles, E., & Tinsley, B. J. (2012). Families coping with natural disasters: Lessons from wildfires and tornados. *Qualitative Research in Psychology*, 9: 314–336.

Mott, J. M., Hundt, N. E., Sansgiry, S., Mignogna, J., & Cully, J. A. (2014). Changes in psychotherapy use among veterans with depression, anxiety, and PTSD. *Psychiatric Services*, 65: 106–112.

Newport, F. (2013). Most Americans say religion is losing influence in U.S. (but 75% say American society would be better off if more Americans were religious). *The Gallup Poll*. See website: www.gallup.com/poll/162803/americans-say-religion-losing-influence.aspx# (last accessed 8/26/16).

Norris, F. H., Kaniasty, K., Conrad, M. L., Inman, G. L., & Murphy, A. D. (2002). Placing age differences in cultural context: A comparison of the effects of age on PTSD after disasters in the United States, Mexico, and Poland. *Journal of Clinical Geropsychology*, 8(3): 153–173.

North, C. S., Smith, E. M., McCool, R. E., & Lightcap, P. E. (1989). Acute post-disaster coping and adjustment. *Journal of Traumatic Stress*, 2(3): 353–360.

Ogden, H., Harris, J. I., Erbes, C., Engdahl, B., Olson, R., Winskowski, A. M., & McMahill, J. (2011). Religious functioning and trauma outcomes among combat veterans. *Counselling and Spirituality*, 30: 71–89.

Pearce, M. J., Koenig, H. G., Robins, C. J., Nelson, B., Shaw, S. F., Cohen, H. J., & King, M. B. (2015). Religiously-integrated cognitive behavioral therapy: A new method of treatment for major depression in patients with chronic medical illness. *Psychotherapy*, 52(1): 56–66.

Perry, R. W., & Lindell, M. K. (2003). Understanding citizen response to disasters with implications for terrorism. *Journal of Contingencies & Crisis Management*, 11(2): 49–60.

Priya, K. R. (2002). Suffering and healing among the survivors of Bhuj earthquake. *Psychological Studies*, 47(1–3): 106–112.

Rubonis, A. V., & Bickman, L. (1991). Psychological impairment in the wake of disaster: The disaster-psychopathology relationship. *Psychological Bulletin*, 109(3): 384–399.

Schuster, M. A., Stein, B. D., Jaycox, L. H., Collins, R. L., Marshall, G. N., Elliott, M. N., Zhou, A. J., Kanouse, D. E., Morrison, J. L., & Berry, S. H. (2001). A national survey of stress reactions after the September 11, 2001, terrorist attacks. *New England Journal of Medicine*, 345: 1507–1512.

Seal, K. H., Maguen, S., Cohen, B., Gima, K. S., Metzler, T. J., Ren, L., Bertenthal, D., & Marmar, C. R. (2010). VA mental health services utilization in Iraq and Afghanistan veterans in the first year of receiving new mental health diagnoses. *Journal of Traumatic Stress*, 23: 5–16.

Shiner, B., D'Avolio, L. W., Nguyen, T. M., Zayed, M. H., Young-Xu, Y., Desai, R. A., Schnurr, P. P., Fiore, L. D., & Watts, B. V. (2012). Measuring use of evidence based psychotherapy for posttraumatic stress disorder. *Administration and Policy in Mental Health and Mental Health Services Research*, 40: 311–318.

Sibley, C. G., & Bulbulia, J. (2012). Faith after an earthquake: A longitudinal study of religion and perceived health before and after the 2011 Christchurch New Zealand earthquake. *PLoS One*, 7(12): e49648.

Smith, B. W., Pargament, K. I., Brant, C., & Oliver, J. M. (2000). Noah revisited: Religious coping by church members and the impact of the 1993 Midwest flood. *Journal of Community Psychology*, 28(2): 169–186.

Smith, T. B., McCullough, M. E., & Poll, J. (2003). Religiousness and depression: Evidence for a main effect and the moderating influence of stressful life events. *Psychological Bulletin*, 129(4): 614–636.

Sosis, R., & Handwerker, W. P. (2011). Psalms and coping with uncertainty: Religious Israeli women's responses to the 2006 Lebanon War. *American Anthropologist*, 113(1): 40–55.

Taylor, A. J. W. (1998). Observations from a cyclone stress/trauma assignment in the Cook Islands. *Traumatology*, 4(1): 30–40.

Taylor, A. J. W. (1999). Value conflict arising from a disaster. *Australasian Journal of Disaster & Trauma Studies*, 3(2): NP. (www.massey.ac.nz/~trauma/issues/1999-2/taylor.htm, accessed 8/26/2016).

Tsai, J., El-Gabalawy, Sledge W. H., Southwick, S. M., & Pietrzak, R. H. (2015). Post-traumatic growth among veterans in the USA: Results from the National Health and Resilience in Veterans Study. *Psychological Medicine*, 45: 165–179.

VanderWeele, T. J., Li, S., Tsai, A. C., & Kawachi, I. (2016). Suicide and religious service attendance among US women. *JAMA Psychiatry (Archives of General Psychiatry)*, 73(8): 845–851.

Weaver, A. J. (1995). Has there been a failure to prepare and support parish-based clergy in their role as front-line community mental health workers? A review. *Journal of Pastoral Care*, 49: 129–149.

Weinrich, S., Hardin, S. B., & Johnson, M. (1990). Nurses respond to hurricane Hugo victims' disaster stress. *Archives of Psychiatric Nursing*, 4: 195–205.

Witvliet, C. V. O., Phillips, K. A., Feldman, M. E., & Beckham, J. C. (2004). Post-traumatic mental and physical health correlates of forgiveness and religious coping in military veterans. *Journal of Traumatic Stress*, 17: 269–273.

Worthington, E. L., Jr, & Langberg, D. (2012). Religious considerations and self-forgiveness in treating complex trauma and moral injury in present and former soldiers. *Journal of Psychology and Theology*, 40(4): 274–288.

Chapter 5

Killing the human being within
Irenaeus and moral injury

Fr John Behr

In his book, *Killing from the Inside Out: Moral Injury and Just War*, Robert E. Meagher draws upon an incident in Sophocles' play *Philoctetes* to illustrate the untold damage done by war to those called upon to fight other people's battles: Odysseus, a man with a "shabby slit-eyed soul," talks the young Neoptolemus into betraying his high moral ground to become an instrument of Odysseus's wiles. Later, looking back, Neoptolemus realizes that, although he survived, he is nevertheless wounded, through a self-inflicted wound, and, as Meagher characterizes it, "the malaise he suffers is that of moral injury, which he self-diagnoses and describes in these timeless words: 'All is disgust when one leaves his own nature and does things that misfit it.'"[1] The "misfitting" deed, in this case, is that of killing another human being, which, even when done in the context of war, remains murder and leaves an indelible imprint, a moral injury, upon the one who committed the act, even if done for a higher cause, and which is not only not wiped clean, but actually exacerbated when defended in the name of a "just war," as Meagher demonstrates so forcefully.

However, there is also another lesson to be learnt from the Greek poets, another way in which the human being might be killed from within; and this is taught by no less than Odysseus himself, though he, ever cunning, avoids the danger. It is exemplified in his decision not to remain with Calypso, to live the untroubled, immortal life of a god with a god, and so transcend his human nature, but to instead return to Penelope, to live as a human in human society, with all the vulnerability, tribulations, and certainty of death that this entails. What justifies this decision? What gives value to, or what value is there in, weakness, suffering, and ultimately death?

Martha Nussbaum raises this question in her essay "Transcending Humanity."[2] She accepts that choosing the life of a god is indeed a desirable and intelligible choice, for such a life does not suffer from any of the constraints that make human life transitory, limited, precarious, and often miserable. Moreover, alongside such negative motivation, there is the positive attraction of transcendence itself. Following a philosophical tradition at least as old as Xenophanes, which held that the sole activity of a divine being was thinking, Plato and those who followed him maintained that the highest, and most proper, activity for human beings was philosophical contemplation. Although we might resemble the lower forms of life, and seem to live in subjection to nature and fate, there is part of us, Plato insisted, that is "divine, immortal, intellectual, unitary, indissoluble, ever unchanging,"[3] and it is this rational element that must govern the rest of our being, thereby securing us against the vicissitudes of fate and bodily life. Similarly, the later philosophical schools of the Hellenistic period, with the possible exception of Skepticism, offered various techniques, based on the domination of reason, for the formation and shaping of the self. Their claim to be *the* "art of life" asserts that they can do more than any other source of *logos* in healing and governing the soul. In contrast to superstition and popular philosophy, where the outcome is always uncertain, true philosophy claims "to remove that element of darkness and uncontrol from human life, making *tuche* subordinate to an intelligent and intelligible *techne*," so offering its adherents the possibility of a "*godlike* life."[4]

However, Odysseus did not stay with Calypso, but chose rather to return to his mortal bride. To have remained with Calypso would have brought Odysseus's story to an end: he would no longer have the opportunity to demonstrate those virtues and achievements which are characteristically human, nor indeed be truly in love, for when even the gods fall in love it is with mortal humans.[5] The Greek poets, according to Nussbaum, understood the fact that "part of the peculiar beauty of *human* excellence just *is* its vulnerability."[6] Human beings are not gods, neither the transcendently anthropomorphized Olympians nor the purely intellectual divinity of the philosophical tradition. Accordingly, the truly good life for human beings is not the immortal life of the Olympians, nor one of contemplation (an acceptable activity when subordinated to other specifically human ends), but one that recognizes and accepts the full range of human values. Nussbaum finds such a position elaborated most comprehensively and consistently in Aristotle. Philosophizing within the confines of the "appearances" of things, Aristotle acknowledged that central human values, such as courage, moderation, generosity, and friendship, can only be found in a life which is subject to risk, need, and limitation; as Nussbaum puts it "Their nature *and* their goodness are constituted by the fragile nature of human life."[7]

Although her work is not concerned with Christian theology, the centrality of this insight is fundamental to Christianity, a point which is recognized, in passing, by Nussbaum:

> For Christianity seems to grant that in order to imagine a god who is truly superior, truly worthy of worship, truly and fully just, we must imagine a god who is human as well as divine, a god who has actually lived out the non-transcendent life and understands it in the only way that it can be understood, by suffering and death.[8]

The life and death of Christ within this world not only endorses the value of the human situation, but refocuses and holds our attention on the world in which we live. What is involved here is more than, in Nussbaum's words, the "thought experiment" which concluded that "a perfect being would perform intellectual contemplation."[9] What is only imagined by Nussbaum is, however, a key conviction for Christian theology, that through a death witnessing to Christ Christians attain to the full status of being human, a son of God in the crucified and risen Son of God.

No one has thought this through more or better than Irenaeus of Lyons in the late second century, who can justifiably be called the first father of the Christian tradition. Living in an age of martyrdom, rather than the supposed peace of a Christian imperial epoch with all the compromises it entails (for as Meagher demonstrates, a state always operates with a view to its own interests, justifying its actions even in theological terms), Irenaeus was a witness to the martyrs, understanding their suffering and death in the broad sweep of the economy of God, which he, for the first time in Christian theology, unfolds, from beginning to end, as a single movement embracing both creation and salvation, together, to see in the death of martyrs not a defeat or a victimization, but rather a witness to the creative and salvific work of God.

Earlier, at the beginning of the second century, Ignatius of Antioch, whose writings Irenaeus knows and cites, already intimates this. On his journey to Rome, to be martyred there, Ignatius wrote to the Christians in Rome, imploring them not to interfere with his impending fate:

> Birth-pangs are upon me. Suffer me, my brethren; hinder me not from living, do not wish me to die. ... Suffer me to receive the pure light; when I shall have arrived there, I shall become a human being [ἄνθρωπος]. Suffer me to follow the example of the passion of my God.[10]

Only by willingly suffering death in confession of Christ, who himself willing embraced the Cross, so showing us the free, self-sacrificial love that is the life of God, that is God, is Ignatius born as a living human being.

I have argued elsewhere that the background of this vision lies in the interplay between Genesis and the Gospel of John, already evident in their opening words.[11] While Genesis begins by God speaking everything into existence by a divine *fiat*, "Let it be!", the only work said to be God's own, the purpose and project of God, is not introduced by a divine imperative, but with a subjunctive—"Let us make a human being" (Gen. 1:26)—a work which is not complete until, in the Gospel of John (and only there), Christ goes to the Cross, with Pilate unwittingly stating, "Behold the human being!", to say, as his last words from the Cross, "It is finished" (John 19:5, 30): the project announced at the beginning is completed at the end. For the only work said to be God's own, "to make human beings in our image and likeness" (Gen. 1:26), we, males and females, must give our own "Let it be!" Having come into existence in this world through no choice of our own, we are thrown into an existence which, again whether we like it or not, culminates in death. Yet Christ ascended the Cross, manifesting the life of God, so that "he might destroy him who has the power of death, that is, the devil, and deliver all those who through fear of death were subject to lifelong bondage" (Heb 2:14–15). We now have open to us the possibility of freely choosing, as did Ignatius, to be born (rather than merely coming into existence) into a life lived as self-sacrificial love, a life that is the very being of God, and so become human beings.

The working out of this overarching scope of the economy of God within the framework of the life span of each, and perhaps its implications for the topic of moral injury, are explored in a most intriguing fashion in three chapters of the fourth book of Irenaeus's major work, *Against the Heresies*. In *haer.* 4.37–39, he provides an exposition from Scripture of "the ancient law of human liberty," the fact that "God created the human being free, having, from the beginning, power over himself."[12] Fundamental to his argument is the point that only creatures created with freedom are capable of initiative and response, and only in this way are they capable of changing the mode or fashion of their existence, growing into the immortality of God.

After citing many passages from Scripture to demonstrate human freedom, a freedom which extends to faith (*haer.* 4.37.5), and the corresponding responsibility and accountability that follows on from this, Irenaeus turns to those who would deny this, representing, he claims, the Lord as destitute of power, unable to accomplish what he willed, or as ignorant that some human beings are merely "material," not able to receive immortality. He draws out the presuppositions of his opponents, as a question:

> "But," they say, "he should not have created angels such that they were able to transgress, nor human beings such that they immediately [*statim*] became ungrateful towards him, because they were created rational and capable of examining and judging, and not like irrational or inanimate creatures which are not able to do anything of their own will but are drawn by necessity and force towards the good, with one inclination and one bearing, unable to deviate and without the power of judging, and unable to be anything other than what they were created."
>
> (*haer.* 4.37.6)

Had this been the case, Irenaeus replies, it would have benefited neither God nor human beings: communion with God would not be precious, desired, or sought after; it would be by nature, and not as a result of their own proper endeavour, care, or study. As such, it would be misunderstood and no pleasure would be found in it.

Irenaeus continues by citing Christ's words that "the violent take it by force" (Matt. 11:12) and Paul's exhortation to run the race (1 Cor. 9:24–27) to emphasize the need for struggle, on the grounds that endeavor heightens the appreciation of the gift:

> as it lies with us to love God the more, the Lord has taught and the apostle has handed down that this will happen with struggle, for otherwise this, our good, would be unknown, not being the result of striving.
>
> (*haer.* 4.37.7)

Irenaeus gives an example by way of explanation: as the faculty of seeing is desired more by those who know what it is like to be without sight, so also is health prized more by those who know disease, light by contrast with darkness, and life by death (*haer.* 4.37.7). For Irenaeus, the whole economy, from beginning to end, as symbolized in the example of Jonah (cf. *haer.* 3.20), has been arranged in such a manner that human beings come to know their own weakness, for it is here that they simultaneously know the strength of God (cf. 2 Cor. 12:9), that having known the experience of death they might thereafter hold ever more firmly to the source of life.

A little later, Irenaeus develops this analysis by contrasting two different types of knowledge: that gained, on the one hand, through experience, and that, on the other hand, learned through hearsay (*haer.* 4.39.1). It is, he points out, only through experience that the tongue comes to learn of both bitterness and sweetness, and, likewise, it is only through experience of both good and evil, the latter being disobedience and death, that the mind receives the knowledge (*disciplina*) of the good, that is, obedience to God, which is life for human beings. By experiencing both, and casting off disobedience through repentance, the human being (as in the case of Jonah) becomes ever more tenacious in obedience to God, growing into the fullness of life. The alternative, Irenaeus says dramatically, is that "if anyone shuns the knowledge of both of these, and the twofold perception of knowledge, forgetting himself he destroys the human being."[13] There is no place, in Irenaeus's understanding of the economy of God, for, as Berthouzoz puts it, "an ethics of preventative abstention."[14] The always "mixed" character of our life upon earth is intrinsic to the pedagogy by which we are brought, through the economy, to become human beings.

Returning to *haer.* 4.37.7, Irenaeus continues that the heavenly kingdom will therefore be more precious to those who have known the earthly kingdom, and, if they prize it more, they will also love it more, and loving it more, they will be glorified more by God. He then concludes this section:

God therefore has borne all these things for our sake, in order that, having been instructed through all things, henceforth we may be scrupulous in all things and, having been taught how to love God in accordance with reason, remain in his love, God exhibiting patience [*magnanimitatem*] in regard to the apostasy of the human being, and the human being being taught by it, as the prophet says: "Your own apostasy shall heal you."

(*haer*. 4.37.7; Jer. 2:19)

Irenaeus immediately continues by placing this particular action of God within the economy as a whole:

God, thus, determining all things beforehand for the perfection of the human being, and towards the realization and manifestation of his economies, that goodness may be displayed and righteousness accomplished, and that the Church may be "conformed to the image of his Son" [Rom. 8:29], and that, finally, the human being may be brought to such maturity as to see and comprehend God.

(*haer*. 4.37.7)

Human disobedience, apostasy, and death is, for Irenaeus, inscribed into the very unfolding of the economy; death results from human action, but it is nevertheless a result which is subsumed and transformed within the larger arc of the economy, as it brings the creature made from mud to share in the very life, glory, and power of the Uncreated, so demonstrating the goodness and righteousness of God. Worked out in and through the life of each individual human being, if they should respond with faith and thankfulness, the conclusion is also corporate, for in this way the Church is conformed to Christ as each human being is brought to see God.

In 4.38, Irenaeus analyzes the question with which he began these chapters, but from a different angle. Here he suggests that God could indeed have created the human being perfect or as a "god" from the beginning, for all things are possible to Him. However, he points out, created things simply by virtue of being created are necessarily inferior to the one who created them, they fall short of the perfect to begin with; as created, they are initially "infantile," and so "unaccustomed to and unexercised in perfect conduct" (*haer*. 4.38.1). Using another example, he points out that while it would be possible for a mother to give solid food to her infant, the infant would not benefit from this, "so also, it was possible for God himself to have made the human being perfect from the first, but the human being could not receive this, being as yet an infant" (*haer*. 4.38.1).

This need not be taken to suggest that the infantile state is itself somehow "imperfect," but simply that it has not yet reached the stature to which growth will bring it; an infant may well be born with "perfect" limbs, but will nevertheless be unable to walk.[15] Nor need it suggest that the omnipotence of God is restricted by the nature of that upon which He is working.[16] By definition the created cannot be uncreated, but more importantly the omnipotence of God *is* in fact demonstrated, for Irenaeus, by the way that the created is brought in time to share in the uncreated life of God, a change in the "fashion" of its existence or the mode of its life, which requires preparation and training, for this is what the whole economy, including disobedience and death, effects.

There is, moreover, no end to this process; never becoming uncreated, the perfection of human beings lies, instead, in their continual submission to the creative activity of God, through which they are brought to share in the glory and power of the Uncreated (*haer.* 4.38.3). As Irenaeus puts it, with musical resonance:

> By this order and such rhythms and such a movement the created and fashioned human becomes in the image and likeness of the uncreated God: the Father planning everything well and commanding, the Son executing and performing, and the Spirit nourishing and increasing, and the human being making progress day by day and ascending towards perfection, that is, approaching the Uncreated One. For the Uncreated is perfect, and this is God.

> Now, it was first necessary for the human being to be created;
> and having been created, to increase;
> and having increased, to become an adult;
> and having become an adult, to multiply;
> and having multiplied, to become strong;
> and having been strengthened, to be glorified;
> and being glorified, to see his Master;
> for God is He who is yet to be seen, and the vision of God produces
>   incorruptibility, and "incorruptibility renders one close to God."
>
> (haer. 4.38.3; Wis. 6:19)

Such is the rhythm and movement of human life, which recapitulates the movement of the economy. We can no more escape its pattern or anticipate its conclusion than we can expect a newborn infant to live in an adult manner. "Irrational, therefore, in every way are those who await not the time of increase and ascribe to God the infirmity of their nature," Irenaeus continues, "knowing neither God nor themselves, being insatiable and ungrateful, they are unwilling to be at the outset as they have been created, human beings subject to passions" (*haer.* 4.38.4: *homines passionum capaces*). Wanting "to be gods from the beginning," rather than "at first human, and only then gods" (*se primo quidem hominess, tunc demum dii*), they blame God and show their ingratitude for what He has given them, "even though God has adopted this course out of his pure benevolence."[17]

Irenaeus then cites the two contrasting verses of Psalm 81.6–7 (LXX) to demonstrate this point: "'I said you are gods, sons of the Most High,' but since we could not sustain the power of divinity, he adds, 'you shall die like human beings.'" This, he says,

> sets forth both truths: by his kindness, he graciously gave good and made the human being self-governing like himself, but by his fore-knowledge he knew the weakness of human beings and what would come of it, yet by love and power he conquered the substance of our created nature.[18]

Finally, Irenaeus concludes by sketching out his analysis of the economy of the growth of the human being, in a few brief strokes:

> It was necessary, first, for nature to be manifest; after which, for what was mortal to be conquered and swallowed up by immortality, and the corruptible by incorruptibility, and for the human being to be made in the image and likeness of God, having received the knowledge of good and evil.[19]

Irenaeus takes the words of God in Genesis 3:22—"Behold, the human being has become like one of us, knowing good and evil"—as spoken without any sense of irony, but rather as a statement reflecting just how it is that the creature made from dust, coming to know both good and evil, and rejecting the latter through repentance, becomes a human being in the image and likeness of God.

To become human in this stature, to become a god, cannot be done by setting our own agenda, "wishing to be even now like God." Such an attempt demonstrates an ignorance of all that we have seen: on the one hand, the fact that God has revealed Himself in Christ as the perfect living human being, dying for others, and, on the other hand, the comprehensiveness of the arc of the economy through which the Creator brings his handiwork to this stature, by the created individuals themselves undergoing the long pedagogy of the economy, culminating in their death and resurrection. To become a living human being, a god upon this earth, then, created males and females must allow themselves to be fashioned by God through being open and responsive to His creative activity. Irenaeus concludes these chapters with a beautiful passage, picking up on various themes that are explored throughout his work *Against the Heresies*: the artistic work of the Word of God, the presence of the Spirit, as Water, enabling this formation, and the response of the human being by trusting in God, letting Him be the Creator:

How then will you be a god, when you are not yet made human? How perfect, when only recently begun? How immortal, when in mortal nature you did not obey the Creator? It is necessary for you first to hold the rank of human, and then to participate in the glory of God. For you do not create God, but God creates you. If, then, you are the work of God, await the Hand of God, who does everything at the appropriate time, the appropriate time for you, who are being made. Offer to him your heart, soft and pliable, and retain the shape with which the Fashioner shaped you, having in yourself his Water, lest you turn dry and lose the imprint of his fingers. By guarding this conformation, you will ascend to perfection; the mud in you will be concealed by the art of God. His Hand created your substance; it will gild you, inside and out, with pure gold and silver, and so adorn you that the King himself will desire your beauty. But if, becoming hardened, you reject His art and being ungrateful towards him, because he made you a human being, ungrateful, that is, towards God, you have lost at once both his art and life. For to create is the characteristic of the goodness of God; to be created is characteristic of the nature of the human.

(*haer.* 4.39.2–3)

And so, Irenaeus urges us, we should offer to Him what is ours, "that is, faith in him and subjection," so that we "receive his art and become a perfect work of God." If, on the other hand, he warns us, we don't accept this, not believing in Him and fleeing from His Hands, "the cause of imperfection will be in you who did not obey, and not in him who called you." For the handiwork of God to be fashioned to the stature of Christ, the truly living human being, rather than hardening himself, trying to be what he wants to be, he must remain pliable, open, and responsive to the creative work of God. As Denis Minns puts it, "What the earth creature needs to learn above all is to relax in the Hands of God, to let God be the creator."[20]

Perhaps the best definition of a human being, at least within the Christian theological tradition, is provided by the *Letter of Barnabas*, written sometime in the second century: "The human being is earth that suffers."[21] Barnabas surely has in mind the image from the second chapter of Genesis, with God taking clay from the earth and molding a human being, clay which thus suffers in His hands. However, it would be extremely short-sighted not to also see in these words our own reality, clay which suffers during the course of life upon the earth, battered, bruised, wounded. The span of our life, as also the economy of God as a whole, from creation to salvation, is understood by Irenaeus as a pedagogy in which we learn to become human, to become malleable clay in the hands of the Creator.

Whether we in fact do so, however, depends upon us and our reaction to our suffering, to the moral injuries that we sustain: whether we offer our hearts with thankfulness to God, who has shown His love to us in the Cross of Christ and invites us to share in that love through and in our own suffering, so that we become the vessel of His working, or whether we choose to harden ourselves and reject the workings of His hands, so becoming brittle and useless clay. The beauty of human beings, as we saw in the case of Nussbaum's analysis of Odysseus, lies precisely in their fragility and vulnerability. To seek to transcend this basic fabric of human life, either by defining the only appropriate activity of human beings as being intellectual contemplation, as with the Greek philosophical tradition, or, as is more likely today, by "an ethics of preventative abstention," would be, as Irenaeus puts it, to destroy the human being, not by a moral injury inflicted by others, but by one's own choice of reaction to what is (and a reaction that is), in more senses than one, all too human.

Notes

1 Robert E. Meagher, *Killing from the Inside Out: Moral Injury and Just War* (Eugene, OR: Cascade Books, 2014), 7–8.
2 In M. C. Nussbaum, *Love's Knowledge: Essays on Philosophy and Literature* (Oxford, 1990), 365–91. See also idem, *The Fragility of Goodness: Luck and Ethics in Greek Tragedy and Philosophy* (Cambridge, 1986, repr. 1989); *The Therapy of Desire: Theory and Practice in Hellenistic Ethics* (Princeton, 1994). See also the various articles on Nussbaum's work, and her response, in R. V. Norman and C. H. Reynolds (eds.), *Symposium on* The Fragility of Goodness, *Soundings*, 72.4 (1989). Oxford University Press, Cambridge University Press, and Princeton University Press.
3 *Phaedo* 80b. Ed. and trans. H. N. Fowler, *Plato*, I, Loeb Classical Library, 36 (Cambridge, MA: Harvard University Press, 1917).
4 Nussbaum, *Therapy*, 50, 497.
5 Note, however, C. Osborne's criticism of Nussbaum's analysis of the role of love in Hellenistic philosophy, in "Love's Bitter Fruits: Martha C. Nussbaum The Therapy of Desire: Theory and Practice in Hellenistic Ethics," *Philosophical Investigations*, 19.4 (1996), 318–28.
6 *The Fragility of Goodness*, 2, original emphasis.
7 *The Fragility of Goodness*, 341, original emphasis.
8 "Transcending Humanity," 375.
9 "Transcending Humanity," 383.
10 Ignatius of Antioch, *Letter to the Romans*, 6. Ed. and trans. B. D. Ehrman, *The Apostolic Fathers*, 1, Loeb Classical Library, 24 (Cambridge, MA: Harvard University Press, 2003); trans. modified.
11 Most fully in J. Behr, *Irenaeus of Lyons: Identifying Christianity* (Oxford: Oxford University Press, 2013), from which much of the following paragraphs are indebted; *Becoming Human: Meditations on Christian Anthropology in Word and Image* (Crestwood, NY: St Vladimir's Seminary Press, 2013), and "Life and Death in an Age of Martyrdom," in J. Behr and C. Cunningham (eds.), *The Role of Death in Life: A Multidisciplinary Approach*, Veritas 15 (Eugene, OR: Wipf and Stock, 2015), 79–95. See also my forthcoming *John the Theologian and His Paschal Gospel: A Prologue to Theology*.

12 Irenaeus of Lyons, *Against the Heresies* (= *haer.*) 4.37.1. Ed. and French trans.
    A. Rousseau et al., *Sources chretiennes* 100 (*haer.* 4) (Paris: Cerf, 1965); Eng.
    trans. A. Robertson and J. Donaldson, *Ante-Nicene Fathers*, 1 (Edinburgh,
    1887; repr. Grand Rapids: Eerdmans, 1987), modified. On the place of 4.37–39,
    the so-called "Treatise on Free Will," in *Against the Heresies* see P. Bacq, *De
    l'ancienne à la nouvelle alliance selon S. Irénée: Unité du livre IV de l'Adversus
    Haereses* (Paris: Editions Lethielleux, Presses Universitaires de Namur, 1978),
    363–88. For a more comprehensive analysis of this section, see R. Berthouzoz,
    Liberté et grâce suivant la théologie d'Irénée de Lyon (Fribourg en Suisse: Edi-
    tions Universitaires; Paris: Cerf, 1980), 189–243.
13 *Haer.* 4.39.1: *Si autem utrorumque eorum cognitionem et duplices sensus cogita-
    tionis quis defugiat, latenter semetipsum occidit hominem.*
14 Berthouzoz, *Liberté et grâce*, 236: "En conséquence, l'humanisation de
    l'homme demande un engagement de sa part, ce qui est évident à l'expérience,
    et comporte l'acceptation corrélative d'un risque, en particulier celui de se
    tromper. Par là se trouvent exclues l'éthique de l'abstention préventive, toute
    valorisation de l'innocence originelle et indifférenciée et, surtout, l'hétéronomie
    comme instance de conduite moral, adulte."
15 Cf. G. Wingren, *Man and the Incarnation: A Study in the Biblical Theology of
    Irenaeus*, trans. R. Mackenzie (London: Oliver and Boyd, 1959), 20, and, more
    generally, 26–45.
16 As D. Minns, *Irenaeus* (London: Geoffrey Chapman, 1994), 73–74, argues. As
    Robert F. Brown points out, "Irenaeus does not accept the Platonic view that
    the recalcitrance of a pre-existent matter constitutes a limit to what God can
    make of it." "On the Necessary Imperfection of Creation, Irenaeus' *Adversus
    Haereses* IV, 38," *Scottish Journal of Theology*, 28.1 (1975), 17–25, at 23.
17 Cf. Jeff Vogel, "The Haste of Sin, the Slowness of Salvation: An Interpretation
    of Irenaeus on the Fall and Redemption," *Anglican Theological Review*, 89.3
    (2007), 443–59, at 443: "This graspingness is the fundamental problem in the
    way that human beings comport themselves in relation to God. Though they
    have an original capacity to be incorporated into the divine life, they lose it
    through their impatience, what I call the 'haste of sin.'"
18 *Haer.* 4.38.4. Bacq (*Alliance*, 384) points out that this implies that God did
    indeed bestow the power of his divinity on the human race, but the human
    being, unable to bear it, lost it, though it can now be regained through Christ's
    work of recapitulation. It must be borne in mind, however, that for Irenaeus
    what God bountifully bestows is set within the whole economy of the arc,
    which includes the loss by human beings of what is given to them in the begin-
    ning, that is, the breath of life, but yet through this loss, dying, and rising,
    comes to acquire something more, the fullness of the Holy Spirit, which the
    breath anticipated.
19 *Haer.* 4.38.4, cf. 2 Cor 5:4; 1 Cor. 15:53; Gen 1:26; 3:5, 22.
20 Minns, *Irenaeus*, 64.
21 *The Letter of Barnabas*, 6.9: ἄνθρωπος γὰρ γῆ ἐστιν πάσχουσα. Ed. and trans.
    K. Lake, *The Apostolic Fathers*, 1, Loeb Classical Library (Cambridge, MA:
    Harvard University Press, 1912).

Chapter 6

Just war and moral injury
Un-telling a lie and envisioning a path to healing

Robert Emmet Meagher

Of all the wounds that war inflicts on those who wage it, wounds to the soul are the deepest and arguably the most resistant to healing. Moral injury—the signature injury of America's recent wars in Afghanistan and Iraq—describes just such a wound. In the words of U.S. Army LTC Douglas Pryer, moral injury "kills the souls of warriors who, having marched off to war ... return home, heads held high while the music plays and their loved ones cheer, yet feeling inside they are forever lost."[1]

"In the end, for me, it is all about properly handling hundreds of thousands of miserable souls, one at a time."[2] These are the words of U.S. Army Major Sean Levine, an Orthodox Christian chaplain who served with the 1st Cavalry Division, and the "miserable souls" he has in mind are men and women in uniform, as well as military veterans, who suffer from moral injury—men and women who, while they have not gone dark in death, either in combat or by their own hand, have gone dark in life. What this means—to go dark in life without going dark in death—is to live in what one former combatant described to me as "impenetrable darkness," to live without light, without hope. This inner darkness may and often does descend slowly, incrementally—stealing up on us—ignored or denied until it leaves us blind. U.S. Marine medic Doug Anderson, however, saw it coming from the start.

> My first day in Vietnam in February of 1967, I knew something was wrong. On my first patrol I saw an old man beaten by a squad leader for no other reason than he was Vietnamese. What I saw in my fellow marines was not the attitude of men who believed they were fighting for a noble cause—protecting the South Vietnamese against communist aggressors. Their behavior was an admission that no one cared what the war was about anymore, and that the civilian population had become the enemy, and the enemy threatened their survival. There was nothing else beyond that, no long view, no strategy. That day was the beginning of my education, and an immense darkness opened under me. What I saw that day in these men was a kind of soul damage.[3]

The very idea of "soul damage" is a stretch for many persons these days. How could it be otherwise in our dismissive, cynical age, when the mind is reduced to a by-product of the brain and "the brain is just a computer made out of meat," as artificial intelligence pioneer Marvin Minsky once so "poetically" put it? Indeed, if the soul is no more than an antique superstition, then how can it suffer injury, much less die (even as brain and breath go on)? Curiously, the all-but-dead language of soul, soul wounds, and soul death has enjoyed (if that is the right word) a resurgence among military veterans, religious or otherwise.

The soul, I would argue, is not an object of faith. It is something we either know or we don't. It is an experience, not a doctrine. When we are in pain and seek understanding or healing, we point to the source and locus of our suffering. Veterans are discovering or rediscovering their souls because, quite simply, they are losing them. It's a matter of triage not metaphysical theory. Anderson puts it this way: "There is nothing ethereal about the soul: it is worldly in a way the mind will never be. Perhaps the strongest argument for its existence is that you can damage it, imprison it. Lose it."[4] Veterans learn the truth of these words in war, not in classrooms or churches.

But where do the rest of us—the over 99% of the American people who never see the face of war—learn the truth that war darkens the soul, imperiling not only the lives and limbs of those who wage it but their humanity and peace of mind as well? We, the seemingly innocent and unscathed, send our sons and daughters, brothers, sisters, husbands and wives, friends and strangers off to fight our wars; but do we have any real sense of what they do, what they endure, what they bring home with them and carry for the rest of their days? I think not. And how could we? America apparently doesn't "go to war" anymore. This, anyway, is the gist of a sign displayed for years at Virginia's MCB (Marine Corps Base) Quantico, known as the "Crossroads of the Marine Corps." The sign reads as follows:

> America is not at war.
> The Marine Corps is at war;
> America is at the mall.

So what is it that we need to know? What is it that our veterans bring home with them from war? Are we prepared to know and to do what that knowledge requires of us? "America," writes former U.S. Army infantry Sergeant Brian Turner, "vast and laid out from one ocean to another, is not a large enough space to contain the war each soldier brings home. And even if it could, it doesn't want to."[5]

That must change, and we need to make a start. However, before we can begin to grasp the dark truth of war, acknowledge the moral pain of our veterans, and embark on what will be a long road to healing, there is an old lie that needs to be untold. Wars often start with lies, false promises, and delusions, and none of these has caused more confusion and carnage than what we know as "Just War theory," or simply "Just War." It is a core doctrine of the U.S. military, taught in our service academies, invoked by presidents and politicians, preached by pastors and chaplains, held tightly by those who go to war and by those who await their return. The late Father Daniel Berrigan, in his memoir *To Dwell in Peace*, called just war a "cornerstone of the Catholic edifice,"[6] while from well outside that edifice Dr. Jonathan Shay, author of *Achilles in Vietnam*, adds that Just War doctrine has become as American as apple pie.[7]

Before launching into a critique of Just War, however, I first need to clarify a few things, lest we set off on false footing here. Firstly, in calling Just War a "lie" or "false promise" I am not denying that in countless instances it has been and remains for many a lie told, a promise made, in deeply good faith. Neither, however, can I deny that for the past 15 centuries it has been used and abused repeatedly in loathsome bad faith, with immeasurable, catastrophic consequences.

Next, my concern to challenge and in the end dismiss "Just War theory" or "Just War doctrine" is not focused, first or foremost, on the multifarious standards of character and conduct invoked and more or less observed by warring parties and polities for millennia, from ancient India and China to the West, from classical Greece and Rome to the streets of Baghdad and the remote villages of the Korengal Valley. If we look to the origins of what we call today the "Law of Armed Conflict," such as the Geneva Convention or our military's fluidly adaptable "rules of engagement," we find that Western Christianity, or more specifically the Latin Fathers of late antiquity, are hardly their earliest or principal source. In fact, the three traditional categories of the Western Just War tradition —*ius ad bellum*, *ius in bello*, and *ius post bellum*—whose collective aim was and is to set somehow acceptable standards for (or limits upon) the launching, conducting, and concluding of wars—each had their counterparts long before and far beyond the Christian West and its wars. Civilized peoples and their warriors (some, not all, just as it is now) have for millennia concerned themselves with justifying their wars, fighting with honor, and crafting a generous peace.

Thucydides' account of the 30-year war between Athens and Sparta and their respective coalitions chronicles in dramatic detail the rhetorical feats of the future combatants to convince themselves and others that, if war broke out, they would be the ones in the right, the aggressed, not the aggressors. Centuries earlier, in the dynastic conflicts of rival kingdoms in north India, as recorded in the *Mahabharata*, we learn that warriors were bound by strict codes of fair, even magnanimous, conduct in battle, dictating, for example, that foot soldiers attack only foot soldiers, elephant warriors attack only those similarly mounted on elephants, and that no combatant without armor—or whose weapon was lost or broken, or whose chariot was disabled, or who was in retreat—could ever be attacked. Consider, too, the unwillingness of the Chinese Duke of Song who, in 638, facing a foe that far outnumbered his forces, refused to take advantage of the enemy's temporary vulnerability while crossing a river. Even after his defeat the Duke defended his actions in these words: "a junzi (gentleman) worthy of the name does not seek to overcome the enemy in misfortune. He does not beat his drum before the ranks are formed."[8] Contrast these words with Sebastian Junger's succinct assessment of war as we know it today:

> much of modern military tactics is geared toward maneuvering the enemy into a position where they can essentially be massacred from safety. It sounds dishonorable only if you imagine that modern war is about honor; it's not. It's about winning, which means killing the enemy on the most unequal terms possible. Anything less simply results in the loss of more of your own men.[9]

Finally, pre-imperial Roman Just War theory and practice, a major source of later Western Just War doctrine, emphasized that the conduct of rulers in war should be guided by the principle of *humanitas* which included the offer and implementation of a generous post-war peace, one that would not nourish the seeds of further enmity and conflict. The point I am making here is that my calling radically into question Western Christian Just War doctrine in no way amounts to or entails the abandonment of any and every humane limit, standard of decency, code of conduct, or measure of sanity and restraint that nations at war or men and women in arms might invoke and enforce. Until we live in a world rid of the plague of war, any and every effort to reduce the extent and duration of conflict, tame its ferocity, prevent unnecessary destruction, and enforce civilian neutrality are to be commended and embraced.

If we are to trace the roots and understand the significance of Christian Just War theory in the 4th century we would do well to realize that, from the outset, "war" was only one of its concerns. "War" is a euphemism, an abstraction, synonymous with struggle, confrontation, and conflict. War is quite simply about killing. "The soldier," writes former U.S. Marine Captain and Iraq War veteran Tyler Boudreau, "kills for a living—it is his reason for being. Killing is not a by-product or some shitty collateral duty like peeling potatoes or scrubbing the latrine. It is the institutional point."[10] U.S. Army LTC Pete Kilner makes the same point in his West Point class on the morality of killing: "there is one absolutely unique and defining characteristic of our profession—we are organized, equipped and trained to kill people."[11]

If war then is about killing, what is "Just War" about? Like "war," "just" is a misleading word to rely on when considering the early Christian abhorrence of and eventual accommodation of killing. "Just," the Latin *ius*, is primarily a legal term connoting legitimacy, action in keeping with an oath taken, a pact made, or a law passed. Just killing would therefore be killing according to accepted rules, killing for which one cannot or should not be prosecuted, decriminalized killing. Just killing, then, is legalized killing, killing within the law, and the law, as recognized by Plato long before the dawn of Christianity, mostly enshrines the self-interest of the powerful.

The "legality" of killing was largely beside the personal point for early Christians, who were convinced to their core that killing, in whatever cause or to whatever end (war, legal execution, self-defense, retribution or revenge), was never justified and always sinful. After all, for several centuries, in periods of state persecution, Christians had been killed wholesale, all quite legally. More to the point, at the very roots of the Christian tradition, we find a Christ unequivocally committed to non-violence. The Jesus that emerges from the proto-evangelical collection of the sayings (*logia*) of Jesus known as "Q," short for "*Quelle*" or "Source"—claimed to be our earliest source of an authentic Jesus tradition—is a teacher whose words advocate love and forgiveness, a man of peace, fearless in the face of death. Later, in the Gospel narratives, where we witness the deeds and not just the words of the God-man whom Christians are called to imitate, we find his essential pacifism confirmed, most convincingly when he offered no resistance to his captors in the garden on the night of his arrest.

The Christian Church of the first three centuries, East and West, reached consensus on this: Christians may not kill. Their calling—to imitate Christ and to heed his teachings—left no room for the taking of life or the exercise of violence, whether in battle or in courts of law. "No uniform," wrote Tertullian, "is lawful among us, if it stands for sinful action";[12] and the "sinful action" in question here was the act of taking human life—always sinful, always to be condemned and eschewed by Christians.

Yet all this has changed, not overnight, but at a pace that even today seems rather startling. To begin to grasp this reality, I suggest that we consider these two quite bold declarations regarding Christians, military service, and killing:

> [1] when God forbids us to kill, He not only prohibits us from open violence, which is not even allowed by the public laws, but He warns us against the commission of those things which are esteemed lawful among men. Thus it will be neither lawful for a just man to engage in warfare, since his warfare is justice itself, nor to accuse any one of a capital charge, because it makes no difference whether you put a man to death by word, or rather by the sword, since it is the act of

putting to death itself which is prohibited. Therefore, with regard to this precept of God, there ought to be no exception at all; but that it is always unlawful to put to death a man, whom God willed to be a sacred animal.[13]

[2] For they ("the passions") are not evil of themselves, since God has reasonably implanted them in us; but inasmuch as they are plainly good by nature,—for they are given us for the protection of life,—they become evil by their evil use. And as bravery, if you fight in defense of your country, is a good, if against your country, is an evil, so the passions, if you employ them to good purposes, will be virtues, if to evil uses, they will be called vices.[14]

In the first instance, the author makes it indelibly clear that God's law forbids all killing and that God's law trumps any other. Not only executioners or soldiers, but judges, magistrates, emperors, and generals—anyone in the lethal chain leading to violent death—are equally guilty of murder. The author of the second statement, however, takes a more equivocal, accommodating position on righteous rage and battlefield courage. Regarding the right and wrong of killing, it all depends on what side you are on, what cause you serve.

The author of the first view was the esteemed late 3rd- to early 4th-century North African philosopher Lucius Caecilius Lactantius, a Christian convert who managed to survive the savage and slaughterous anti-Christian persecutions under the emperor Diocletian. The author of the second view, also named Lactantius, enjoyed the friendship and patronage of Emperor Constantine the Great, who eventually appointed him to the imperial court to tutor his son Crispus. As it happens, these two authors are, in fact, the same person! Lactantius, it seems, underwent two conversions, one to the Christianity of the non-violent Jesus and the other, and later, to an emergent imperial Christianity. For Lactantius and many if not most of his contemporaries, there was no contradiction here, only fulfillment; for they saw in the Christian conversion of Constantine the hand of their crucified and risen Savior and the dawn of his promised kingdom.

The Christian Church of the 4th century had turned a corner. Christians were no longer imperial outsiders or bystanders, much less scapegoats. No longer anticipating the imminent end of the *saeculum*, most Christians recognized life's necessities, a list led by security of life, freedom, and property. They were no longer prepared, if indeed they ever had been, to look to the lilies of the field and live without care. As Romans became Christians, Christianity became Roman. Far from an intimate circle of disciples, Christians by the 4th century numbered in the millions. The Church was no longer simply *in* the world; day by day it was more and more adamantly *of* the world. Those who dissented from this ever-deeper investment in the worldly order, with its incumbent necessities, responsibilities and anxieties, followed Anthony and Pachomius into the desert, or climbed and perched above it all like Simon Stilotes, while the majority played an ever greater and more central role in the governance and preservation of the empire in an increasingly threatening world. In a word, Christians were now stakeholders, and the Church's "stake" in the world expanded in the ensuing centuries to the point that Pope Boniface VIII summed up the primacy of the Church and his own papal reach in these words: "we declare, state, define and pronounce that it is altogether necessary to salvation for every human creature to be subject to the Roman Pontiff."[15]

The imperial church and its commitment to clout are no secret to anyone who reads the past. What may be less known and recognized is the fact that Just War theory and doctrine made it all possible, or at least morally palatable. At the core of this deviation from previous Christian tradition was the claim that war, with all of the destruction and death it entails, is itself morally neutral. It all depends—on the authority endorsing it, the cause driving it, the intentions of those who wage it, and ultimately on the blessing of the Lord above, the once and future Prince of Peace. War—not necessarily evil—can be useful, redeemable, meritorious. Just War all but inevitably led, and still leads, to holy war in one or other of its endless permutations. When, in the Crusades, taking up arms became the preferred and preeminent way to take up the cross and follow in the footsteps of Christ, the justification of war took full form and revealed its limitless potential. The pacifist Christian communities of the first three centuries lost—though they would have seen it differently—no more than a few thousand of their number to martyrdom at the hands of the Romans. Armed with the moral assurances of Just War or holy war in the ensuing centuries, militant and righteous Christians slaughtered countless millions of even their own number and never looked back. Consider the St. Bartholomew's Day Massacre of August 23, 1572, when French Catholics murdered somewhere approaching 10,000 French Protestants over a matter of theological dispute.

> When the pope in Rome heard the news from France, he was so overcome by joy that he organized festive prayers to celebrate the occasion and commissioned Giorgio Vasari to decorate one of the Vatican's rooms with a fresco of the massacre ... More Christians were killed in those twenty-four hours than by the polytheistic Roman Empire throughout its entire existence.[16]

With Just War doctrine installed, no war, it seems, is beyond the pale of justification, even celebration. In our own day, we have seen that even nuclear war is morally defensible, for some as a policy and for others as a deterrent.

The contested core of Just War theory is the claim that war can be waged without moral violation and the destruction of character. There are many ways of putting this same question: can we kill without guilt, without shame, without stain, without being haunted by the souls of the dead, without sin, without (in today's currency) "moral injury"? In his philosophical masterwork, *The Rebel*, Albert Camus summed it up this way: "We shall know nothing until we know whether we have the right to kill our fellow men, or the right to let them be killed."[17] Camus, in 1951, against the immediate backdrop of history's two most devastating wars— wars that took the lives of 60–80 million lives—and confronting the imminent threat of nuclear annihilation, argued that the justification of murder was the most grave issue we face, and nothing in the last 65 years would challenge that assessment. In *The Rebel*, Camus drew no distinction between killing and murder, because he was convinced there is none to be made. The act is the same in either case and has the same consequences. What we call "killing," as distinguished from what we call "murder," amounts to a murder that we would somehow attempt to justify, even condone or commend, and as such it is an evasion. The early Christian Church made no such distinction, until Augustine and Ambrose found it necessary or useful, or both, to create a new category of killing, one that a church with civil powers and responsibilities required. Denying that distinction, as Camus did, especially in an age like ours of "forever war" clears the head and allows us to confront the reality of moral injury, the reality of what 15 years (and counting) of continuous war is doing to our men and women in uniform and to the rest of us as well. "Long wars," writes U.S. Marine veteran Doug Anderson,

> create a level of depravity among servicemen that is never understood by the public. If you continually expose people to legal murder, it makes them numb and cynical. This depravity is increased if the reasons for the war are murky. Human life becomes worth even less.[18]

To those who have taken life or watched it taken on the indiscriminate scale of war, "Just War" makes no convincing sense out of what they have seen and done. "A walk across any battlefield shortly after the guns have fallen silent is convincing enough," wrote WWII veteran J. Glenn Gray: "A sensitive person is sure to be oppressed by a spirit of evil there, a radical evil which suddenly makes the medieval images of hell and the thousand devils of that imagination believable."[19] James Hillman, a noted Jungian analyst, echoed Gray's words when he described "the return from the killing fields" as "a slow ascent from hell."[20] Hillman learned this from working with Vietnam veterans, whose post-war agony has been painfully inscribed in the national consciousness and carved into the very soil of the National Mall.

The inescapable truth is that war leaves no one unaltered. Michael Yandell, a former U.S. Army explosive ordinance specialist in Iraq, writes how, in his descent into war's netherworld, what he lost was

> a world that makes moral sense … I was 19 when I left for war. I did not know I was leaving a world that made sense—a world where people respected one another's lives and dignity, a world where violence and murder were understood to be wrong and punished by laws —and entering a world where all bets were off.[21]

"None of us were like this before …" recalls Daniel Keller, a former tanker in Vietnam. "No one thought about dragging people through concertina wire or beating them or strangling them or anything like that … before this."[22] "This is the shit that you live with for a year," contributes Vietnam veteran Don Dzagulones, "and it becomes routine—it's part of your life. You come back to the world, and it's criminal. So where does that leave you?"[23]

Exactly. Addressing the moral burden that her haunted son Sergeant Adam Gray carried to his death, Cindy Chavez, Adam's mother, reflected that "Nobody can do things like that to people without some reflection at some time. You're born with a soul, and then they take it and restructure it. And your soul is telling you, 'this is wrong.'"[24] On August 29, 2004, Adam was found dead in his barracks in Alaska with a plastic bag tight around his neck. The Army ruled his death an accident. Perhaps the only less appropriate ruling would have been to call it an act of God.

There is, however, a road out of this hell, out of even impenetrable darkness. It may be as yet unmarked, unpaved, uphill, perilous, and uncertain, but it is there and trodden daily by veterans displaying a courage and commitment equal to or beyond any that was demanded of them in war. Their full recovery and return must concern and occupy us all, not only as a moral imperative but also as a matter of sheer survival. In the aftermath of our wars, the stakes, not only for our veterans but for our nation and world could not be higher. Appealing to the deep human instinct to resist destruction and chaos, J. Glenn Gray wrote these words after World War II:

> If our wars were to make killers out of all combat soldiers, rather than men who have killed, civilian life would be endangered for generations or, in fact, made impossible. … (but) no modern war has until now lasted long enough to contract this preservative love to mere survival of the individual naked life or to make large numbers unregenerate killers. Such wars are possible in the future. But the civilizing impulse is

strong indeed, and frequently carries us along after reason and will have been temporarily overpowered.[25]

We may well wonder (and worry), however, whether our most recent wars, already prolonged well beyond any in the history of our nation and offering no promise of closure or confinement, might not be realizing the fears expressed by Gray over half a century ago. Fixation on "the individual naked life" is already here in the age of "selfies," while arguably "unregenerate killers" appear to own the header "Breaking News." If we imagine that our wars are safely distant and that the "home front"—apart from brief, random bursts of violence—remains at peace, we need to think again and listen to what veteran war reporter Sebastian Junger would have us ponder:

> I know what coming back to America from a war zone is like because I've done it so many times. First there is a kind of shock at the level of comfort that we enjoy, but that is followed by the dismal realization that we live in a society that is basically at war with itself. People speak with incredible contempt about—depending upon their views— the rich, the poor, the educated, the foreign-born, the president, or the entire US government. It's a level of contempt that is usually reserved for enemies in wartime, except that now it's applied to our fellow citizens. Unlike criticism, contempt is particularly toxic because it assumes a moral superiority in the speaker. Contempt is often directed at people who have been excluded from a group or declared unworthy of its benefits. Contempt is often used by governments to provide rhetorical cover for torture or abuse … People who speak with contempt for one another will probably not remain united for long.[26]

If we as a nation, as a community, admit that we are in crisis, we must resist for once what has become our default response to threat—to declare war on it. With mixed results at best we have declared war on poverty, crime, racism, homelessness, cancer, illiteracy … the list goes on. Now we are on the brink of declaring war on each other. "The United States is so powerful," says Junger, "that the only country capable of destroying her might be the United States herself, which means that the ultimate terrorist strategy would be to just leave the country alone."[27] It may just be time to declare not war but peace, to come together in search and celebration of what we have or might have in common. "If you want to make a society work," argues Dr. Rachel Yehuda, Director of the Traumatic Stress Studies Division at the Mount Sinai School of Medicine, "then you don't keep underscoring the places where you're different—you underscore your shared humanity."[28] Humanity, like soul, however, is an idea in which we as a society have largely lost faith. Our one hope may be that we will come to know it again as we experience its loss.

This may be exactly what happens in war, when you realize that someone just like yourself—someone who could in another world, another
place, another time be your friend—is, as Brian Turner described the
experience, "hunting for your soul."[29] The irony is that veterans, who have
seen how easily humanity is lost and how difficult it is to recover, may be
just the ones to lead or at least point our nation back to its senses. Military training and discipline, after all, are not only to do with learning to
kill. They are also to do with survival, not the "mere survival of the individual naked life" that Gray wrote about but the survival of the "we," the
unit, what Junger refers to as the "tribe." It is to this communal survival
that one unreservedly commits, subordinates, even sacrifices, oneself. The
"war of all against all" to which Hobbes consigned us and to which we
moderns and post-moderns have so unstintingly given ourselves must be
renounced; and the common humanity, in which Hobbes had so fully lost
faith, must be reaffirmed, blindly if necessary. It may even be time to
revive and repurpose the long discarded axiom of Anselm—*credo ut intelli-
gam*—"I believe so that I might know." Our world is replete with far stranger and surely worse counsel than this.

"Today's veterans often come home," Junger points out,

> to find that, although they're willing to die for their country, they're
> not sure how to live for it. It's hard to know how to live for a country
> that regularly tears itself apart … It's complete madness, and the vet-
> erans know this. In combat, soldiers regularly all but ignore differences
> of race, religion, and politics within their platoon. It's no wonder
> many of them get so depressed when they come home.[30]

This depression, we know, is not unique to veterans. We are a nation
exhausted by our wars and lacerated by our divisions. But we can change.
We can do something different. This, affirmed President Barack Obama, as
he laid a wreath at the Hiroshima Peace Memorial on May 27, 2016, "is
what makes our species unique."

> We're not bound by genetic code to repeat the mistakes of the past.
> We can learn. We can choose. We can tell our children a different
> story, one that describes a common humanity, one that makes war less
> likely and cruelty less easily accepted.[31]

The first step, I would argue, must be to refuse to justify war, which is not
precisely the same as not to wage it, though it is a decisive step in that
direction. "People like myself," wrote Camus in 1946, amidst a Europe in
ruins, "want not a world in which murder no longer exists (we are not so
crazy as that!) but rather one in which murder is not legitimate."[32] In
saying this, Camus knew he was caught in contradiction. "For we do live,

it is true, in a world where murder is legitimate (and) it appears that we cannot change it without risking murder."[33] The Catholic Church, the historical matrix and traditional mainstay, of Just War theory and doctrine, is caught today in the same contradiction. Recent popes, from Pope John XXIII to Pope Francis have categorically repudiated war while upholding the right of self-defense and the moral imperative of defending the innocent. Pope Francis has made clear his position that war brings on war and violence breeds violence, and yet he acknowledges that ISIS and other sowers of violence must be stopped. To just say "no" to war and violence remains, of course, as it always has, a personal option; and it is very possible that that option, however radical and perilous, is the only one that could ever lead to universal and lasting peace.

In the meantime, many or most people probably suspect that Euripides got it right when he put these words into the mouth of war-weary Hecuba, queen mother of Troy: "No more can be hoped for, by anyone in any life, than to elude ruin one day at a time." And this would appear to be true so long as we live and act from fear, fear of the worst that could happen, fear of ruin. There is, however, an alternative. We actually have a choice to make, as a country but first as individuals and as communities. "The most basic way [people are] divided," wrote Abraham Heschel,

> is between those who believe that war is unnecessary and those who believe that war is inevitable; between those who believe that the sword is the symbol of honor and those to whom seeking to convert swords into plowshares is the only way to keep our civilization from disaster.[34]

In a moment in our national history reminiscent of the turbulence of the 1960s, exhausted by war and lacerated with division, we could do worse than to consider the challenge with which Senator Robert Kennedy concluded his unforgettable reflections to a largely African American crowd in Indianapolis minutes after learning that Martin Luther King had been shot and killed:

> Let us dedicate ourselves to what the Greeks wrote so many years ago: to tame the savageness of man and make gentle the life of this world. Let us dedicate ourselves to that, and say a prayer for our country and for our people.[35]

Notes

1 Excerpt from book blurb for *Killing from the Inside Out: Moral Injury and Just War.*
2 Personal email, 3.15.15 (with permission).

3 Anderson, "Something Like a Soul," 491.
4 Ibid., 492.
5 Turner, *My Life*, 173.
6 In April, 2016, a landmark Vatican conference met in Rome to re-consider the just war tradition and called upon the pope to write an encyclical, challenging just war and embracing non-violence and just peace.
7 Afterword, in Meagher, *Killing*, 151.
8 Quoted in Armstrong, *Fields of Blood*, 86.
9 *Junger*, War, 140.
10 Boudreau, *Packing Inferno*, 78.
11 Kilner, "A Moral Justification," 55.
12 Tertullian, *On Idolatry*, 19.318, 321. Adapted from the 1885 translation by S. Thelwall.
13 Lactantius. *Divine Institutes*, VI.20.15–17.
14 Lactantius, *Epitome*, LXI.3–4.
15 Bettenson, *Documents*, 161.
16 Harari, *Sapiens*, 216.
17 Camus, *The Rebel*, 4.
18 Anderson, "Something Like a Soul," 491.
19 Gray, *Warriors*, 51.
20 Hillman, *A Terrible Love of War*, 33.
21 Yandell, "The War Within," 13.
22 Phillips, *None of Us*, 186.
23 Ibid., 181.
24 Ibid., 185.
25 Gray, *Warriors*, 86–87.
26 Junger, *Tribe*, 125–26.
27 Ibid., 127–28.
28 In Junger, *Tribe*, 127.
29 Turner, *My Life*, 15.
30 Junger, *Tribe*, 124–25.
31 Obama, Hiroshima speech, https://obamawhitehouse.archives.gov/the-press-office/2016/05/27/remarks-president-obama-and-prime-minister-abe-japan-hiroshima-peace.
32 Camus, "Neither Victims," 4.
33 Ibid., 4.
34 Quoted in Dear, *Abraham Heschel's*.
35 Kennedy, Indianapolis.

Sources cited

Anderson, Doug. "Something Like a Soul," *The Massachusetts Review* LII, 3&4 (2011): 489–494.

Armstrong, Karen. *Fields of Blood: Religion and the History of Violence*. New York: Anchor, 2015.

Bettenson, Henry, ed. *Documents of the Christian Church*, 2nd ed. Oxford: Oxford University Press, 1963.

Boudreau, Tyler. *Packing Inferno: The Unmaking of a Marine*. Port Townsend, WA: Feral House, 2008.

Camus, Albert. *The Rebel*. Translated by Anthony Bower. New York: Vintage, 1956.

———. *Neither Victims nor Executioners*. Translated by Dwight Macdonald. Berkeley: World Without War Council, 1968.

Dear, John. "Abraham Heschel's Prophetic Vision." *National Catholic Reporter*, June 14, 2011. Online: www.ncronline.org/blogs/road-peace/abraham-heschels-prophetic-judaism.

Gray, J. Glenn. *The Warriors: Reflections on Men in Battle*. Lincoln, NE: Bison Books, 1998.

Harari, Yuval Noah. *Sapiens: A Brief History of Humankind*. New York: HarperCollins, 2015.

Hillman, James. *A Terrible Love of War*. New York: Penguin, 2004.

Junger, Sebastian. *War*. New York: Twelve, 2010a.

———. *Tribe: On Homecoming and Belonging*. New York: Twelve, 2010b.

Kennedy, Robert F. Speech. Indianapolis, Indiana, April 4, 1968. John F. Kennedy Presidential Library and Museum. Online: www.jfklibrary.org/Research/Research-Aids/Ready-Reference/RFK-Speeches/Statement-on-the-Assassination-of-Martin-Luther-King.aspx.

Kilner, Pete. "A Moral Justification for Killing in War." *Army Magazine*, February, 2010. Online: www.usma.edu/caldol/siteassets/armymagazine/docs/2010/cc_army_10-02%20(feb10)%20morality-of-killing.pdf.

Lactantius. *The Divine Institutes*. Translated by William Fletcher. In vol. 7 of *The Ante-Nicene Fathers*. Edited by Alexander Roberts and James Donaldson. Peabody, MA: Hendrickson, 1996.

———. *The Epitome of the Divine Institutes*. Translated by William Fletcher. In vol. 7 of *The Ante-Nicene Fathers*. Edited by Alexander Roberts and James Donaldson. Peabody, MA: Hendrickson, 1996.

Meagher, Robert Emmet. *Killing from the Inside Out: Moral Injury and Just War*. Eugene, OR: Cascade, 2014.

Obama, Barack. Speech. Hiroshima Peace Memorial. *New York Times*, May 28, 2016. Online: www.nytimes.com/2016/05/28/world/asia/text-of-president-obamas-speech-in-hiroshima-japan.html.

Phillips, Joshua E.S. *None of Us Were Like This Before: American Soldiers and Torture*. New York: Verso, 2010.

Tertullian. *On Idolatry*. Translated by S. Thewall. In Roberts, *The Ante-Nicene Fathers*, vol. 3.

Turner, Brian. *My Life as a Foreign Country: A Memoir*. New York: W.W. Norton, 2014.

Yandell, Michael. "The War Within: A Veteran's Moral Injury." *The Christian Century*, January 2, 2015. Online: www.christiancentury.org/article/2014-12/war-within.

Chapter 7

What is moral about moral injury?

A virtue approach

Aristotle Papanikolaou

Recent discussions on the newly constructed category of "moral injury" have not given sufficient attention to how "moral" is understood, which ultimately shapes an understanding of the experience that this category attempts to name. I will argue that the experience of what is being named "moral injury" points to a morality understood in terms of "virtues," but only if "human-nature-as-it-could-be-if-it-realized-its-*telos*" is defined in terms of learning how to love. For such an understanding of the "moral," I will turn to the ascetical writings of the Byzantine theologian, Maximus the Confessor (580–662).

Understanding the lingering effects of war

There are accounts of war replete with the language of glory, honor, and courage. The military once served as a means for those in poorer classes to obtain status and prestige, and combat afforded the opportunity, regardless of class, for one to achieve the eternal recognition of being a hero within one's community or nation. Those paralyzed by the fear of combat either before or after battle were often condemned as cowards, sometimes even executed for treason.

The images of the Vietnam War elicited a more complicated picture of war, and the experience of veterans returning from combat provoked some psychologists to develop a more nuanced understanding of the lingering effects of combat violence on veterans. In large part due to the medical community's experience with Vietnam veterans, post-traumatic stress disorder (PTSD) was introduced in 1980 into the third edition of the *Diagnostic and Statistics Manual for Mental Disorders*, or the *DSM-III*. It is classified as an anxiety disorder caused by exposure to real or threatened death, injury, or sexual violence. For combat veterans, causes for PTSD may include having killed an enemy combatant, having killed a non-combatant, seeing a comrade killed or injured, seeing non-combatants killed, handling remains of the dead, seeing non-combatants that could not be helped. One need not necessarily be physically present in combat to suffer from PTSD. As reported in the *New York Times*, drone-aircraft pilots experience depression, anxiety, and post-traumatic stress at the same rate as those of manned aircraft deployed to Iraq or Afghanistan (Dao, 2013).

The experience of the drone operators reveals that PTSD does not simply result from being in situations of bodily fear or threat, or in physical proximity to death and injury through violence, but from being the agent of violent acts of injury and death.

This clinical assessment, however, still does not tell the full story of the lingering effects of war and violence in PTSD. Symptoms of PTSD include startled reflex, memory loss, fear, flashback, anger, depression, anxiety, insomnia, nightmares, and self-medication with alcohol and/or drugs. What is most damaging to combat veterans who suffer from symptoms of PTSD is the destruction of their capacity to trust, which inevitably renders impossible any forms of bonding with others that are meaningful (Herman, 1992; Shay, 1994, 2002).

Since the introduction of the diagnostic category of PTSD, two other significant developments have occurred in relation to the existential effects of violence on trauma victims, including combat veterans. First, improved technology has led to tracing the neurological impact of violence on the brain (van der Kolk, 2014). Trauma, in particular, can interfere with healthy brain development, decision-making, memory, and the type of sequential thinking needed to work through problems (Bornstein, 2014). Violence can affect the brain in such a way as to negatively affect learning (Bornstein, 2014; cf. Walker et al., 2007, 2011) and the regulation of anger (van der Kolk, 2014).

A new category is also emerging in order to distinguish a certain state of being that is effected by the combat veteran's participation in war and which is no longer thought to be identical to PTSD, even if many of the symptoms are similar. This state of being is now referred to as "moral injury," which is distinguished from PTSD in the sense of not being induced through a fear response (Litz et al., 2009; Drescher et al., 2011; Brock and Lettini, 2012; Meagher, 2014). In PTSD, the amygdala and the hippocampus—areas of the brain that regulate fear and memory—and the relation between them are affected; conversely, the category of moral injury has a short history and no conclusive linking with a specific area of the brain exists, even if a lot of the symptoms appear similar. While PTSD has been described as a mental disorder (a label that many veterans reject), moral injury has been called a "dimensional problem" (Maguen and Litz 2012).

Moral injury refers to a state of being in which the combat veteran experiences a deep sense of having violated his own core moral beliefs. It may occur as a result of either combatants or non-combatants torturing prisoners, abusing dead bodies, or failing to prevent such acts; it may also ensue even if there was no way the combat veteran could have avoided doing such acts (MacNair, 2002; Grossman, 2009; Maguen et al., 2009, 2010, 2011). In the experience of moral injury, combat veterans may judge themselves to be worthless, unable to live with an act he or she committed that can never be erased. Some symptoms are similar to those of PTSD, such as isolation, mistrust of others, depression, addiction, emotional detachment, and negative self-judgments. There are countless stories of combat veterans who admit that they are afraid to speak of all that they did in combat situations for fear that the one to whom they speak will deem him or her unlovable. One story that sums up well the experience of moral injury appeared as a *New Yorker* article entitled "The Return." In the article, an Iraqi war veteran says: "I don't want her to know that her husband, the person she married, has nightmares about killing people. It just makes me feel like a monster ... That she'll hate me" (Finkel, 2013).

Injuring virtue

As the psychological literature on the existential effects of violence become more nuanced, and as neuroscience on the brain expands our knowledge on the impact—short- and long-term—of violence, there has been little from philosophical or theological ethicists to amplify the category of "moral injury." The initial definition itself comes from psychology, where Jonathan Shay first defined it as a transgression of one's deepest moral convictions, often associated with a betrayal by leadership (Shay, 1994). The term has since been expanded to involve a loss in one's sense of personal morality and capacity to act justly (Litz et al., 2009). While studies have confirmed the adequacy of the category relative to the particular experiences of combat veterans, there is also an indication that the current definitions are inadequate (Drescher et al., 2011).

A question that arises, however, is how a diagnostic category such as "moral injury" is possible without having already decided what counts as morality? If, in fact, the three reigning theories within philosophical ethics are deontological, consequentialist, and virtue—which of the three apply when thinking about moral injury? At first, it would seem as if the background moral theory for understanding moral injury is deontological, which defines morality in terms of rules or principles. In a deontological sense, moral injury might involve a transgression of one's absolute sense of right or wrong either by committing an act in war that constitutes such a violation, or participating in such an act, or being betrayed by leaders whom one trusted to abide by such principles. Both the symptoms and the narratives of those identified as suffering from moral injury reveal that what is being experienced cannot be fully explained by a moral theory whose focus is exclusively on rules and principles. When a veteran proclaims that he fears his wife seeing him as a monster, the anguish is not reducible to his sense of right or wrong being disrupted. Neither does consequentialism fully capture the dilemma, since the concern voiced is not about an act that leads to happiness or maximizes the greatest good for the greatest amount of people. In fact, one could imagine a consequentialist logic guiding a soldier's actions in combat and still exposing him or her to experiences that lead to moral injury. A soldier could very well be convinced that a war is just and that the outcome of combat is good, resulting in, as an example, freedom from oppression; but it is still possible for this soldier to have killed innocent non-combatants, or have been the perpetrator of friendly-fire casualties, or to have witnessed a friend's decapitation from a bomb blast. Regardless of the outcome, these types of experiences can still result in moral injury.

If deontological and consequentialist moral theories are ruled out, then that leaves virtue ethics. Although G. E. Anscombe is credited with reviving virtue ethical theory, it is questionable whether the discussion that followed fell short of her call to challenge modern moral philosophy. Insofar as much of virtue ethics fails to risk making claims about "human-nature-as-it-could-be-if-it-realized-its-*telos*" (MacIntyre, 1984, p. 53), it seems stuck on debates about right action, motivation, or moral judgment—the very terms of the debate that defined modern moral theory. Put another way, virtue ethics continues to lack a "rich anthropology, one that includes an explicit teleology and robust theory of practical reasoning" (Sanford, 2015, p. 257). If we are to take the cry of the veteran who is fearful of being seen as a monster because of acts committed during war, who wishes the nightmares to stop, whose bodily symptoms make relationships of trust and intimacy difficult, then the "moral" aspect of "moral injury" must have something to do with being and not simply doing; it must have something to do with virtue as the realization of "human-nature-as-it-could-be-if-it-realized-its-*telos*"; it must have something to do with not seeing oneself as—or fearing being seen as—a monster.

One could see a step in this direction with Robert Merrihew Adams' distinction between virtue ethics and the ethics of virtue, where virtue ethics is concerned with virtue for the sake of right action, while ethics of virtue is about being for the good for the sake of the good. As Adams claims, one can be virtuous and still commit a wrong action. For Adams, being virtuous entails being for the good in a way that is persistently excellent. He further defines "being for the good" as

> loving it, liking it, respecting it, wanting it, wishing for it, appreciating it, thinking highly of it, speaking in favor of it, and otherwise standing for it symbolically, acting to promote it or protect it and being disposed to do such things.
>
> (Adams, 2006, p. 15)

One could see Adams' understanding of virtue at work in the training of soldiers for combat situations. Although the training involves an increased effectiveness in killing, the being for the good is not killing *per se*, but defense—of country, and more concretely of fellow comrades and of innocent non-combatants within the vicinity of combat soldiers, who are also threatened by those seen as the enemy. Toward this end, the military is one of the most effective institutions at training in the virtues. Beyond forming habits that would incline the soldier to act in reaction to a particular sound or image, the military trains soldiers to relate to fellow soldiers in terms of loyalty, integrity, and camaraderie; there is also training in discipline and trust to higher-ranking officers. This training in particular virtues and habits is to enable a being for the good that manifests itself as courage in life-threatening situations both for protection of self, but especially for protection of fellow soldiers and innocent non-combatants. I want to be clear here—I am *not* presenting a defense of war grounded in the ethics of virtue. Whether the good for which the military trains soldiers to be *is* actually good or not is debatable; but it would be unfair to see this training in virtue as simply for killing, even if it involves killing.

Real problems begin to occur when combat veterans return home, because what has not been recognized is that the combat soldier has indeed been formed in habits, inclinations, tendencies, dispositions, and character, and that such a training and the kind of momentum generated by such a training cannot simply be reversed by switching geography. The problem is that while the military understands the importance of virtue in training for combat, it falls back on deontological ethics for the return home. It treats the soldiers as if they simply need to will the good when they return home, even though it took the military months to train them for a particular kind of being for the good. It fails to recognize that there is a different kind of being for the good that requires the soldier to engage in a different kind of training with a different set of practices. The kind of military training the soldier experienced may, in fact, get in the way of the being for the good at home. This is especially evident when soldiers cannot sleep, react to sounds of birds chirping as if they are in combat mode, and/ or have difficulty being in crowds for fear of threat. These particular habits cannot simply be turned off. What the military especially fails to consider is the lingering effect of images of violence that induces states of fear, anger, depression, guilt, and shame. While the military is very good at understanding the training involved in being for the good that involves defense, it expects the soldiers to simply will the good that is subsequently required for civilian life. Well-known stories and statistics indicate that such willing of the good is not so easy for many combat veterans.

Let us return to Adams for help to further specify exactly how what is "moral" about moral injury involves the virtues. For Adams, ethics of virtue is distinguished from virtue ethics by focusing on good character and not good action. He argues that one can be of good character and still do the wrong action. Good character has to do with the interrelation of what he terms structural (courage and temperance), cognitive (wisdom), and motivational virtues (love). In the end, what is important is the good for the sake of the good, and not right action or the consequences. The structural, cognitive, and motivational virtues constitute an

> excellence in being for the good [that] involves having feelings and desires that respond appropriately to the good, as well as acting well and thinking well about the good. Virtue's integration needs to involve all these types of response. In pursuit of such holistic integration it is reasonable, I think, to seek resources in practices that are not purely intellectual; various forms of psychotherapy and of religious mediation come to mind.
>
> (Adams, 2006, p. 222)

If we interpret this passage in light of the experience of combat veterans, what we notice is that the combat veteran desires the good, especially in terms of personal well-being which involves being able to sleep, not having nightmares, being able to be in public spaces and thus in various forms of relationships, having good relationships with friends and family, being able to keep a job, and other related goods. What often interfere with the realization of such goods are feelings pulsating throughout the body that make it difficult for the combat veteran to act in ways that attain the goods desired. In the context of PTSD and moral injury, such feelings often involve fear-induced anxiety to particular images, sensations, and situations. Anger is another feeling associated with PTSD and moral injury, often resulting in rage provoked by minor arguments. Finally, if part of the experience of moral injury is the experience of worthlessness, then feelings of hatred, especially self-loathing, will make difficult the fulfillment of the desire for personal goods, as well as contributing to the goods of the other. The self-loathing of the combat veteran is sometimes the result of having performed an act, such as the killing of innocent people, that is irrevocable and for which there can be no reciprocal compensation. How does one live with such an act being an eternal part of one's own narrative?

In terms of Adams' language, fear, anger, and hatred do not necessarily disrupt one's desire for the good, as these combat veterans have a palpable, bodily sense of the good that is eluding them; these feelings diminish the capacity for the structural and cognitive virtues, which, according to the neuroscience of the brain, has something to do with the impact and traces of violence on wiring and forming the brain to respond to particular situations. These particular insights resonate with the understanding of virtue by the Christian thinker, Maximus the Confessor, who, rather than using the language of structural, cognitive, and motivational virtues, uses the classical tri-part understanding of the soul in terms of the concupiscible (desiring), irascible, and rational. Much like Adams, Maximus sees the interrelation of virtues associated with these various parts of human psychology as having to be operative in order to manifest excellence in being for the good.

What Maximus specifies more clearly than Adams is the *telos* to which humans aspire, and this *telos* is to learn how to love. Motivated by his Christian conviction in a God who became human, Maximus affirms that humans can indeed become God, can be deified. This deification—*theosis*—has, however, nothing to do with being Zeus or Thor, but is about loving as God loves, even the stranger and the enemy. Virtues, thus, are not simply a moral category in that they allow for right action or right moral assessment; the manifestation of a virtue, such as patience, engenders other virtues, all of which together rightly order the desiring and irascible parts of the soul, thus making love possible to a greater degree. It is not uncommon for Maximus to assert that "[Love] springs from the calm of detachment, detachment from hope in God, hope from patience and long-suffering; and these from all-embracing self-mastery; self-mastery from the fear of God, fear of God from faith in the Lord" (Berthold, 1985, p. 36). Indeed, faith as a virtue could set off a chain reaction of virtues leading to love.

Maximus further amplifies that vices block love, and the three at the top of Maximus's list are fear, anger, and hatred.

> He knew well that this **fear** [of the Lord] is different from the fear which consists of being afraid of punishments for faults of which we are accused, since for one thing this (fear of punishment) disappears completely in the presence of love, as the great Evangelist John shows somewhere in words, "Love drives out fear."
>
> (1 Jn 4.18) (Berthold, 1985, p. 101, emphasis added)

> When you are insulted by someone or offended in any matter, then beware of angry thoughts, lest by distress they sever you from charity and place you in the region of hatred.
>
> (Berthold, 1985, p. 38)

> The one who sees a trace of **hatred** in his own heart through any fault at all toward any man whoever he may be makes himself completely foreign to the love for God, because love for God in no way admits of hatred for man.
>
> (Berthold, 1985, p. 37, emphasis added)

We can, at this point, combine Maximus's insights on pride and the affective trio of fear, anger, and hatred in a way not evident in Maximus, and with the help of basic psychoanalytical categories. If pride consists of the self-conscious inflation of the self, we know from psychoanalysis that our conscious sense of self masks unconscious emotions and desires that we simply do not want to confront. In this sense, pride could be a mask for self-loathing in the form of self-assertion. What then blocks love goes beyond selfish impulses, but probably has something to do with unconscious fears, anger, and hatred, formed in particular ways according to each person's unique history.

In identifying the *telos* of human-nature-as-it-could-be in terms of love, Maximus helps us to see that what is "moral" about moral injury is the diminishment of one's capacity to love, both oneself and the other as family, friend, stranger, or enemy. We also discern that what is injured morally can only be understood in terms of the virtues, especially since what is diminished is one's capacity for realizing the good; the self-loathing that ensues as a result of particular experiences is a diminished capacity for self-love, which affects one's ability to love and receive love. The anger and fear that can accompany PTSD and moral injury, and which now can be traced in the brain, make love difficult, especially since they diminish the capacity for the virtues related to the concupiscible part of the soul, most notably temperance. In addition to concretizing what is morally injured as a result of particular combat experiences, defining the human *telos* thickly in terms of learning how to love allows for an interdisciplinary approach to understanding this "dimensional" or existential mode of being; it also troubles the too-easy distinction between the ethical, the spiritual, and the psychological. In fact, to reduce this "dimensional problem" to either of these disciplines would restrict understanding of the complexity of moral injury at the expense of the morally injured.

Rewiring the self to love

There is hope amidst the suffering of violence. Neuroscientists have discovered that the plasticity of the brain lasts throughout our lifetime. This means that the brain can, indeed, be rewired, that new pathways can be formed that one might describe in the language of virtues. They are discovering that spiritual practices, such as yoga and certain forms of prayer, can rewire the brain, because, as explained by one of the leading specialists in treating trauma, Bessel van der Kolk, such practices allow "the body to have experiences that deeply and viscerally contradict the helplessness, rage, or collapse that result from trauma" (van der Kolk, 2014, pp. 3, 217, 267–69). According to van der Kolk,

> twenty weeks of yoga practice increased activation of the basic self-system, the insula and the medial prefrontal cortex. This research needs much more work, but it opens up new perspectives on how

actions that involve noticing and befriending the sensations in our
bodies can produce profound changes in both mind and brain that can
lead to healing from trauma.

(van der Kolk, 2014, p. 275)

In response to this problem of the effects of violence on learning, the Head
Start Trauma Smart program has students engage in such practices as
breathing exercises to help regulate anger and enable learning, even issuing
breathing stars as rewards, realizing that traditional disciplinary methods
based on fear, such as timeouts, are ineffective (Bornstein, 2014). Moreover,
Maximus gives concrete practices, along the lines of cognitive behavioral
therapy or positive psychology, for manifesting the virtues related specifically to the desiring and irascible parts of the soul. For example, he says
"For fornication, fast, keep vigil, work hard, keep to yourself. For anger
and hurt, disdain reputation and dishonor and material things. For
grudges, pray for the one who has hurt you and you will be rid of them"
(Berthold, 1985, pp. 62–63). One of the practices that wires the body for
openness to love is truth-telling, and one can see the importance of truth-
telling in treatments for both PTSD and moral injury, such as exposure
therapy, where the patient speaks repeatedly to the therapist about his or
her trauma in order to reduce the fear reaction to the memories; or adaptive disclosure therapy, where patients engage in "imaginal conversation
with the deceased or a compassionate and forgiving moral authority"
(Maguen and Litz, 2012, p. 3).

The fact that yoga and breathing practices are proving to be so helpful
to those who have suffered trauma—child abuse, rape, combat violence—
should motivate more studies on the effects of various spiritual practices
on the body for healing the effects of violence, such as the Jesus Prayer,
which recites "Lord Jesus Christ, Son of God, have mercy on me,
a sinner" according to rhythmic breathing patterns. There is clearly
potential in these spiritual practices to wire the body to mitigate the feelings of fear, anger, and hatred; and, thus, toward openness to loving and
being loved. The language of virtue most adequately captures the dynamics of this wiring, but diligence is required so as not to overlay this formation with deontological categories of right or wrong, and correlative
notions of penance, atonement, or guilt. The virtues are not primarily
about right or wrong but about forming the body so as to receive the
presence of God, which means toward loving and accepting love. As
Maximus states, "The essence in every virtue is the one Logos of
God … Which is to say that anyone who through fixed habit participates
in virtue, unquestionably participates in God, who is the substance of virtues" (Constas, 2004, p. 103).

Primary sources

Berthold, G. C. (trans.) (1985), *Maximus the Confessor: Selected Writings* (Mahwah, NJ: Paulist Press).
Constas, N. (trans. and ed.) (2004), *Maximos the Confessor, On the Difficulties in the Church, The Ambigua*, vol. 1 (Cambridge: Harvard University Press, 2014).

Secondary sources

Adams, R. M. (2006), *A Theory of Virtue: Excellence in Being for the Good* (Oxford: Oxford University Press).
Bornstein, David "Teaching Children to Calm Themselves," *New York Times*, 20 March 2014. http://opinionator.blogs.nytimes.com/2014/03/19/first-learn-how-to-calm-down/?_r=0, last accessed 11 July 2016.
Brock, R. N. and Lettini, G. (2012), *Soul Repair: Recovering from Moral Injury after War* (Boston: Beacon Press).
Dao, James (2013), "Drone Pilots Are Found to Get Stress Disorders Much as Those in Combat Do," *New York Times*, 23 February. www.nytimes.com/2013/02/23/us/drone-pilots-found-to-get-stress-disorders-much-as-those-in-combat-do.html?_r=0
Drescher, K. D., et al. (2011), "An Exploration of the Viability and Usefulness of the Construct of Moral Injury in War Veterans," *Traumatology* 17:1: 8–13.
Finkel, D. (2013), "The Return: The Traumatized Veterans of Iraq and Afghanistan," *The New Yorker*, 9 September.
Grossman, D. Lt. Col. (2009), *On Killing: The Psychological Cost of Learning to Kill in War and Society* (New York: Little, Brown and Company).
Herman, J. (1992), *Trauma and Recovery: The Aftermath of Violence from Domestic Abuse to Political Terror* (New York: Basic).
Kerr, N. A. (2007), "St. Anselm: *Theoria* and the Doctrinal Logic of Perfection," in.
Litz, B. T., et al. (2009), "Moral Injury and Moral Repair in War Veterans: A Preliminary Model and Intervention Strategy," *Clinical Psychology Review* 29: 694–706.
MacIntyre, A. (1984), *After Virtue* (South Bend: University of Notre Dame Press).
MacNair, R. M. (2002), *Perpetration-Induced Traumatic Stress: The Psychological Consequences of Killing* (Westport: Praeger).
Maguen, S., et al. (2009), "Killing in Combat, Mental Health Symptoms, and Suicidal Ideation in Iraq War Veterans," *Journal of Anxiety Disorders* 25: 563–567.
Maguen, S., et al. (2010), "The Impact of Reported Direct and Indirect Killing on Mental Health Symptoms in Iraq War Veterans," *Journal of Traumatic Stress* 23: 86–90.
Maguen, S., et al. (2011), "The Impact of Killing on Mental Health Symptoms in Gulf War Veterans," *Pychological Trauma: Theory, Research, Practice, and Policy* 3: 23–26.
Maguen, S. and Litz, B. (2012), "Moral Injury in Veterans of War," *PTSD Research Quarterly* 23:1: 1–6.
Meagher, R. E. (2014), *Killing from the Inside Out: Moral Injury and Just War* (Eugene: Cascade Books).
Sanford, Jonathan J. (2015), *Before Virtue: Assessing Contemporary Virtue Ethics*. Washington, DC: Catholic University Press.

Shay, J. (1994), *Achilles in Vietnam: Combat Trauma and the Undoing of Character* (New York: Scribner).

Shay, J. (2002), *Odysseus in America: Combat Trauma and the Trials of Homecoming* (New York: Scribner).

van der Kolk, B. (2014), *The Body Keeps the Score: Brain, Mind, and Body in the Healing of Trauma* (New York: Penguin Publishing Group).

Walker, S. P., et al. (2007), "Child Development: Risk Factors for Adverse Outcomes in Developing Countries," *The Lancet* 369 (9556): 145–157.

Walker, S. P., et al. (2011), "Inequality in Early Childhood: Risk and Protective Factors for Early Child Development," *The Lancet* 378:9799: 1325–1338.

Chapter 8

The psychic counterpoise to violence towards the human other

Romano Màdera

It is well known that killing a member of one's own species requires overcoming an inhibition that is phylogenetic in nature. One hypothesis that may explain this inhibition is that the natural empathy that functions as the basis of this recognition could be attributed to the operation of mirror neurons and the implications of their operation to other areas and systems of the brain. As the American psychologist Cozolino tells us,

> Measuring neural firing in a monkey's brain while she observes another monkey grasping a grape is relatively straightforward when compared to examining the complexities of human emotional experience. Not only do we lack a clear definition for complex emotions, but we also lack the technology to directly measure human brain activity in naturalistic settings. Although we are just beginning to explore the neurobiology of empathy, some clues are beginning to emerge. Given that the cortex first evolved to guide motor behavior, it makes sense that more primitive somatic and motor activation serve as the infrastructure of emotion, cognition, and abstract thought. Utilizing mirror circuitry as a core system and expanding it to include additional systems of the social brain, we may be able to begin looking for a fundamental network of resonance and empathy.
>
> (Cozolino, 2014, pp. 231–232; see also Botvinick et al., 2005)

Among mammals, murderous behaviour towards others of the same species only occurs under exceptional circumstances. Violence is typically ritualized, and the instinct to act violently is neutralized as soon as the opponent accepts defeat. It is for this very reason that, conversely, the most diverse of human cultures produce specific rituals that help to modify communal perceptions and thus overcome this inhibition. Such a line of reasoning led Konrad Lorenz (1966) to attribute to the invention of firearms, which have made it possible to kill at ever-greater distances, a key role in facilitating war.

Both behaviour and the use of substances aimed at altering states of consciousness are invariably situated within a cultural construction that transforms the image of the other who becomes the object of attack. This other must be distorted to the extent of no longer resembling a human other. Such a transformation, which appears to be a feature of all cultures, as theorized by Eibl-Eibesfeldt (1989), may be termed "pseudo-speciation". The other becomes a member of a different species, and may therefore be killed. In other words, the constraints applying to behaviour among members of the same species no longer hold. From here, it is a downhill ride to the "mutual demonization" of rival groups, or to the "monsterization" of scapegoats, whether they be individuals or collectives.

It is at this deep level, which is still ethological and pre-psychic, that we need to consider moral injury. Arguably, we are touching here on a dimension that we might call the dimension of "anthropic constants", or, in Jungian terms, an archetypal dimension. Mutual demonization of rival groups as well as the projection of the image and function of scapegoats can be understood as a "network of interactions" that comprehends both victims and perpetrators:

> Instead of having one single archetype organizing the network of interactions, there is a cluster of archetypes ("Network of Archetypal Images") because archetypes are closely interrelated; it is seldom that only one, single archetype is activated without other archetypes also participating in the relational network with other individuals. Moreover, even in the context of one individual, one archetype does not act on its own but it triggers the activation of related archetypes (in a compensatory or supplementary way). This means that, mostly, archetypes affect individuals and groups not in isolation but in clusters, networks, constellations.
>
> (Papadopoulos, 2006, p. 32)

This archetypal dimension indeed proves to be deeper and more stable than any attempts to be overridden by other processes. Occasionally, certain cultural and ritual forms promote processes that violate the phylogenetic tendency to regulate violence among members of the same species. However, invariably, these are met with resistance. Analysis of this persistent resistance to acts of destructive violence leads us to formulate the hypothesis that it is in the nature of the species to oppose the operational tactics of cultures and their ability to influence and transform these archetypal sanctions. The retroactive consequence suffered by those who treat others with violence is the paradigmatic illustration of the fact that it is human nature itself that is violated whenever one human is violated. It appears that the moral law that commands us not to kill another human being is within our nature. Then, progressively, through history, this law became a universal commandment reaching far beyond the confines of a particular group of people or collective. Therefore, I contend that while the universality of this moral law has developed across history, it is solidly founded on our phylogenetic heredity. This is why transgression of the law often gives rise to a backlash against the aggressors – a backlash that we may term "counterpoise", to draw on a notion used by Dante in "The Divine Comedy". In Dante, the expression "*contrappasso*" refers to the general form of punishment received in Hell, according to which the evil deeds of a person come back to haunt him. Contrapasso simply means "suffer the opposite", and Dante borrowed it from Thomas Aquinas who developed the idea in his *Summa Theologica*. According to Dante, this type of punishment involves the sinner receiving punishment that relates directly to, and in a sense mirrors and reflects, the sin committed. For example, those who perpetrated violence against others are condemned to be thrown into a river of boiling blood (in the "Seventh Circle" of the "Inferno").

Counterpoise is the process that intervenes when compensation, in Jungian terms, fails to restructure a conscious attitude. Then, a person would be led to some form of one-sidedness, some form of violation of one's own psyche, because a conscious stance would overrule any indications from the unconscious. We might say that due to counterpoise, it is impossible for human beings to harm others without the offense falling back on the perpetrators in a circular fashion. What takes place in the poetic and symbolic universe of Dante's "Inferno" is a good metaphor for what happens beneath the surface of human consciousness, in the deep and dark psyche of those who violate this fundamental law based on the common membership in the human race. This struggle is both unconscious and conscious, individual and collective, inside and outside, and can be enlightened by the dialectic of "recognition and misrecognition", which Hegel introduced and recently was developed further by Axel Honneth, in relation to the themes that this chapter addresses. Honneth maintains that, fundamentally, moral injury has its origin in the experience of misrecognition.

As Flynn put it succinctly, Honneth (1995) identified three forms of social recognition:

> The emotional concern and support found in the intimate relationships of love and friendship, the equal respect accorded to rights-bearing individuals, and the social esteem granted to individuals based on their abilities. Thus, there are three types of recognition – love, respect and esteem and these stand in opposition to three corresponding forms of disrespect: physical or psychological abuse, denial of rights or exclusion, and denigration or insult.
>
> (Flynn, 2008)

In this sense we can understand moral injury as every form of disrespect that tends to destroy the possibility of being an object of love by others, which prevents self-esteem and erases self-respect because it cancels the victim's human rights.

Inspired by Honneth, J. M. Bernstein (2005) claimed that the theory of recognition, with its central concept of misrecognition or social disrespect, provides a comprehensive account of all forms of moral injury. In fact, for Bernstein this theory represents a universal foundation for legitimizing various forms of social and political struggle. But what precisely is meant here by the term "misrecognition"? And what is the nature of moral injury, which is developed as a result of the experience of misrecognition?

Honneth emphasizes the way that misrecognition disrupts a subject's basic forms of self-relation, hindering the development of social self-identity and of moral-practical autonomy. Misrecognition, comprising a variety of forms of social disrespect, ultimately has a bodily basis. This bodily basis consists of the possibility of bodily injury – a violation of the vulnerable physical self – and such physical vulnerability presents an image of the comparable possibility of violation that can be inflicted on the integrity of the equally vulnerable human psyche. From the perspective of misrecognition, moral injury is understood as the possibility of a violation that harms essential forms of practical self-relation and that can result in various forms of psychic regression.[1]

The consequences of moral injury deeply affect both victims and perpetrators: the suffered misrecognition is internalized involuntarily. The victim is united with the perpetrator because he cannot get rid of his hatred of him. Identifying himself with the perpetrator means that some parts of oneself will be hated by other parts of oneself. This is another form of the dynamics of counterpoise: if the process does not become conscious and the possibility of compensation is not properly elaborated, both victim and perpetrator will "suffer the opposite", which is what Jung referred to as "enantiodromia" (literally meaning: opposite ways). According to this principle, any extreme tendency will activate its opposite so that some form of equilibrium is maintained.

Clinical vignettes

In order to clarify these dynamics further, some examples from clinical practice might be useful.

The first case concerns a young industrial manager, intelligent and sensitive, who, most inconsistently with his overall personality, had an impulse to want to shoot "gypsies". At the end of an analytical session he remains silent and then, as though taking up a thread from much farther back, says: "I like changing city, nation, job, environment".

ɪ: "Do you remember when you used to hate gypsies: the ones in your dreams and the ones on the street?"

ANALYSAND: "Yes. I've become a gypsy myself in a certain sense. Travelling around Europe has released me from staying here just to scrape a living, in situations without future prospects. My teenage desire to run away, to get away from my mother's suffocating control. And my father's."

ɪ: "The gypsy has saved you".

After many years of analytical work, it emerged that this impulse was directed at freeing himself from his own gypsy shadow – which had been stigmatized in childhood by his pervasively and anxiously controlling mother, but which contained the freest and most creative aspects of his aspirations to self-realization as an adult man. The gypsy redeemed through the analytical process was the analysand himself, who successfully overcame his partial and unconscious identification with the superego prescriptions of his family. Victim and perpetrator were found to be two dynamic and dialectical figures within the same, internalized, and projected complex. In the course of the analytical work, it became clear that this young man's impulse to destroy "the gypsy" was actually directed against himself, against his own potential for self-liberation.

In this case, "gypsies" as possible victims, reduced to a kind of "human game" – as otherwise really happened in the darkest moments of colonialism in the Americas, Africa, and Australia – resumed their human feature through the elaboration of the shadow of the analysand. So, the "perpetrator" recognized himself in the victim and the moral counterpoise that persecuted him through the interiorized figure of his mother ceased to work. It is evident that the lack of recognition of the rights of gypsies, the absence of respect corresponds to the projection of the feeling of not being respected by the mother.

The second case is that of a young homosexual Turkish man who had emigrated to Italy. His life story combined paradoxes, contradictions, and the double-bind of the victim–perpetrator relationship, in a way that was both particularly complex and, at the same time, illuminating. The young man had been abused psychologically throughout childhood by his mother, who had made her son and daughter pay for their father's hurtful betrayal of her with a sister-in-law, a relationship that subsequently led to the birth of a baby girl. In a dream, this young man first tried to disappear, and later locked himself into a safe from which he called to his mother to release him. The safe in which he is hidden may also have contained jewels – the dreamer's job was in reality to create jewellery. Is he the mother's jewel, and does he want his desire to be discovered?

Immediately after, he related another scene: a very big man is strangling him, and he is choking. At this point he is not able to continue the story in Italian, and says in English, a language he knows better than Italian, "can you mother me?" In another dream, he found himself transformed into a jellyfish, later recognizing the power to sting, which characterizes this animal. This is a powerful mythical resonance, which relates both to his hurt and to his way of connecting with others. The image was a hybrid between Medea and Medusa that seemed to evoke scenarios in which a frustrated desire for recognition is turned against a victim, who remains caught up in the world of the persecutor. In a certain sense, this case is the opposite of the first and yet, similarly, presents the same dyad in which victim and perpetrator provide a mirror image of one another. Misrecognition calls misrecognition.

The dreams show that it is impossible not to recognize that the role of perpetrator has unconsciously become part of the victim, that the transformation into a monster of another human being remains at the level of consciousness, but that this misrecognition has its counterpoise in the nocturnal dimension of the psyche where the opposites merge one into the other.

The third case is that of a social worker in an Italian city, involved in the reception of refugees and immigrants. In a dream, the period of the struggle against Nazism emerged as an alienating memory mixed with the contemporary conflicts encountered by the analysand in the context of his daily work.

The dream's landscape is that of Monte Sole, a place in which the Fascists and the Nazis had massacred hundreds of people. In the cemetery dedicated to the victims hides a shabby man with torn clothes; he is Hitler's brother. This shabby man was not well; he was psychologically fragile, antisocial, and very bashful. But even so, he exuded the air of an artist. The dreamer felt he had a social and political role in relation to the shabby man. And then in the dream, the dreamer noticed a wall but, looking closer at it, noticed that it was in fact a parallelepiped-shaped building dominated by a triangle, altogether appearing like a pyramid, a memorial. Inside that memorial-pyramid was a person who was like a stone and, perhaps, was the shabby man's brother, Hitler. In this case, the dreamer's usual framework of political and moral values had become uncertain and confused; a vicious circle seemed to dominate whereby there was no longer a clear boundary between criminals and victims who blended indistinctly with one another.

This story tells us that even the monster *par excellence*, Hitler, has a brother who restores him to the humanity of the victims murdered by the Nazi terror. Here, the dreamer's ideals that have supported his sense of freedom and justice are confronted by the need not to lose their own humanity; and this possibility exists if he does not undergo the counterpoise that would make him look like those whom he opposes.

Finally, we have a life story that was tragic but straightforward in its dynamics, which was recounted by another analysand. Her mother had killed her younger brother, and sometime later, despite having received medication and undergone institutional care, her mother took her own life in a way that was reminiscent of how she had killed her son. The mother had drowned her son in the water of the bathtub, and she drowned herself in a river, on the anniversary of her son's death.

Here the dialectic of counterpoise is evident: the mother didn't succeed in working through and expiating her crime, she was not able to consciously compensate her feelings of guilt, to forgive herself and to move forward with her own life story. She "balanced" her killing of her child by killing herself. In this vicious circle, injuries of love, respect, and esteem continue to reproduce themselves without being transformed.

This circularity of injury to the human person appears to bear out each person's shared belonging to the species, which is psychically present as the archetypal dimension of the bond, and therefore as a field that contains and influences the individuals who are situated and move within it.

This is a characteristic that may be theoretically viewed as a convergence, and a partial reciprocal translatability, between systems theory and analytical psychology, as suggested by Renos K. Papadopoulos (2006).

Jung himself wrote:

> The clinical standpoint by itself is not and cannot be fair to the nature of a neurosis, because a neurosis is more a psychosocial phenomenon than an illness in the strict sense. It forces us to extend the term "illness" beyond the idea of an individual body whose functions are disturbed, and to look upon the neurotic person as a sick system of social relationships.
>
> (Jung, 1993, p. 24)

We can understand the dynamics of what happens between victim and perpetrator only if we put them in a context which differentiates social, historical, biographical, and archetypal dimensions. At the same time, what affects the psychological state of the subject has to be carefully analysed as a point of the system that has its own proper characteristics. In doing so we assume that everyone is a part of a bigger whole. Interdependence from outside and from inside is the relational pattern that governs history and psychology, willingly or unwillingly.

The parallel with the spiritual, and specifically Christian conception of the unity of whole humankind, symbolized in Adam, is clear, as Kallistos Ware writes in his essay in this same volume quoting St. Mark the Monk: "In this way the whole universe is held together in unity, and through God's providence we are each assisted by one another".

The Golden Rule and enantiodromia

This leads us straight to the anthropological foundation of what is often called the Golden Rule: "Do not do unto others what you would not wish them to do unto you" is a principle rooted in the interdependence of human beings. Whether in terms of enacting self-punishment, projective "acting out", or inner conflict, the evil inflicted on an other demands that a price be paid by the one inflicting it. This is paradoxical but not absurd, especially if we consider the complexity of the psyche of the offending subject in relation to his or her victim and their mutual environment.

For further key theorizing about these connections, we are indebted to the work of E. Neumann (1973). His reconstructive work commented on the human tendency – both on the individual and group levels – to create scapegoats by projecting an evil felt within onto certain categories of "other", mostly chosen from the lowest or highest strata of society. Members of a minority group of any kind, be they handicapped or exceptional individuals, innovators, reformers, revolutionaries (such as Socrates, Jesus, and Galileo), are all alien to "ordinary" people who are considered representatives of general social norms. Every difficulty can be projected onto such a member of a minority, in order to save and calm the majority of people. Both Neumann and Jung suggest psychological and spiritual ways to cope with the temptation of attempting to rid ourselves of conflicts by projecting them onto somebody who has to take the role of the scapegoat.

In a passage of great intensity in *The Red Book*, Jung (2009) writes:

> No one rises above himself who has not turned his most dangerous weapon against himself. One who wants to rise above himself shall climb down and hoist himself onto himself and lug himself to the place of sacrifice. But what must happen to a man until he realizes that outer visible success, that he can grasp with his hands, lends him astray. What suffering must be brought upon humanity until man gives up satisfying his longing for power over his fellow man and forever wanting others to be the same. How much blood must go on flowing until man opens his eyes and sees the way to his own path and himself as the enemy, and becomes aware of his real success. You ought to be able to live with yourself, but not at your neighbour's expense.
>
> (p. 309)

In this passage, Jung implies that if you do not become aware of your own destructive tendencies and you do not sacrifice the willpower of the ego, inevitably countless others will be sacrificed as scapegoats. Again, the interdependence between individuals and between groups is at stake, but also the interdependence between what is external and what is internal.

In the spiritual sphere, this awareness of the function of scapegoats and of the systemic interdependence of victims and perpetrators has surfaced in contexts of extreme suffering, and is compatible with a wide variety of religious and philosophical paths, as borne out by vivid accounts and writings.

It is really remarkable to follow this golden thread of compassion and mercy disentangling itself in horror-filled places: Etty Hillesum, a Jew who was imprisoned and killed in a Nazi concentration camp; Simone Weil, a philosopher, in the midst of the Spanish Civil War; Pavel Florenskij, a victim of the Stalinist Gulag; Thich Nhat Hahn, a Zen monk during the Vietnam War; Dietrich Bonhoeffer, a Lutheran pastor and theologian, hanged in a Nazi prison, all of them were able to forgive their torturers and assassins. All of these are bright examples of the possibility of avoiding continually reproducing the dialectic that transforms the victims into perpetrators and *vice versa*. It is this dialectic that makes it impossible to put an end to perpetuation, generation after generation, of violence and moral injury, caused or suffered. This is the race of opposites, the essence of *enantiodromia*. It is an illusion that the culture of war and destructive violence can stop the course of revenge; it is an illusion that the evil of the oppressor does not infect the oppressed. Certainly, there are different responsibilities, different roles, but the mutual implications somehow bring in something of the opposite side; and sooner or later, through actual acts or psychologically suffering, this opposite will emerge.

In the final analysis, I believe that we may escape the enantiodromic implications of the opposition between victim and perpetrator by postulating the mercy principle as a dynamic dialectic, both external and internal, which continuously offers us the possibility of forgiveness.

The mercy principle

I would formulate the "mercy principle" as follows:

> Behave towards others and towards yourself as though you were the instrument of a mercy that is so broad and deep as to be capable of forgiving every horror, pain and error. Since we will all certainly continue to commit every kind of horror and error, never let condemnation be the last word, but go on forgiving others and forgiving yourself. Only that which we are incapable of forgiving is unforgiveable.
>
> (Màdera, 2012, p. 285)

The rationale of this principle lies in the fact that it brings together procedure and content. No matter what error, crime, or sin the other party is guilty of – according to a definition that will vary as broadly as the outlooks of those making the judgement – they may be forgiven, and they must be allowed the possibility of a future. It is useful to reflect on the etymology and composition of the word "forgive". It is astonishing that in most European languages, the word has an identical composition "for" and "give"; in Greek "syn-horo", in French "par-donne", in Italian "perdonare", in Spanish "per-donar", and even in German "ver-zeihen". The "for" that precedes "give" intensifies the "give" considerable. Moreover, in Greek, "syn-horo" (Συγ-χωρώ) literally means sharing space with another person, being together in the same space. A humanity that adhered to the regulative criterion of mercy would be bound together by a higher-level universal agreement, going beyond differences in culture, ideology, or political orientation and sharing space together, co-existing. This does not mean renouncing judgement and punishment, but situating them within a horizon that remains open to and ultimately points to mercy.

One might object to or even deride these pious intentions, arguing that they may lead to a "crocodile tears morality", or to the "blessing of crimes by the Holy Inquisition": that is, an idea that no matter what evils a person commits they are entrusted to divine mercy. I believe that the Taoist saying – which was born through meditation on the art of war and government, and recommends behaving on one's day of victory as if one were going to a funeral – cannot be dismissed easily. A political power that followed this maxim to some extent would certainly not allow itself to be taken over by the desire for vengeance once victorious. It would not behave, for instance, as the winners of the First World War behaved towards Germany, a behaviour which contributed to the rise of Nazism. This example is common to most wars, both international and civil. The principle is dynamic, and restores itself after each denial of its truth, thus continuously re-proposing a fundamental harmony with life that looks to the future.

This harmony is comprised of a variety of native and natural human capacities for recognition, empathy, and trust, re-elaborated to the point of understanding and overcoming, each time afresh, the equally natural but less native inclination to destroy the enemy. That destructive inclination is less native because it is derived from the need to safeguard and defend ourselves from threats to the primary needs of a community of recognition, empathy, and trust in which the memory and therefore the identity of both group and individual are structured. It may also be argued that the mercy principle carries overtones that relate more to Judeo-Christian traditions, or perhaps Mahayana and Vajrayana Buddhist traditions, than they do to other religious or philosophical traditions. However, it would be irrefutable that the Judeo-Christian and Buddhist version of this principle comprehends the universal love of humanity that is at the core of all the ancient philosophical schools. It is this love that inspired Socrates in the *Apology* and Plato in his *Euthyphro*.

Spirituality and psychology

In the religious language of the Christian tradition we might speak of "divine mercy", a possible and, in my view, appropriate understanding of faith in a God of Love, or in Love that is God. In such an understanding, the only thing that is unforgiveable is to sin against the Spirit, where the

Spirit of God, revealed in Jesus of Nazareth as the Christ and continuously at work, is Divine Mercy. This framework also fits with the idea of God who sends rain on the just and the unjust, and the idea that neither the man born blind nor his parents have sinned, but that his healing is a manifestation of God's salvation. It also fits the statement of Jesus that "I judge no one", and the verse in the New Testament in which Jesus was "stirred with compassion".

A strong counterargument to this reading, but in reality to any claims about the identity of God and of love itself, is the doctrine of creation, or of God as the creator of the physical world. This doctrine is also at the root of theodicy's difficulty in accounting for natural evil and the suffering of the innocent. In the present context, I shall only point out that the force of the objection depends on how one interprets the opening chapters of the book of Genesis. Carlo Enzo's (2010) reading of them excludes that the Genesis account of creation regards the physical world, because otherwise it would lose the status of a "sacred text", that is to say a text that is composed in keeping with the language and canons of the Hebrew Scriptures. If creation is therefore understood as regarding the moral-spiritual world of a particular type of Adamic man who is called to follow and complete the path shown to him by his God, then the issue of nature appears in a very different light. I might even say that divine mercy allows us to look at nature as though it had been given to us so that we might contemplate it in another or second way, in a certain sense as though it were "forgiven". I mean this in the sense that it was justified by this other or second nature, which is "divine" or supernatural, and which represents the good freedom of the fulfilment of desire; a desire that is born of the first nature and which wants – though still blindly, contradictorily, and destructively – what is good.

How to reconcile our naturally mortal and sometimes horrific existence with our equally natural desire for good is a question that inevitably recurs, independently of our religious or philosophical inclinations, and this is eloquently expressed by Enzo Paci (1961). Although he was not remotely thinking of the dead and risen Christ, this is what he wrote in his *Phenomenological Diary*: "because temporality is consumption and death, life has meaning if it succeeds in turning death into life". In the symbolic life, mercy proclaims that every death, and every end – even the most hateful – may be redeemed. Its giving may be renewed in for-giving, in which death opens up a new perspective, a new direction, a new meaning.

In the world of Christocentric symbolism, mercy as the revelation of the divine life is identified with the crucified one who is the risen one, and the risen one who is the crucified one. The cross represents life that fulfils the supreme expression of mercy and the essence of forgiveness. Lack of recognition, shame, blame, betrayal, and revenge, which are the intolerable barriers that cut us off from the possibility of forgiveness – thereby imprisoning us in a finite life, condemned to replicate the past because we remain under the power of the past – are overcome. This utterance of Christ: "forgive them, for they know not what they do" is the sacrament, continuously renewed, of life after death – after the death that our lack of conscious awareness of our bond with the other who co-institutes us and condemns us to. In contrast, in Michelangelo's *Pietà* or in Mantegna's *Lamentation of Christ*, the figure of the mother represents the potential to undergo recognition in failure and ignominy – the only guarantee, in truth, of any substance in our ephemeral and unreliable attempts at recognition. The son gave himself up with the words of Psalm 22 on the cross: "my God, my God, why have you abandoned me?" – and this to the hope of a recognition that would reach beyond his absence. Thus, we have these two, mother and son, who communicate in death, who recognize one another in unconditional love, when all, truly all, is irreversibly lost. This awareness of love without limits is true understanding, and in this true understanding resides mercy. In this sense, Mary is the Mother of God, if God and Divine Mercy are one and the same: because in the *Pietà*, which is the symbol of Mary embracing Jesus, the dead Christ is born, that is to say, rises from the dead as Divine Humanity. A more complex figure of a new feeling and thinking about God as Mercy fulfilled.

As I see it, in order to think about the resurrection, it is not necessary to dwell on the juxtaposition of witnessing to the early Christian faith, in its sapiential narrative (whose purpose is to teach a way of life), mythical themes, and historical elements. All of these layers are clearly present in the Biblical text, but in order to access the meaning that is feasible for us, we only need to seek out its essence, the symbolic essence that is preserved within each cultural-historical framing of the symbol. This is an essence whose creative vitality manifests differently in each of its variations. In contemplating the image of the dead Christ, we may realize our regretful longing for the one we have lost and our desire to have him back, and this may ignite life in our image of the corpse. Because of our wish for reparation, in effect, the image of the dead person still lives in us and this represents a form of resurrection. The universal greatness of the resurrection lies also in this – in the complete reprocessing of bereavement.

Furthermore, completion of the mourning process is equivalent, in the resurrection of he who was crucified, to the assimilation and integration of the heaviest and darkest symbols of evil. The radical humanization of the risen one, and the resurrected body, coincides with the resurrection of the divine in ourselves and its universality beyond the confines of any religion. It belongs to the ecumenical spirituality of cosmic humanity. The divine lives in the human life of Christ and by identifying with Christ we also partake of the divine spirit. It takes place in the ascension to heaven, the descent of the spirit, the communion of languages at Pentecost, and even right up to the last events of the Apocalypse and the coming of the new heavens and the new earth – which is the ultimate conciliation of the divine-human cosmos. Again, this final conciliation comes to pass after the ascension to heaven and the entrusting of the disciples to the Spirit who will teach all truth, in that the ascension of Jesus of Nazareth, recognized as a crucial stage in the coming of the Christ, implies a distancing from any personifications identifying the Spirit of the Master with a particular historical moment. The announcing of a possible liberation from any form of fetishistic idolatry lies in this movement of ascent and descent, of separation and of birth, to the life of the symbol. However, we cannot progress in this direction without consciously sacrificing our empirical self-centredness: we must necessarily undergo its symbolic death as the cost of redeeming the self in the risen life of the spirit.

Making the transition through *failure*, going through the experience of *forgiveness*, discovering a self that is transfigured in its *communion* with the human and the cosmos, and offering *thanksgiving* as acceptance and affirmation of life even in death: these are the four great words of a renewed *Philosophia Christi*. What do redemption and resurrection of the self, in a transfigured and transformed form, mean? Certainly, they mean that the self must learn to follow that part of itself that conjoins it to the universal cosmos and the history of humanity, where its very end becomes an episode in its cosmic story of meaning, and a page in its mythobiography.

For many people today, psychology can contribute substantially to the transition to spirituality through a process of psychological interiorization. Psychology could overcome the danger of subjectivist closure in order to open up to the spirit. Psychotherapies and psychoanalysis dig into biographical history to uncover its unconscious determinants but are often lacking in an orientation and in concrete exercises – such as those practised in all spiritual traditions and even in ancient Greek-Roman philosophy – to foster the transcendence of egotistical interests, thus running the risk of exacerbating even further the leading illness of our world by making exploration of the depths of the psyche yet another pretext for narcissism.

On the other side, spirituality could be freed of residuals of objectivistic exteriority, otherwise, without psychological interiority, its meaning could remain obscured by devotional practices or by literal beliefs in their mythological aspect.

In the possible synthesis of depth psychology and spirituality, mercy does not mean cancelling out what is negative, or sentimental acquiescence to all wickedness. The negative must be transfigured and therefore transformed. We are able to see it from a different – anamorphic – perspective. We need to comprehend that hunting down external or internal scapegoats is a response to our unattainable desire to expel anger and vengeance and to eliminate suffering. It is the inefficacy of this condemnation of the presumed guilty party – condemnation which at best will only fuel the infinite circuit of resentment – that underpins the transfiguration of the scapegoat into our shadow twin, of whom we must be aware and with whom we must negotiate, so as to be able to finally make the transition from acting out to symbolic dramatization.

An ethics that undergoes a serious course of analysis and is based on the mercy principle can work out an individual position that does not in any way imply the affirmation of an ethic of particularism. It does not mean doing whatever we like, and it does not mean that we are exempt from justifying our conduct to ourselves and to others. On the contrary, it is a process aimed at developing the most responsible and coherent of ethical positions, as interpreted within the mercy principle.

In response to the dilemmas posed by moral injury, the mercy principle can represent a resumption, at the highest level of ethics and spirituality, of the phylogenetic inhibition of killing a member of one's own species. Mercy can be the process of overcoming the inevitable backlash, the counterpoise, that inside the psyche or in acting out chases both the perpetrators and the victims who remain trapped in the prison of resentment and vengeance, repression, and unquenchable feelings of guilt. A process that implies a difficult and delicate intertwining of depth psychology and spirituality.

The age of wars and destruction between different cultures, peoples, and societies is fading away, even if the pains of birth of a new possible world will last for a long time. But there is no alternative to the increasing international interdependence. The historical and cultural conditions that have created our attitudes to pseudo-speciation are losing their cogency more and more: only forgiveness, compassion, and mercy can offer a possible answer.

Note

1 M. Sharpe, M. Noonan, J. Freddi, *Trauma, History, Philosophy*. Cambridge: Cambridge Scholar Publishing, Cambridge University Press, 2009, p. 283. See also J. M. Bernstein, "Suffering Injustice: Misrecognition as Moral Injury", *Critical Theory. International Journal of Philosophical Studies*, 13 (3), 305–309, 2005. These essays discuss the theory of A. Honneth, *The Struggle of Recognition. The Moral Grammar of Social Conflicts*, Cambridge UK: Polity Press, 1995.

References

Bernstein, J. M., "Suffering injustice: misrecognition as moral injury", *Critical Theory. International Journal of Philosophical Studies*, 13 (3), 305–309, 2005.
Botvinick, M., Jha, A. P., Bylsma, L. M., Fabian, S. A., Solomon, P. F., and Pukachin, K. M., "Viewing facial expressions of pain engages cortical areas involved in the direct experience of pain", *Neuroimage*, 25 (1), 312–319, 2005.
Cozolino, L., *The Neuroscience of Human Relationships*. New York and London: W. W. Norton & Company, 2014.

Eibl-Eibesfeldt, I., *Human Ethology*. Chicago: Aldine Transactions, 1989.

Enzo, C., *La generazione di Gesù Cristo nel vangelo Secondo Matteo. II. La Legge*, vol. 3. Milano-Udine: Mimesis, 2010, pp. 206–215.

Flynn, J., "Review of *Disrespect: The Normative Foundations of Critical Theory*, by Axel Honneth. (Cambridge UK: Polity, 2007)", *International Philosophical Quarterly*, 48 (4), 552–555, 2008.

Honneth, A., *The Struggle of Recognition. The Moral Grammar of Social Conflicts*, Cambridge UK: Polity Press, 1995.

Jabbi, M., Swart, M., and Keysers, C., "Empathy for positive and negative emotions in the gustatory cortex", *Neuroimage*, 34 (4), 1744–1753, 2007.

Jung, C. G., "What is psychotherapy?", in *Collected Works*, Vol. 16. London: Routledge, 1993.

Jung, C. G., *The Red Book*, New York: Norton, 2009, p. 310.

Lorenz, K., *On Aggression*, London: Methem Publishing, 1966 (the first German edition was published in 1963), pp. 133–236.

Màdera, R., *La carta del senso. Psicologia del profondo e vita filosofica*. Milano: Cortina Editore, 2012.

Neumann, E., *Depth Psychology and a New Ethic*. New York: Harper Torchbooks, 1973 (first published in German in 1949).

Paci, E., *Diario fenomenologico*. Bompiani, Milano, 1961, p. 61.

Papadopoulos, R. (ed.), *The Handbook of Jungian Psychology*. Hove: Routledge, 2006.

Chapter 9

Moral injury and forgiveness

A theological and psychoanalytic approach

Vasileios Thermos

Moral injury pertains to the impact of enacting or enduring an assault upon or from another human being, and this impact encompasses the entirety of a person's spiritual world, including religious beliefs, emotions, conscience, and moral standards. Moral injury can and does occur for both victims and perpetrators of assault, because both are creatures of God with a spiritual vocation. This is a crucial point, because in life any one of us may become a victim or a perpetrator under certain sets of circumstances. In this chapter, I will combine psychoanalytic and theological perspectives in addressing moral injury with an emphasis on the place of forgiveness for potential healing for both victims and perpetrators.

Impact on victims and perpetrators

Moral injury is not a mere religious problem; it also raises psychiatric concerns. Fontana and Rosenheck (2004) found that among a group of 554 veterans receiving outpatient psychiatric care and 831 receiving inpatient care through the U.S. Department of Veterans Affairs (VA), those who had killed others or failed to prevent death often experienced a weakened religious faith. Thielman (2011), commenting on Fontana's and Roseheck's work, concluded later that

> weakened religious faith and guilt contributed significantly to more extensive use of VA mental health services, whereas severity of PTSD symptoms and social functioning did not ... [Fontana and Roseheck] conceded that veterans' use of mental health services under these circumstances seemed to be connected with their search for meaning and purpose, suggesting a greater role for pastoral counseling or the inclusion of spiritual issues in traditional psychotherapy.
>
> (p. 109)

It has become clear that the loss of meaning, cynicism, post-traumatic religious doubts, and moral disintegration that many veterans experience are also connected with higher levels of anxiety, depression, substance abuse, and other pathologies which indicate the need for psychiatric or psychotherapeutic treatment. Thus, it is evident that secular concerns (public health and economics included) stress the necessity not only to avoid the effects of traumatic experiences but also to effectively treat moral injury in its entirety, which includes the moral and ethical dimensions.

Traumatizing events can be said to provide a shock to the psyche. However, the religious, spiritual, and moral apparatus of the human psyche does not structurally contain religiously specific thoughts and emotions; rather, it borrows them from ordinary thoughts and emotions, which are then recruited to serve such purposes. In this sense, traumatic experiences, which can be said to result in some form of injury to a person, affect not only the religious, spiritual, and moral dimensions of the human being but, inevitably, also the cognitive, affective, and volitional aspects of mental life. Moreover, in so far as these realms are interlinked, there is a strong inter-relationship among all of them, each one of them affecting the others. This means that, in effect, for a person with a traumatized mental life, the meaning of the world is not the same anymore.

When a person's sense of meaning and order is undermined, an impact on faith and spirituality is inevitable. Judith Herman wrote that

> traumatic events undermine the belief systems that give meaning to human experience. They violate the victim's faith in a natural or divine order and cast the victim into a state of existential crisis ... When this cry is not answered, the sense of basic trust is shattered.
>
> (1997, pp. 51–52)

This results in a form of existential insecurity, a type of "woundedness" that develops states of moral destabilization or moral indifference.

Comparable forms of "woundedness" also occur in the perpetrator. The act of inflicting violence on others casts aside moral principles. The perpetrator may use rationalizations in order to create an alibi and other forms of justification for the atrocities that he or she commits. Such rationalizations, which often produce a sense of omnipotence generating a God-like position, would eventually distort the person's conscience. This resulting damage to conscience, combined with the nature of the accompanying thoughts which are actioned (e.g. those of omnipotence) shape the severity and the particular type of moral injury sustained.

Further complicating the situation of perpetrators is a certain degree of a state that can be called "moral obscurity," which tends to precede and follow the actual violent or unjust actions that harm others. Saint John Chrysostom says:

> During the night we are unable to discern even our friend; the same happens with hostility ... also in winter, the clouds do not allow us to enjoy the beauty of the sky ... this is the way hostility acts: it distorts views and voices. But if we put it aside we are able to see and listen with correct and fair thought.
>
> (*Third Homily on David and Saul*, 5–6, P.G. 54, 702)

These vivid images clearly depict the haze that descends upon the perpetrator's psyche, affecting most of his or her mental and emotional functions.

In this haze, a tendency develops in the perpetrator to dehumanize his or her victim, and it seems that the degree of dehumanization is proportional to the harm inflicted; the more harm, the greater and more severe the dehumanization. The victim is not perceived as a distinct, individual human being; instead, in the perpetrator's eyes the victim does not exist at all as an individual but is downgraded to being an object of the perpetrator's fantasies. This is one of the core elements of moral distortion. Indeed, persons who are targeted by perpetrators to become victims must first be considered less than human. By devaluing and stripping victims of their humanity, perpetrators are able to enact their persecutory acts, breaking away from their own human conscience. Accordingly, any later attempt by perpetrators towards repentance and reparation requires them to follow a path of recognizing who the victims really are and were and to restore them to their full and complete humanity, which also implies the restoration of equality as human beings, undoing the earlier denial of this equality. Actually, such a task amounts to nothing less than a restoration and structural repair of the perpetrator's own humanity, complete with the reinstatement of their psyche – of their own mental and emotional world.

This begins to address the question of how moral (self-)injury can be repaired and undone. Is it a matter of punitive justice or of cognitive reformulation? Authors such as Muse (2011) and Prager (2008) dare to suggest that healing for perpetrators cannot exist outside of a loving community. Moral injury can only be healed by the enormous potential of love which has the power to reconstruct a personality. Winnicot (1963) once suggested that "moral education is no substitute for love," and it is in a network of corrective pedagogical relationships that one can come to re-acknowledge humanity in the face of others and to discern one's own inhuman traits for what they are.

Although justice requires its own route, and although special therapeutic groups are sometimes necessary, something more is needed to restore perpetrators to wholeness. A proper and meaningful community, an *ecclesia*, is required. Such an *ecclesia* should be composed of not only victims who are struggling to forgive but also of perpetrators willing to repent, potential perpetrators who would be willing to be preventively assisted to empathize, and of ordinary persons who would become aware of these complexities thus avoiding developing a vulnerability to become victims themselves.

Shifting focus, now, what about the moral injury of victims? Their healing from moral injury is based on their capacity to restore their trust in humanity and humankind by regaining their ability to risk loving encounters with others, and by moving past cynicism and enduring impulses to withdraw into themselves. If a victim was once a person of deep faith, which was then shaken following victimization, faith and zeal would have to warm up again, or even build up, together with a possible reconsideration and restructuring of their religious beliefs.

Types of forgiveness

Such a healing obviously includes forgiveness. However, forgiveness is not easy. It is quite remarkable how common the inability to forgive is, even among those who strongly wish to forgive. Additionally, the true content and nature of forgiveness remains fairly elusive, given that we quite often encounter unreliable forms of forgiveness. Many people of faith are willing to swear that they have completely forgiven the persons who had offended them, but their forgiveness proves rather fragile under problematic circumstances, or merely with the passage of time. Psychoanalysis has contributed to the undoing of certainties by articulating its theory of illusion-building defence mechanisms, such as repression, denial, reaction formation, and rationalization.

Many people, religious or not, persuade themselves that they have forgiven someone who has hurt them, whereas in reality they have simply forgotten one specific act, e.g. the attack, or do not feel that they "hate" the perpetrator any longer. However, are these expressions sufficient and adequate for proper forgiveness? What is true forgiveness, essentially? What is the most appropriate context within which to appreciate the value of forgiveness? But there are more crucial questions. Is ineffectual forgiveness simply a matter of personal sinfulness and imperfection or is it perhaps a shortcoming to which the collective ecclesiastical mentality contributes? Finally, why should a victim forgive at all? Starting from this last question, there have been various answers, which can be grouped into the following three categories.

1   *Conventional* forgiveness: this refers to the belief that if we are pragmatic and far-sighted, we have no other choice but to forgive in order to avoid turning our lives into chaos.
2   Forgiveness out of *empathic mutuality*: this refers to the experience whereby if we become aware of our own sins, shortcomings, and faults, we are inclined to also forgive others.
3   Forgiveness as a means to acquire *inner peace*: this refers to the belief that we have to forgive in order to find relief and serenity, whereas if we do not forgive, then we are the ones who will suffer.

All these three types of forgiveness can be found among both those persons with religious beliefs as well as those without them. However, a fourth type can also be differentiated, and this is encountered among religious persons only: *submission to a divine commandment*.

According to this fourth category of forgiveness, we should forgive because God asked us to do so. Very often all four of these types of forgiveness are endorsed by spiritual guides. Although they are not trivial and meaningless, each one of them promotes forgiveness out of a motivation to profit something, in some way or another. I find it appropriate for those interested in Christian spiritual life to search for a more elaborate theological reason than what would best profit oneself. Yes, we must forgive, but out of what *ontological* understanding of forgiveness?

It may seem paradoxical that, in order to explore theological ontology as applied to moral injury, I would start with the psychoanalyst Donald Winnicott and his remarkable thoughts on *destructiveness*. However, although he develops them in an analytical context, they can also be applied to interpersonal relationships, because, I would argue, comparable processes prevail. In 1969, Winnicott writes along lines analogous to Saint John Chrysostom, that prior to an act of destruction, a perpetrator does not have a clear and proper idea about his object (i.e. a fellow human being), and this is why he proceeds with the victimizing act. Then, Winnicott adds a remark of important teleological significance: "It is the destruction of the object that places the object outside the area of omnipotent control" (1969, p. 712), namely outside the realm of the subject's distorted imaginary perceptions. By "destroying" the object[1] in the imaginary domain, the subject is enabled to use the object in a functional and constructive way. This use means that the perpetrator becomes capable of reconstructing him/herself by virtue of the victim's reaction. The necessary presupposition for this outcome is that the object *survives* the attack.

It is interesting to note what Winnicott understands by this survival of the object. In addition to the idea that the attacked object must not be damaged, to "survive in this context means *not to retaliate*" (1969, p. 713). He explains this idea more fully in a different context, namely the residential care for violent children:

> Your job is to survive. In this setting the word *survive* means not only that you live through it and that you manage not to get damaged, but also that you are not provoked into vindictiveness. If you survive, then and only then you may find yourself used in quite a natural way by the child, who is becoming a person and who is newly able to make a gesture of a rather simplified loving nature.
>
> (Winnicott, 1970, p. 227)

The critical challenge for the victim is to avoid both revenging and collapsing. To the degree that a victim avenges him/herself, he or she remains entrapped in the attacker's imaginary net – in the unreal world of shadows – and thus a genuine encounter has not yet taken place between them. The attack offers the attacked person the opportunity to change things into a real relationship, and in this sense, it may express a cry of help from the perpetrator: "I need you."

I cannot ignore the fact that Winnicott equates revenge with *death*. Obviously, this is a death of psychological (more precisely: *imaginary*) nature. When the victim collapses, his or her mental representation in the perpetrator becomes deprived of its vital energy and appears to have been "killed," whereas if the victim responds with vindictiveness, the perpetrator becomes assured of his or her own killing power and the real world "dies" to him or her once more. In the perpetrator's unconscious imagination, he or she has "exterminated" the victim and, therefore, can no longer benefit from the victim.

I would argue that these Winnicottian considerations are comparable with the Christian tradition, i.e. *lack of love and forgiveness is death*.

Life as forgiveness and communion

Although resentment and revenge are often accompanied by the dark burden of psychological death – that is, by a depressive core of the psyche or by other equivalent depressive states – in this context the problem is nevertheless what we would call the *ontological* level of death, which is the absence of *communion*.

My claim is that today we have lost the distinction between the psychological and the ontological level. According to the current Western understanding, death and life are approached as states of psychological experience. If I feel alive, I am alive; if I feel loving, I love; if I feel peaceful, I am peaceful. However, one may feel peaceful by recruiting various psychological mechanisms, while simultaneously remaining alienated from real peace because true forgiveness has not taken place. A person may be certain that he or she loves, but this "love" is achieved by disdaining or depreciating the poor sinner in a way similar to that of Pharisee.

The moral injury of the victim, by undermining his or her capacity for communion because of hatred, induces a type of death that we can characterize as ontological.

In the Christian tradition, communion is accepted as one of the central purposes of spiritual life. For human beings to be ontologically alive, an experience of loving communion with others is required. To help us comprehend the need for a deep unity, Saint John of Sinai provides us with the following diagnostic criterion of forgiveness:

Putrefaction (of the soul) will go away, not when you pray for the person who offended you, not when you give him presents, not when you invite him to share a meal with you, but only when, on hearing of some catastrophe that has afflicted him in body or soul, you suffer and you lament for him as if for yourself.

(*The Ladder of Divine Ascent*, P.G. 88, 841CD)

In other words, sanctity occurs when the victim perceives the attacker as belonging to the same "body," i.e. the body of Christ. The important issue here is that victims may spiritually die not because of an attack, but because of their resentment of and vengefulness toward the perpetrator, regardless of whether or not the perpetrator is ontologically dead: "Be merciful to the evil-doer because he destroys himself ... This is the nature of wickedness" (Saint John Chrysostom, *Homily on Psalm 7th*, 6, P.G. 55, 89).

Therefore, the victim's ontological death does not depend on the perpetrator's acts or intentions; instead, it is based solely and absolutely on the victim's own will and spiritual way of dealing with the entire process of victimization and forgiveness. In the light of this idea, victims must seek a forgiveness which is neither reduced to *condescension* nor to *extenuation*. Forgiveness where motives of arrogance or vindication lie behind it is not proper forgiveness.

Theologically speaking, forgiveness blossoms out of the notion of communion, upon the ground of the one and common nature of humanity which has been assumed by Christ. Actually, Christ is the source of fullness of life: "He is the *Life*" (John 14:6) because He is the archetype of this *double survival*, as He both literally resurrected and forgave His persecutors. Resurrection becomes the tangible sign, appropriate for this metaphorical survival, referring to the ontological death. Christ's Resurrection is the source of every person's life, forgiveness, and resilience.

From a certain psychoanalytic perspective, and under certain circumstances, the act of hating and causing harm to others can be understood as an unconscious attempt to create a better and healthier relationship with them. Unconsciously, perpetrators wish to rid themselves of the psychological projections that they have of others (projections that entrap them), resulting in distortions of both their lived reality as well as of their experience of others. In this sense, by attacking others, unconsciously, perpetrators make it possible for their victims to free them from their own omnipotent imaginary control (of their victims). Whether this possibility will be realized or not will depend on the victim's reaction. Revenge of any type will constitute a perfect failure. In the history of the Church, there are many impressive examples of sinners, torturers included, who convert to Christianity when they are granted forgiveness by the martyrs whom they were persecuting.

Based on the grounds of the one and common nature of humanity, the Church has always seen the very essence of human beings expressed through communion with others; and this communion refers to much more than mere human interpersonal relationships.

Through the Incarnation, Jesus Christ entered human territory and became part of human unity. Accordingly, the nature of humans is bound to the Deity in God. Starting from these two unities – the horizontal (amongst humans) and the vertical (humans with Christ) – as a basis, Saint Maximus explains why Christ put the forgiveness we offer to those who trespass against us as a presupposition of forgiving our sins. At first glance, it seems paradoxical that we are taught in the Lord's Prayer to bring ourselves to God as models. Maximus's interpretation, however, sheds further light on the teaching:

> And for God he makes himself an example of virtue, if one can say this, and invites the inimitable to imitate him by saying, "Forgive our trespasses as we forgive those who trespass against us," ... so as not to be accused of dividing nature by his free will (γνώμη) by separating himself as human from any other humans. For since free will has been thus united to the principle (λόγος) of nature, the reconciliation of God with nature comes about naturally, for otherwise it is not possible for nature in rebellion against itself by free will to receive the inexpressible divine condescension. And it is perhaps for this reason that God wants us first to be reconciled with each other, not to learn from us how to be reconciled with sinners and to agree to wipe away the penalty of their numerous and horrid crimes, but to purify us from the passions and to show that the disposition of those who are forgiven accords with the state of grace. He has made it very clear that when the intention (γνώμη) has been united to the principle of nature, the free choice (προαίρεσις) of those who have kept it so will not be in conflict with God, since nothing is considered unreasonable in the principle of nature, which is as well a natural and a divine law, when the movement of free will is made in conformity with it. ... In these words the Scripture makes us see how the one who does not perfectly forgive those who offend him and who does not present to God a heart purified of rancour and shining with the light of reconciliation with one's neighbour will lose the grace of the blessing for which he prays. Moreover, by a just judgment, he will be delivered over to temptation and to evil in order to learn how to cleanse himself of his faults by cancelling his complaints against another.
> (Maximus Confessor, *Commentary on the 'Our Father ... '*, P.G. 90, 901–905. Translation retrieved from *Selected Writings of Maximus Confessor*. New York: Paulist Press, 1985, pp. 99–126)

This long excerpt explains why the petition for forgiveness precedes the petition for redemption from temptation. However, above all, it interprets the Lord's commandment: "First be reconciled to your sister or brother, and then come and offer your gift" (Matthew 5:24). Evidently, resentment disrupts the unity of human nature, so it is also impossible to be united with God – no matter how many prayers one recites or how many good works one performs – unless one forgives. Unity with God takes place only in Christ, Who took on human nature; thus, by resentment or hostility and the like, humans are separated from God as well as from each other. We would be right in saying that a genuine forgiveness can eliminate all sins and lead to salvation, not merely by virtue of a moral superiority, but because of its ontological potential.

Spiritual healing

Moral injury is a serious spiritual problem. In the ancient Church it seems that there was awareness of this and, consequently, there was greater vigilance to avoid it, as was expressed in the worship. Saint Cyril of Jerusalem informs those to be baptized that in the Liturgy in which they will participate "the Deacon cries aloud, 'Receive ye one another' and 'let us kiss one another' … this kiss blends souls one with another, and courts entire forgiveness for them" (*23rd Catechesis*, 3, P.G. 33, 1112A).

Also, in the ancient Liturgy of the Apostolic Constitutions, forgiveness was indispensable for receiving Holy Communion:

> If, therefore, you have anything against your brother, or he has anything against you, neither will your prayers be heard, nor will your thanksgivings be accepted, by reason of that hidden anger … but you remember injuries, and keep enmity, and come into judgment, and are suspicious of His anger, and your prayer is hindered … wherefore, O bishop, when you are to go to prayer after the lessons, and the psalmody, and the instruction out of the Scriptures, let the deacon stand near you, and with a loud voice say: "Let none have any quarrel with another; let none come in hypocrisy"; that if there be any controversy found among any of you, they may be affected in conscience, and may pray to God, and be reconciled to their brethren.
> (*Apostolic Constitutions*, 2: 53–54, P.G. 1, 717A–720A)

In the quoted writings of Saint John of the Ladder and Saint Maximus it is implied that the necessity for forgiveness is founded on the need for unity of our common human nature and on its reception by Jesus Christ, Who has become the archetype of humanity. By loving us as members of His own flesh, He indicates a quite new way of being which does not tolerate any disruption of the communion among us and with Him. He introduces a perspective and a mentality that both have forgiveness as their natural consequence.

Exercising forgiveness in daily life is useful not only for the healing of moral injury but also for preventing its onset when trauma strikes.

Practising forgiveness in minor circumstances providentially facilitates the tendency towards forgiveness in major circumstances.

It is the same mode of being, i.e. being as communion, which leads to higher spiritual achievements, such as the practice of praying for others as if for oneself, or even repenting for others' sins as if they were one's own. Archimandrite Sophrony Sakharov (1992) has commented on Christ's Prayer on the night He was arrested, making the important remark that everybody can imitate Christ in His prayer to the degree that one prays for the entire world and for forgiveness, viewing and feeling one's enemies as members of one's own flesh. He adds that this is precisely the nature of laity's priesthood, the fulfilment of human destiny, the achievement of the fullness of life.[2]

Forgiveness becomes a topic of paramount importance when reassessing the meaning we give spirituality. It forces us to decide whether we privilege the individualism of psychological experiences over the ecclesiological virtue of love for all. Love is the essence of the Church because it is the ultimate quality of God; this is how God is defined (1 John 4:8).

The ontological exercise of love has to be emphatically distinguished from psychological soothing or subjective happiness. The former focuses on communion, while the latter is inspired by individualism and is a kind of spiritual hedonism where one seeks merely a state of well-being, avoiding reality. In fact, it is reality that calls for love. The "psychological spirituality" that is extremely prevalent today is actually a secular spirituality, an egocentric one which uses God as an *alibi*. The main motivation is thirst for power, and God is considered as the best means to achieve this. Such "spirituality" does not constitute care for the other and for love, but only for oneself; if there are any acts of love, these would be reduced to external behaviour. This is why Saint Paul says that you can give your body to be burned, but if you have not love, you are nothing. Not only does it profit you nothing but, in fact, you *are* nothing (1 Corinthians 13:3).

Love is the only eschatological virtue, the only virtue that will survive death, and the nature of the Kingdom to come will be that of love. Love for enemies represents the peak achievement of love. As Metropolitan John Zizioulas (2016) writes:

> No form of love is freer than this one, and no greater form of freedom than love of one's enemies ... Love that does not expect reciprocation – or better, that is directed at those who do us harm – is truly full of grace, i.e., free. The love of God "in Christ", "while we were yet sinners" (Rom. 5:8) and enemies of God, this love for sinners is the only free love. In brief, we only have healing when love coincides with freedom. Love without freedom and freedom without love are pathological conditions which themselves require treatment.
>
> (p. 39)

Psychological presuppositions for forgiveness

My contention is that in order to achieve the ecclesiological notion of communion one first has to succeed in achieving communion which also includes its intrapsychic dimension: by this I mean the harmonious integration of all mental faculties (reason, feelings, desire). To the degree that they do not function in unity and integration, the person will face difficulties achieving fully interpersonal communion. This is one of the domains that, I would argue, proves necessary the cooperation between psychology and theology, where the former helps clarify the conditions and terms which assist with the fulfilment of the latter.

One problematic human condition, typical of our postmodern era, is what psychologists call "borderline personality disorder," which is characterized by a certain lack of coherence. The inner disorganization of persons suffering from this syndrome cannot enable them to develop forgiveness. Worse, such persons easily misinterpret others' behaviours and see attacks where there are none. Either through exaggerated perceived assaults or because of a lack of resilience against real traumas, a person with a borderline personality disorder may easily consider him/herself victimized and would be more prone to moral injury.

Another kind of psychological difficulty can be found in the phenomenon that Winnicott (1960) called *false self*, i.e. the self who is alienated from body, feelings and desires, through inflation of the intellect. Often, such persons appear to be religious, although, at the deep ontological level, they are almost atheists; they denounce the very core of religiosity, which is communion, by their own sense of self-sufficiency.

Persons with a false self do not need to forgive, because they think that they have no complaints or that they have already easily overcome them. Those entrusted with spiritual direction would not be well prepared to identify such psychological conditions; instead, they would become fascinated by such persons, surrendering to perceiving them as being assiduous and cooperative Church members. Spiritual directors should become equipped to discern the harsh superego and its interference in interpersonal life, which consists of illusions about the innocence of oneself or about the sadistic bitterness towards others.

On the other hand, there are psychological conditions and structures that, by facilitating maturity, can prevent moral injury and increase resilience when trauma is inflicted. The psychoanalyst Otto Kernberg writes:

> The capacity to forgive others is usually a sign of a mature superego, stemming from having been able to recognize aggression and ambivalence in oneself and from the related capacity to accept the ambivalence that is unavoidable in intimate relations. Authentic forgiveness is an expression of a mature sense of morality, an acceptance of the pain that

comes with the loss of illusions about self and other, faith in the possibility of the recovery of trust, the possibility that love will be recreated and maintained in spite of and beyond its aggressive components.

(Kernberg, 1995, p. 103)

Therefore, psychological conditions affect spiritual progress. My argument is that it is of paramount importance to remember that, whilst attending to people pastorally, we should not merely apply high-demanding theology without taking into consideration the psychological developmental level of the faithful, who may not be capable of easily overcoming moral injury due to their psychological difficulties. Adjusting our spiritual diagnosis and guidance according to each person's psychological developmental stage should be a basic principle of Church life; this should be an expression of true and caring love for the faithful. It is in this manner, I argue, that psychology and theology can collaborate fruitfully. Accordingly, appropriate psychotherapy may be a valuable additive to spiritual guidance for overcoming moral injury. Psychotherapy does not directly aim at spiritual goals, yet it can heal psychological conditions and thereby support spiritual goals.

Future perspectives

Both theology and psychology converge in preventing and healing moral injury. To the degree that moral injury eventually occurs, it undermines fulfilment, leaves human potential unaccomplished, makes human relations toxic, and undoes hopes for an improvement in society. Psychological maturity and spiritual development can and should go hand-in-hand in lessening the evil in the world.

I would like to finish with some points for further consideration:

• What idiosyncratic psychological traits make some people more vulnerable to moral injury? Can more systematic research on personality dimensions and structure contribute to a psychology of morality?

• How can real healing be implemented for perpetrators? What role can justice and the mission of religious communities play?

• When clergy (pastoral practitioners and confessors) encounter persons with distorted conscience, how can they discern an underlying injured conscience, and contribute to its healing?

• How can military training prepare soldiers for their service in a way that helps prevent moral injury?

• How can clergy and mental health professionals better collaborate for treating moral injury and promoting forgiveness?

• What would a proper pastoral practice be which would promote resilience and prevent moral injury?

Notes

1 The reader should keep in mind that in certain psychoanalytic theories the "object" refers to a person who contains emotional investment from the subject, either with a positive or a negative effect. Moreover, the idea is that the "subject" and the "object" are involved in an interactive relationship which is not only significant but also constitutive of both of them.
2 Here I paraphrase Elder Sophrony's text (1992) on pages 370 and 371, in my translation. The chapter from which this passage has been taken appears in the Greek original edition but is not included in the English edition of the same book.

References

Fontana, A., & Rosenheck, R. (2004). Trauma, Change in Strength of Religious Faith, and Mental Health Service Use Among Veterans Treated for PTSD. *Journal of Nervous and Mental Disease*, 192, F579–F584.

Herman, J. (1997). *Trauma and Recovery: The Aftermath of Violence – From Domestic Abuse to Political Terror*. New York: Basic Books.

Kernberg, O. (1995). *Love Relations*. New Haven, CT: Yale University Press.

Muse, S. (2011). *When Hearts Become Flame: An Eastern Orthodox Approach to the διά-Λογος of Pastoral Counseling*. Rollinsford, NH: Orthodox Research Institute.

Prager, J. (2008). Healing from History: Psychoanalytic Considerations on Traumatic Pasts and Social Repair. *European Journal of Social Theory*, 11(3), 405–420.

Sakharov, S. (1992). *Οψόμεθα τον Θεόν καθώς εστι*. Ιερά Μονή Τιμίου Προδρόμου Έσσεξ *We Shall See Him As He Is*. Essex, UK: Saint John the Baptist's Monastery, 1987.

Thielman, S. (2011). Religion and Spirituality in the Description of Posttraumatic Stress Disorder. In Peteet, J., Lu, F., & Narrow, W. (Eds.), *Religious and Spiritual Issues in Psychiatric Diagnosis. A Research Agenda for DSM-V* (pp. 105–113). Arlington: American Psychiatric Association.

Winnicott, D. (1960). Ego Distortion in Terms of True and False Self. *The International Psycho-Analytical Library*, 64, 1–276. London: Hogarth Press and the Institute of Psycho-Analysis, 1965.

Winnicot, D. (1963). Morals and Education. *The International Psycho-Analytical Library*, 64, 1–276. London: Hogarth Press and the Institute of Psycho-Analysis, 1965.

Winnicott, D. (1969). The Use of an Object. *The International Journal of Psycho-Analysis*, 50, 711–716.

Winnicott, D. (1970). Residential Care as Therapy. In Winnicott, C., Shepherd, R. & Davis, M. (Eds.), *Deprivation and Delinquency* (pp. 220–228). London: Routledge, 1994.

Zizioulas, J. (1999). *Illness and Healing in Orthodox Theology*. Alhambra, CA: St. Sebastian Press, 2016.

Chapter 10

From theory to impact

Expanding the role of non-psychiatric moral injury theorists in direct veteran care

D. William Alexander

The moral injury discourse is rapidly expanding. In the four decades since Jonathan Shay's landmark (1994) exposure of the incapability of existing psychiatric categories to adequately approach his generation of distressed combat veterans, there have been a number of new armed conflicts involving Western coalition forces in foreign theaters. Veterans of these new conflicts have returned with unusual forms of morally related distress, just as the previous generation had. Although few psychiatric professionals have followed Shay's lead in leveraging outside discourses to expand their epistemology in understanding and treating these new veterans, there is evidence they have paid more attention to issues of morality in combat.[1] At the same time, an increasing number of new moral injury theorists arising from the disciplines of philosophy, political science, cultural anthropology, literature, journalism, poetry, and theology have joined the social conversation about veteran care.

Realizing that direct care to distressed veterans is still dominated by the psychiatric community, the new moral injury theorists have refreshed Shay's challenge about the dangers of *medicalization* of veteran distress. They have especially warned against the linking of unusual features of moral concerns in order to press them into psychiatric categories, regardless of whether or not they fully meet the criteria for such categories.[2] This is indeed a danger. While the physiological dimensions of morally related veteran distress are becoming increasingly understood through recent advances in neuroscience, the moral, social, meaning-attributive, and other existential dimensions of this distress are often neglected. This enhances the probability that the care veterans receive upon homecoming will be unidimensional, and may therefore actually inhibit their reintegration.

Despite the important ideas expressed by the new moral injury theorists, their contributions have typically been practically limited insofar as they have not often led to direct collaboration with psychiatric professionals in developing new approaches that can be applicable to actual therapeutic care interventions. As a result, even those voices that have developed a novel approach to some specific phenomena of morally related veteran distress often discuss their ideas in the margins, without sufficient opportunity to impact direct treatment. As a recent research solicitation for *Frontiers in Psychiatry: Mood and Anxiety Disorders* stated clearly, theorizing about moral injury is on the rise, but it is nevertheless often ignored in current psychotherapeutic treatments, and few psychiatrists are sufficiently familiar with the contemporary moral injury literature to make use of it in diagnosis and treatment planning (Koenig et al. 2017). This "despite the millions of veterans and active duty military personnel that often come to them for treatment [for mental health issues] which may often be driven by moral injury symptoms that have not been addressed" (Koenig et al. 2017, p. 1).

The contemporary moral injury discourse faces an internal limitation that demands serious consideration. By retaining epistemological positions outside of the psychiatric paradigm, it has been able to freely and successfully challenge reductive presuppositions of psychiatry. However, as a collective discourse, it represents a wide variety of theoretical orientations and presuppositions – each one of which contains its own philosophical limitations. This has complicated the potential for an inter-disciplinary unity that might strengthen challenges to the dominant model of care. Relatedly, it has very likely contributed to the tendency for moral injury theorists to work alone, or primarily with theorists residing within their own particular professional orientation. For instance, within the literature, theologians tend to focus on the spiritual aspects and implications of moral injury, and literary scholars tend to work with connections between distressed veterans and various figures in ancient poetry and mythology. Since these preoccupations do not often clearly overlap, theorists from these two discourses seldom work together.

Unfortunately, oppositional stances between psychiatry and any other single theoretical paradigm on how best to understand distressed veterans tend to result in impasse, with each perspective dismissing the other, and the dominant paradigm remaining unchanged. In order for the moral injury discourse to further mature, and to elevate its relevance and impact on direct veteran care, moral injury theorists must first find a collaborative stance from which they can engage with the psychiatric paradigm with richness and complexity.

There already exists a collaborative potential in the shared human concern for the plight of veterans, and in the recognition that the psychiatric paradigm needs input from other discourses in order to expand its understanding of morally distressed veterans. However, there is not yet active multi-disciplinary collaboration, through which key non-psychiatric theoretical paradigms, recognizing their own limitations, appreciate the importance of the strength of other theoretical paradigms in the area of those limitations. For instance, continuing the example above, there is much that theology and literary scholarship have to offer each other in understanding human distress. There are themes regarding the nature of being human that are powerfully expressed in various ways throughout the history of literature, and yet which are perhaps most distilled within sacred theology. Theologians would benefit from seeing the wide variation of the human experience of distress as expressed in world literature. Likewise, literary scholars would benefit by interacting with fundamental teachings on suffering as it relates the nature of being, and as contained within sacred theology.

Theology and literary scholarship are but two theoretical paradigms currently participating in the moral injury discourse. If it happened that a large number of such relevant paradigms came to appreciate their own limitations, and to encourage input from others, such a movement could activate the potential for collaborative contribution at all levels, i.e. not only theoretical but also in relation to actual practice at local, regional, and societal levels. The effects of this activation would be especially powerful if the resulting group of collaborating multi-disciplinary theorists could agree to approach the psychiatric paradigm not as an enemy, but as a partner, which, although being dominant, also carries the weight of a majority of the responsibility for the care of distressed veterans, and has accomplished much good for many people.

In this chapter, I would like to offer two concrete and crucial opportunities for the formation of such expanded and collaborative multi-disciplinary moral injury discourses in veteran care. These opportunities arise in relation to two particularly unusual forms of morally related distress which cannot be adequately addressed by psychiatry alone. They also cannot be easily categorized together with the classic moral injury symptoms, i.e. entry into unpredictable episodes of exhilarating rage, extreme mistrust of authority figures and leadership hierarchies, and the consistent sense that one has done something "unforgivable" in combat.[3] For the sake of illustration I will make use of two vignettes which have arisen in my own 20-year work as a combat veteran and caregiver to veterans, and in these vignettes I will attempt to rely on the original language of the interviewees. In my experience, this is important in order to maintain theoretical neutrality in the first hearing, so that the meaning these men have assigned to their experiences will remain intact as a part of their narrative. Readers should note that these accounts were collected in private consultations and in no way reflect the opinion of any active military member or institution. Moreover, the names and certain circumstances surrounding the experiences of these warriors have been changed in order to protect their identities.

First-hand accounts

Nathan's account

A U.S. Marine Sergeant we will call Nathan returned from Iraq after participating in intense urban combat operations for over seven months, losing a significant number of his comrades to injury and death. Upon his return from Iraq, he held various positions at home in garrison, and gained a reputation as a loner, speaking seldom and often instigating sudden physical confrontations with peers and subordinates. He visited a counselor nearly five years later, in the aftermath of an incident in which he walked through his barracks room with a fighting knife, threatening every person he saw with murder and closely watching their reactions while seeming otherwise calm and curious. His peers had reported that it wasn't the first time he had acted in such a manner, and that they were all quite scared for their lives. "It's true, you know, I wanted to kill every God-damned one of 'em that time," he later recalled, but the only reason he could mention for wanting to kill them was that he sometimes thinks "killing more people again would make me happier ... or not exactly happier, but it'd feel more easy to get along, more normal."

When Nathan discusses his impulses to kill, and especially when these impulses seem to invigorate him and bring him pleasure, he shakes his head. "I know it ain't supposed to be like this," he says, and he discusses a gap between what he has always been taught about right and wrong and how he actually "feels" about right and wrong. He describes the military emphasis on values such as honor and duty as "completely bullshit to me," and comments that the things he has seen have made him question whether there is anything true, honest, or even real in the world, and whether anything has any real meaning. On his impulses to kill people and mutilate bodies, he says

> there is a crazed animal inside, which I try to keep calm ... not because I think it's wrong. I don't feel like anything is wrong anymore. I only stop it because I don't want to be in jail. Although sometimes I don't care about that either.

Nathan senses that he is losing his humanity and "becoming like an animal," and he traces this sense to the first time he killed a man in combat. His conclusion is that he has lost contact with what he calls "the good side" of himself, and on the occasions when he has entered into a wild rage since homecoming, his experience of himself has been that "I get much worse then. Then there is no human-ness in me, and there are no rules, only blackness and blood and death ... only evil. I'm evil."

Nathan also reports large portions of his life, since homecoming, in which he feels far from rage, or any other emotion. In fact, in these periods he feels disconnected from any embodied sensations, and this leaves him with a sense, in his own words, of being "spaced out ... living outside of my skin ... feeling like a ghost in my own body." He once described this experience as having a part of himself "locked away from the world," but he also noticed that this part could watch his life happen as if from a distance. Nathan explains that when he is not in a rage, he usually defaults to this state of "ghost-likeness." About these times, he comments, "I barely exist then, and that's kind of a relief."

Harold's account

A paratrooper whom we will call Harold, as a member of a special operations team in Iraq, conducted high-risk raiding operations in a politically and militarily unstable environment and came into daily close contact with the enemy. According to Harold, in battle he was considered by his peers to be a "good-luck charm," because he fought with reckless abandon, and performed physical feats that astonished others. He received valorous awards for his actions, and remembers his teammates expressing surprise after certain engagements, being in awe of his fury and athleticism in attacking the enemy. He also remembers hearing comments about his apparent lack of perspiration in the desert heat. As he describes it, "I did three things for that year – sleep, eat, and fight. I don't remember breathing. It was all a high, and I was flying."

Upon Harold's return home, he claims to have felt like "a stranger to himself." He became verbally and physically brutal with his wife, necessitating a formal separation from her and from his children under a court-issued protective order. Now, less than ten years later, he feels as if she and the children actually "belong to a different time"; to him it is as if they "lived a hundred years ago," and he remarks that sometimes he cannot recall their faces or the many times when they were together. Harold says: "there was my life before the deployments, and now there is another life. Two different lives ... the two aren't the same and they have nothing at all in common." His sense of distance between the "two lives" is sweeping and to him seems all-inclusive:

> what was true then isn't true now, what was allowed then isn't allowed now, what I had to keep away from then I don't have to keep away from now. I died over there but I kept on living, too ... it's like I live in another dimension, like in [the movies].

Harold describes a further self-realization that occurred in the months following his return, which caused him some concern: when he was not feeling "keyed up" or intensely energized, he was feeling "nothing." Harold was involved in two high-speed automobile crashes in the first two years after his return, contributing to the eventual end of his military career. As he understands it,

> I can only feel when I'm flying. Otherwise I feel nothing. Like my soul is covered under something. I'm in my body but I'm not. I'm like a tiger in a fucking cage, that's what my whole life feels like ... I hate

it, though. I have no interest in my own kids ... they are so boring to me and I don't feel anything for them at all, even though I know I'm supposed to. I can't feel for shit, for anyone. I'm damaged goods.

Aside from feeling like "damaged goods," Harold experiences something that he considers to be far more disconcerting:

I became some kind of predatory animal out there, I guess. Or maybe the animal is in me. [I'm] not the same since the Iraqi hunting trip ... I did things over there that are unforgiv.able, and I'm glad my kids don't know me now. I would fuck them up. I'm fucking evil. I am bad now. That shit started in the killing maze in [Fallujah]. We were doing some shit then. Something bad has happened I can't shake.

Harold's sense that "something bad has happened" to him serves as a self-summary for his experience of life after combat. He does not claim to only see his current behavior or condition as "bad," or his decisions in combat to have been "bad," but rather he feels as if he has become actually and personally bad, as the result of a personal transformation in and after combat.

From two stories, two unique and shared phenomena

As I reflected on these vignettes, two central themes emerged as common to both. These themes actually represent substantial personal transformations for both Nathan and Harold, which they believe were instigated in the war. I would characterize these changes in the following manner: (1) a perceived absorption of evil in combat that seems to interfere with their ability to relate to common structures of value, and (2) a perceived loss or diminishment of being fully alive and present in the world, marked by a sensation of internal deadening and a question of whether they have become less than human. It is important to address each of these phenomena separately.

The perceived absorption of evil in combat

The first transformation that Nathan and Harold hold in common is an experience of self-horror in the aftermath of combat which cannot be reduced to a sense of guilt over something they have done. Both men believe that they have personally and actually become connected with an evil entity that surfaced within the combat zone. Their experiences are supported by a number of examples in the available literature, including personal veteran narratives discussed by Hoop (2010), McLay (2012), Muruzabal (1996), Segrest (2008), Sherman (2011), and Wizelman (2011).

Among the most notable examples in the literature, Tim Segrest, in his personal reflections of homecoming after serving in combat as a sniper in the Middle East, describes how, upon trying to reintegrate with his friends and family, he found an "evil" lurking in him, which he feels took up residence in him during the war (2008, 198). During his daily interactions with people, he experienced this sense of violent and implacable evil within, encouraging him to murder and dismember others. He expressed self-horror at this tendency, and wrote at length about his difficulty in restraining the impulses he believed were generated by this resident evil: "I can feel my anger come – anger at all this damned evil … [does it want me to] just fucking kill them all? Burst their heads open?" (p. 198). Tim's main concern during treatment, as voiced to his caregivers, was the containment of this internal evil: "[you] can't train me how to reverse this mother fucking sadistic fucker hiding within my mind" (p. 198). Throughout relating his experiences, he expressed a hopelessness that this condition could not be reversed.

Nathan, Harold, and Tim have each described direct encounters with a personal form of evil in combat which followed them home from war, and because of which they feel they must remain isolated in order to protect others from that evil. It is important to note that Nathan's and Tim's use of the term "evil" does not seem to be intentionally metaphorical, but rather seems to arise from their attempts to describe a powerful experience that for them feels as real as any other form of reality that they have known. The latest edition of the American Psychiatric Association's *Diagnostic and Statistical Manual of Mental Disorders* (*DSM-5*) (2013) includes several diagnoses that account for persons claiming contact with evil entities, but such experiences are conceptualized as delusions or hallucinations, and placed within the schizophrenia spectrum. This fact highlights the psychiatric paradigm's epistemological limitations when approaching certain unusual forms of distress, since neither Nathan nor Harold meet the other diagnostic criteria for any diagnosis in the spectrum. If they were to receive a working diagnosis of schizophrenia based on this single conceptualization of their experiences, it would profoundly complicate their lives and chances for growth.

In conjunction with the perceived absorption of evil, Nathan and Harold have difficulty subscribing to existing hierarchies of values in everyday life, in which certain actions or ideas should be judged as "good, true, or meaningful" and other actions judged as "bad, false, or meaningless." This does not mean that they are unable to reliably predict what wider society would call "good" or "bad," but rather that such distinctions are not meaningful to them personally, nor do such distinctions motivate their behavior. In Nathan's case, this phenomenon certainly resists the explanation that his time in combat shattered previously held beliefs about "good and evil" that were naïve and inherently vulnerable.

Nathan does not believe that he had been particularly naïve about the nature of the world before his deployment, having worked in coal mines for years prior to his enlistment, and having been exposed to numerous forms of difficulty and pain. He does, however, remember previously having a strong hierarchy of values which guided his behavior and provided meaning for his life. This structure has now been emptied of meaning, leaving him unwilling to subscribe to any essential principles of good and evil. In fact, he claims that at times the moral norms which inform his community's way of life seem absurd to him, leaving him unable to share common social foundations for relationships, trust, and cooperation.

This experience is also supported by a number of examples in the relevant literature, including Becsey and Haggis (2007), Boal (2004), McCain (2009), Sledge (2007), and Tick (2005). Notable is an account related in both Boal and McCain concerning the 2003 murder and dismemberment of specialist Richard Davis by four of his teammates after they returned from combat in Iraq. They had been involved in intense action during their deployment, including a street battle known as the "Midtown Massacre" that one reporter called "one of the most hellish engagements of the war" (Boal 2004, p. 3). After an argument upon homecoming, one of Richard's teammates stabbed him in the chest 33 times. Others dismembered him, poured lighter fluid over his body and lit him on fire. The teammates then left the scene and casually dined at a chicken restaurant. During the ensuing investigation, detectives struggled to discover a traditional motive for murder. As one of the accused dispassionately discussed the most gruesome parts of the altercation, one investigator claimed that of all the murder suspects he had ever investigated, none had seemed so distant from human compassion (McCain 2009, p. 52). Perhaps most unusual is the murderers' corporate inability to place their actions into a value hierarchy, or to understand them as morally wrong. What judges, reporters, military leaders, the wider community, and their own family members considered outrageous and bizarre criminal behavior, the defendants seemed to consider to be understandable and normal. Indeed, a number of observers noticed that the accused seemed to be just as confused about the public response of outrage over their actions as the public were over their apparent lack of remorse (Boal 2004). Later, two of the guilty teammates discussed the murder as insignificant in the light of the "evils" they had known in combat. This certainly portrays the complexity of their experiences, since the only "evil" or "good" they seem able to articulate is their own "evil" experience in combat.

When asked how they know that the "evil" they have absorbed is actually "evil" and not "good," given their disability or disinterest in using value hierarchies, Nathan and Harold have identical responses. As they each describe it, the sense of "evil" within seems to be visceral and embodied, and so full of hatred and murderousness that it renders morally reasoned arguments about what is "good" and "evil" abstract to them, and as unimportant or weightless as their previously rejected military core values. This certainly resonates with the sentiments of Davis' murderers, above. The lack of relationship of this phenomenon to human morality is clear. Both Nathan and Harold attribute its origins to a time when they were engaged in intense and prolonged action in combat. Harold hints at having changed permanently while participating in some act of inhumanity in the midst of combat action. Nathan remembers a clear transition from feeling *obliged* to kill to a feeling of excited anticipation towards killing in the middle of his tour and identifies this transition as being concurrent with his sense of contact with evil. Both of these experiences are related to conscience, in that both Harold and Nathan feel that their contact with evil is connected with freely participating in actions which they themselves would have abhorred and condemned on moral grounds before entering the war. Both also sense in the aftermath that they began to directly collaborate with evil in those moments, and now cannot escape the connection. In the aftermath of this coupling, they continue to feel an evil within, and to viscerally experience its murderous impulses as evil.

This phenomenon desperately needs development within a collaborative, multi-disciplinary discourse. Theorists from fields that prominently feature the philosophical origins and metaphysics of conscience – and their damage or disorientation under certain extreme existential conditions – are of particular value to the psychiatric professionals tasked with primary care for veterans such as Nathan and Harold. This would likely include theorists from the fields of classical literature, Golden Age Greek philosophy and medical history, who together could explore the construction and function of human conscience in the works of Homer, Plato, Aristotle, and Galen. This collaboration would also strongly benefit from insights offered by the Jungian psychoanalytic community, who might help by investigating the nature and structure of value hierarchies within the collective, and inquiring under what circumstances such hierarchies are most vulnerable to collapse. Lastly, discussion of the potential for long-lasting and unwanted connection with "evil" after a person has willingly participated in evil action might be explored within the constructivist and experimental social psychological discourses, and also within the symbolic theology and social philosophy discourses.[4] Particularly helpful would be input from those discourses that are willing to treat personal evil as "real" within their own theoretical orientation. Obviously, this could also include religious scholars from a variety of traditions, who could provide input on contact with evil as a particular phenomenon and provide context for how such phenomena are activated and deactivated within their schemas of "knowing."

Since the psychiatric community does not often pursue such collaborative discourse, it is appropriate for such collaboration to initially develop outside of the psychiatric discourse, at the initiation of concerned non-psychiatric theorists. Once the conditions can be met for the multi-disciplinary challenge to develop properly, and in the right spirit of disciplinary humility and collaboration, theorists from the discourses mentioned above can approach their psychiatric colleagues with a unified voice. Mental health and psychosocial professionals at the ground level of care may prove even more open to such challenges, as they are often more aware of their own limitations in relation to the needs of their clients. I have been fortunate in my own context in veteran care to have a small group of philosophers and theologians who are willing to challenge my assumptions about care, and who have constructively impacted my work with veterans such as Nathan and Harold. In my case, this challenge began with a single outside theorist, who gathered other voices to strengthen our dialogue once she sensed my openness. I will expand below on the nature of her direct impact on my work.

Perceived loss or diminishment of ensoulment accompanied by inner deadening

The second substantial transformation that Nathan and Harold hold in common is the loss of being fully alive and present in the world, marked by a sensation of internal deadening or loss of inner vitality. This develops with a sensation or fear that they have become animal-like, soul-less, or less than fully human. Nathan describes feeling internally dead while remaining physically alive, and therefore describes his daily life as "ghost-like." Harold describes the deadening of inner vitality and a feeling that he is no longer human in the way he once was. Now he experiences himself as a *sub-species* of man or as an animal, perhaps only to be categorized with other killers. Nathan and Harold believe these experiences are distinct from their perceived absorption of "evil," but that the experiences may be related in the following way. When they feel most agitated by their internal sense of evil, they get into a murderous rage, and are motivated to frenetic activity of some kind. When this rage subsides, it seems to be replaced by the "ghost-likeness," during which time life seems surreal and normal human preoccupations seem insignificant or absurd.

These experiences of the degradation of ensoulment and of alternating ghost-likeness and rage are present in the moral injury and veteran care literature, including in Beckner and Arden (2008), Blake (2008), Egendorf (1985), Friedman and Lindy (2001), Segrest (2008), and Tick (2005). Of these examples, especially notable is Tick's work with a client named Art, who was an infantryman in Vietnam:

> You can feel the connection between your soul and body when it starts to break. It's like a thread that starts fraying. I tried so hard during those long nights, the earth shuddering, my hands over my ears.

> I concentrated to keep that thread from snapping. But I could feel it getting thinner and thinner. One day the enemy was coming up the hill. They were thick that day ... they were [overrunning our position]. I was shooting and screaming. I called for more ammo belts. I looked around. I was the only one left ... I flew out of that foxhole. My feet were pounding the mud. Bullets were whizzing by me, and I was a goner for sure. That's when it happened ... I felt it, Doc. The cord snapped. My soul ran right out of my body. It ran faster than me ... I saw my soul shake its head. There was no way it was going to move back inside my body.
>
> (Tick 2005, p. 15)

Art claims to have subsequently lived without a soul for 30 years. The description of this condition bears remarkable resemblance to Nathan's sense of existing as a ghost and Harold's sense of having lost the part of himself that distinguishes man from beast.

This phenomenon cannot be adequately conceptualized within the psychiatric paradigm, even by leveraging the category of *dissociative depersonalization*. In the latest edition of the *DSM* (APA 2013), this category serves as both a working diagnostic label for a severe feature which occasionally accompanies PTSD, and also as the cardinal symptom of a stand-alone dissociative disorder, which is characterized by a persistent sense of disembodiment. The *DSM-5*, published in 2013, was the first edition of that manual to suggest a direct connection between the phenomenon of perceived disembodiment, the clinical construct of dissociation, and the traditional symptoms of PTSD. Nevertheless, the theoretical formulation for this innovative series of connections is not undisputed.[5] Neziroglu and Donnelly (2010), Steinberg (2004), and van der Kolk (2002), are among the authors in the psychiatric literature whose recent descriptions of dissociative depersonalization most resemble the transformation Harold, Nathan, and Art have endured, in that they each discuss the potential for veterans to experience a detachment from the self which they can consciously detect. However, labeling this phenomenon as "dissociative" represents a departure from the original construction of that term, which traditionally featured a division in consciousness which thereafter rendered certain parts of the self undetectable to others.[6] Dorahy and Hart notice this change, commenting that the concept of "dissociation" has now been widely expanded and reconstructed in the psychiatric discourse under the pressure of "accounting for many and various ... psychological phenomena," some of which do not include breaks in conscious experience at all (2007, p. 4). Indeed, American military medical handbooks published as recently as the year 2000 link depersonalization not primarily with dissociation but with extreme emotional exhaustion and moral confusion (Wilcox 2000). That point aside, even if this most recent category of dissociative depersonalization is used to comprehend the conditions of veterans such as Nathan and Harold, such an attempt would need to reinterpret or dismiss the language they use to describe their own distress. After all, they discuss their experiences as relating to "ensoulment" and "humanness," which are philosophical and theological terms that cannot easily be converted to terminology within physiological, psychiatric, and psychological discourses.

The relationship of this phenomenon to human morality is evident. Both Nathan and Harold connect the experience of dehumanizing the enemy in combat to the experience of feeling less than human themselves in the aftermath of war. This "circularity of dehumanization" is perhaps underexplored in most moral injury discussions today. Contemporary dehumanization of the enemy no longer focuses on cultural and physiological belittlement through cartoon caricatures, as it once did in the mid-20th century. One potent form of dehumanization today is manifested in first-person-shooter (FPS) video games – games that many warriors have not only played from childhood but are playing *in combat zones in-between combat patrols*. FPS is a genre of video game which is played from the perspective of the player being the protagonist in combat, using guns and/or other weapons. Most such games are extremely realistic in terms of their graphics and action. These games functionally separate the gravity of killing human persons from the sights and sounds of military combat, and render young warriors unprepared to bear the existential weight of their actions in war.[7]

Although the function and impact of such war video games is beyond the scope of this chapter, it should be mentioned that this type of "virtual reality" eventually serves *as both* a cause and effect *of both* the dehumanization of others and self-dehumanization. Our young warriors – while far from home – are predisposed to kill without hesitation by the preconditioning of the "virtual" killing they have accomplished over thousands of hours in the privacy of their own bedrooms. This preconditioning is implanted in part by the distance of the actual reality of war from the home-front, and in part because of Western society's increasing hunger for *virtual* experiences which do not carry the same existential weight or personal cost as the real experiences they aim to simulate and imitate. The warrior participates in something real but far away, and his disconnected countrymen at home hunger to experience that reality in "virtual" measure. Perhaps the greater the cost of the real and distant encounter, the greater the hunger from the disconnected and protected countrymen for a similar virtual encounter. In turn, some of these disconnected countrymen will themselves become the new class of young warriors, and will be "virtually" prepared for a costly reality that far exceeds their preparation. Both Nathan and Harold played FPS video games from the time they were in primary school, and both spent much of their free time in the combat zone playing them on portable small devices. Then, on their return home, they still play them. Living in this constant cycle of dehumanization and self-dehumanization contributes substantially to progressively losing embodied sensation, emotional stamina, and eventually the very sense of being fully human.

It must be obvious to the reader that I have already begun to conceptualize this phenomenon beyond the psychiatric discourse. This phenomenon could bear much further consideration from collaborating theorists working from a wide array of orientations, and beginning in the manner I suggested in the section on the phenomenon of absorbing evil. Certainly, the fields of existential philosophy, inter-personal philosophy, and theological anthropology could contribute meaningfully to this discussion. Especially important would be any work of metaphysical inquiry involving the essential interconnectedness between people, and the activation and deactivation of the "self" in proximity to the "other."[8] Psychologists, sociologists, and other theorists investigating the impact of virtual reality on relationships and interpersonal sacrifice would also add an important component to the discussion. As mentioned in the previous section, even one interested theorist who gathers a small, multi-disciplinary cohort of voices can make a direct impact on the local level of care.

Learning from theology and classic studies

I first met Demetra (not her real name) at a community event, during a time when I was working with Harold, Nathan, and other morally distressed veterans. At the time, I was consulting a competent and experienced psychotherapy supervisor, while also making use of a number of assessment and treatment resources for veteran care published within the psychiatric paradigm. However, as illustrated in their vignettes, above, there were aspects of their distress which I did not understand, and which were not clearly understood by my supervisor. Demetra is a classical educator and theologian who was trained at the doctoral level at one of the world's most prominent universities. As we drew away from the gathering that evening, and I began to describe some of what I was seeing – remaining careful to protect my clients' privileges of confidentiality – I was surprised to hear her respond with a theoretical understanding of their unique features, using concepts and quotations from ancient literature, classical metaphysics, Christian monastic wisdom, and theological anthropology.

After obtaining informed consent from three or four of my clients to bring some themes of our work together into "wider supervision" with a group of non-psychiatric colleagues, Demetra and I began to meet weekly to discuss her perspectives on unusual forms of veteran distress, and we included two mutual friends: a professor of kinesiology and occupational therapy, and a professor of public health. The four of us already shared roles in a local community organization, and so we trusted each other and held many social principles in common. However, as we intentionally joined our various professional perspectives together to focus on the moral distress of my clients, we collaborated on an entirely new approach to their care, which included elements of proprioception, classical metaphysics, theological anthropology, moral education, monastic spiritual care strategies, and traditional psychotherapeutic treatment methods.

Although these clients continued to struggle with their unusual forms of distress, we made progress together over the following year. Through my discussions with Demetra and our two companions, I was better able to relate to my clients as they spoke of encountering personal evil, and this powerfully reoriented my therapeutic relationship with both of them. For instance, Demetra introduced the idea that – in both classical Greek literature and contemporary Christian Orthodox monastic teaching – morality is *activated and deactivated interpersonally*. This is different than saying that morality is socially constructed. Rather, in this construction, morality is a universal which exists not in abstraction but in relationship to others and to the divine. From this perspective, once a person engages in killing another person, and especially when this action is avoidable in some way, that person's conscience fragments into its component parts of moral intuition and moral reasoning.[9]

To briefly explain these terms, the Homeric and Platonic literature assumed that humans can be oriented toward the good through both intuition and reason. Moral intuition implies a knowledge of the good that is distinct from conscious reasoning, but which is felt instinctively. Shirley Sullivan (1988) notices that, in Homer's usage, moral intuition can (a) ally with reason to pursue the good, (b) struggle against reason to pursue the good, when reason has been compromised, or, tragically, (c) struggle against reason to pursue something other than good, when moral intuition has been compromised.[10]

Our small group of multi-disciplinary consultants discussed ancient Homeric, Platonic, and Aristotelian examples of conceptualizing conscience as the collaborative unity of these two component parts. We also discussed examples of the implication of the disruption of this collaborative unity under extreme pressure, a phenomenon found in both Classical Greek and contemporary Orthodox Christian monastic writings.[11] In such cases, while moral reasoning can continue to operate in abstraction, moral intuition is deactivated. This helped me understand better veterans like Nathan and Harold when they described being able to predict what others would characterize as "right" or "wrong" without themselves considering such constructs as personally relevant.

Similarly, Demetra introduced the Classical Greek philosophical teaching that once conscience is fragmented, and moral intuition is deactivated, the resulting condition features extreme mistrust of oneself and others, diminished bodily sensation, and on rare occasions, even develops a sense that *the good in oneself has died and has been replaced by evil*. According to her understanding of both the Classical Greek and contemporary Orthodox

Christian monastic teachings, this state is not irreparable. She suggested that moral intuition can be reactivated in the context of developing a relationship to a wise and loving other that would facilitate the eventual reconnection with moral reasoning to effect a repair of conscience. In her view, this will always include elements of mirroring and mimesis between a client and a trusted caregiver. The conditions for such elements are created by the caregiver's enduring love and commitment to the relationship even if strongly tested by the client, and by the caregiver's authentic modeling of morality in the presence of and in relationship with the client.

Demetra's new perspectives provided a substantial enrichment of my therapeutic approach. I began to perceive the possibilities of new dimensions in my work with Harold and other clients. The distinction between moral intuition and moral reasoning as well as a classical understanding of the fragmentation of conscience enabled me to see my clients' predicament from a new angle, from perspectives that are beyond the psychiatric or even psychological conceptualizations of these phenomena. I came to view Harold's and Nathan's struggles and descriptions of their agony in a different way, outside of the narrow psychiatric parameters, and in the context of age-old human dilemmas. Inevitably, this also must have changed the way I was relating to my clients, which led to a greater trust developing between us.

Gradually my enriched approach enabled my therapeutic interaction with my clients to address themes about "right" and "wrong," using relational ideas from pragmatic philosophy. This led the distressed veterans I was working with to not only refer to their predicament in different ways (informed by moral dilemmas) but to also develop a new sense of responsibility in relation to morality and ideals. My new approach was strengthened by the small group of multi-disciplinary consultants that we developed, meeting regularly and discussing these issues. As my clients began discussing certain actions as "good enough to keep relationships together" and "bad enough to destroy relationships," they began to piece together a functional morality that depended on the state of their own relationships as guideposts – including their relationship with me. In time, they began to intuitively *feel* moral direction in certain circumstances, and in a few cases they began to experience a relationship with the divine. Harold indeed returned to a worshipping Church community and became involved in a long-term relationship which later led to a stable marriage. Perhaps none of this would have been possible without the help of our multi-disciplinary team of concerned non-psychiatric consultants.

A paradigm shift for treating morally related veteran distress

It is evident that the local, multi-disciplinary "moral injury focus group" which helped me care for Harold, Nathan, and others need not be a rarity. In fact, I believe it can be reproduced in various forms well beyond the traditional veteran care settings. It is certainly and undoubtedly the case that local multi-disciplinary focus groups have facilitated change for complexly distressed and disoriented persons in many places in the past, even in cases where change seemed extremely improbable.

For instance, in my home state of Alaska in the late 1990s, after detecting troubling trends of oversimplification in the development of psychiatrically formulated treatment approaches for substance abuse in their remote village, local community leaders successfully effected a paradigm shift in their own care. Leveraging professional involvement from Alaska Native linguists, poets, traditional Native healers, religious care professionals, and artists with expertise in traditional Native dance, weaving, woodworking, and songwriting, these local leaders met with their primary care providers and psychosocial professionals to construct a wider, more complete way of understanding (1) the people being seen for treatment, in all of the complexities of their lives and circumstances, including their own ways of viewing their difficulties, and then (2) every aspect of care as it was being currently offered, in view of what they had discovered in examining the people in new ways.

Needless to say, such innovations changed the models of care immediately and produced far more productive outcomes with far greater patient satisfaction. In 1997, agreement was reached with the government for Alaska Native peoples to obtain complete ownership and management of a group of clinics in that region, and within two years a philosophical overhaul of the complete system of medical care was completed. This new model has garnered acclaim regionally, nationally, and globally in the last 20 years.[12]

I write this chapter in the hope that such a radical and collaborative philosophical shift might occur in many other places where combat veterans are experiencing morally related forms of distress. It is time for theorists from any discourse who have an interest in the well-being of veterans to find ways to directly and concretely join together with psychiatrically oriented professionals in order to collaboratively build rich and complex bridges of understanding the veterans in their communities. Only in this way will the work of the contemporary moral injury discourse reach its full potential: to positively impact direct care, one community at a time.

Notes

1 For instance, see the commentary on the rise of awareness of moral issues among mental health providers in the U.S. Veterans Administration in Litz, B. T., Stein, N., & Delaney, E. (2009). Moral injury and moral repair in war veterans: a preliminary model and intervention strategy. *Clinical Psychological Review*, 29(8), 695–706.
2 While I interact with "moral injury paradigm" in this chapter, given its common acceptance in the discourse, I hesitate to discuss morally related features of veteran distress as "symptoms of moral injury." I hesitate because I am

not convinced of the ultimate precision and efficacy of the term "moral injury." I am not certain, for instance, that all phenomena associated with "moral injury" in the literature should be reduced to their component dimensions of pain and loss, and summarized as "injury."

3 This formulation is informed by the "berserk" and post-berserk conceptualizations found in Shay's 1994 work *Achilles in Vietnam* and his 2002 work *Odysseus in America*. It is also influenced by the contemporary focus on persistent guilt and shame in the contemporary moral injury discourse. It first appeared in print as part of a five-symptom construction in my chapter entitled "Gregory is my friend: on the absorption of evil in combat," *War and moral injury: a reader*, R. Meagher, Ed. (Cascade Books, 2018).

4 Regarding symbolic theology, Quebecois theologians Jonathan and Mattieu Pageau have developed a significant approach to the moral dimensions of the meta-narrative of the collective unconscious, as detailed in Mattieu's *The language of creation* (Create Space, 2018).

5 Depersonalization is not listed as a type of dissociative disorder at all in the ICD-10, but is instead listed independently as a rare condition not necessarily related to any other classification.

6 For more on the original psychoanalytic construction of depersonalization, see Ulman, R. B., & Brothers, D. (1993). *The shattered self: a psychoanalytic study of trauma*.

7 There is an increasing amount of compelling discussion emerging in the psychological literature, and it is likely that the moral injury discourse will pay it greater focus in the near future. Examples of these discussions include Greitemeyer, T. & McLatchie, N. (2011). Denying humanness to others: a newly discovered mechanism by which violent video games increase aggressive behavior, *Psychological Science*, *22*(5), 659–665; Bastian, B., Jetten, J., & Radke, H. R. M. (2012). Cyber-dehumanization: violent video game play diminishes our humanity, *Journal of Experimental Social Psychology*, *48*(2), 486–491.

8 Certainly Martin Buber's concept of "I-Thou" would apply here (Touchstone, 1971), as would John Zizioulas' concept of "Being as Communion" (St. Vladimir's Press, 1997) and the Hypostatic Theology of Archimandrite Sophrony (see *Man, the Target of God*, Archimandrite Zacharias, Mt. Thabor Press, 2016).

9 Similar ideas can be found in the moral philosophy literature. Shirley Sullivan suggests in her 1988 work *Psychology and activity in Homer* (McGill Press) that Homer, Plato, and Aristotle understood the rational dimension of morality to be separate (but ideally complementary) to the *thymic* and embodied dimension of morality, and that understanding this distinction is crucial to understanding constructions of "conscience" in Classical Greek thought.

10 Sullivan, S. (1988). *Psychological activity in Homer: a study of phren*. Montreal: McGill University Queen's Press.

11 Again, similar ideas may be found in the moral philosophy and social philosophy literature. For example, see Dellantonio, S., & Remo, J. (2012). Intuitions vs. moral reasoning: a philosophical analysis of the explanatory models intuitionism relies on, *Philosophy and Cognitive Science: Studies in Applied Philosophy, Epistemology and Rational Ethics*, 2239–262.

12 For more context or further information on the Southcentral Foundation and its "Nuka System of Care," readers are encouraged to visit www.southcentral foundation.com.

Sources cited

APA (American Psychiatric Association). (2013). *Diagnostic and statistical manual of mental disorders (DSM–5)*. 5th Ed. Washington DC: APA.

Beckner, V., & Arden, J. (2008). *Conquering post-traumatic stress disorder*. Beverly, MA: Quayside Publishing Group.

Becsey, L., (Prod.), & Haggis, P., (Dir.). (2007). *In the Valley of Elah* (Motion picture). Burbank, CA: Warner Independent Pictures.

Blake, S. (2008). *A journey with PTSD*. Essex, UK: Chipmunka Publishing.

Boal, M. (2004). Death and dishonor. *Playboy, 2003*(5), 1–3.

Brock, R. N., & Lettini, G. (2012). *Soul repair: recovering from moral injury after war*. Boston, MA: Beacon Press.

Burgett, D. R. (1967). *Currahee: a screaming eagle at Normandy*. New York: Random House.

Currier, J. M., Holland, J. M., Drescher, K., & Foy, D. (2015). Initial psychometric evaluation of the Moral Injury Questionnaire – Military Version. *Clinical Psychology and Psychotherapy, 22*, 54–63.

Dellantonio, S., & Job, R. (2012). Moral intuitions vs. moral reasoning: a philosophical analysis of the explanatory models intuitionism relies on. *Philosophy and cognitive science: studies in applied philosophy, epistemology and rational ethics*, Vol. 2, L. Magnani & P. Li, Eds. Berlin: Springer Publications, 239–262.

Dorahy, M. J., & Ven der Hart, O. (2007). Relationship between trauma and dissociation: a historical analysis. *Traumatic dissociation: neurobiology and treatment*. E. Vermetten, M. Dorahy, & D. Spiegel, Eds. Arlington VA: American Psychiatric Publishing, 3–30.

Egendorf, A. (1985). *Healing from the war: trauma and transformation after Vietnam*. Boston, MA: Houghton Mifflin Publishing.

Frankfurt, S., & Frazier, P. (2016). A review of research on moral injury in combat veterans. *Military Psychology* (Public Domain). doi: 10.1037/mil0000132.

Friedman, M. J. & Lindy, J. D. (2001). *Treating psychological trauma and PTSD*. New York: The Guilford Press.

Hoop, D. C. (2010). *PTSD, the struggle from within: from Saigon to Baghdad*. Raleigh, NC: Lulu Press.

Koenig, H., Ames, D., Nash, W., & Bussing, A. (2017). *Frontiers in psychiatry: mood and anxiety disorders*. Online solicitation for special topic: Screening for and treatment of moral injury in veterans with PTSD. (www.frontiersin.org/research-topics/7377/screening-for-and-treatment-of-moral-injury-in-veteransactive-duty-military-with-ptsd).

McCain, C. (2009). *Murder in Baker Company: how four American soldiers killed one of their own*. Chicago, IL: Chicago Review Press.

McLay, R. (2012). *At war with PTSD*. Baltimore, MD: Johns Hopkins University Press.

Meagher, R. (2014). *Killing from the inside out: moral injury and just war*. Eugene, OR: Cascade Books.

Meagher, R., & Pryer, D., Eds. (2018). *War and moral injury: a reader*. Eugene, OR: Cascade Books.

Muruzabal, A. M. (1996). The monster as a victim of war. *Hosting the monster*. At the Interface / Probing the Boundaries series. L. H. Baumgartner & R. Davis, Eds. New York: Editions, 23–42.

Muse, S. (2015). *When hearts become flame: an Eastern Orthodox approach to the dia-logos of pastoral counseling*, 2nd Ed. South Canaan, PA: St. Tikhon's Seminary Press.

Nash, W. P., Marino Carper, T. L., Mills, M. A., Au, T., Goldsmith, A., & Litz, B. T. (2013). Psychometric evaluation of the Moral Injury Events Scale. *Military Medicine, 178*(6), 646.

Neziroglu, F., & Donnelly, K. (2010). *Depersonalization disorder: a mindfulness and acceptance guide to conquering feelings of numbness and unreality*. Oakland, CA: New Harbinger Publications.

Segrest, T. (2008). *Reflections of PTSD: with my perfect flaws*. Bloomington, IN: Indiana University Press.

Shay, J. (1994). *Achilles in Vietnam: combat trauma and the undoing of character*. New York: Maxwell Macmillan International.

———. (2002). *Odysseus in America: combat trauma and the trials of homecoming*. New York: Scribner Press.

———. (2014). Moral injury. *Psychoanalytic Psychology, 31*(2), 182–191.

Sherman, N. (2011). *The untold war: inside the hearts, minds, and souls of our soldiers*. New York: W. W. Norton Publishers.

———. (2015). *Afterwar: healing the moral wounds of our soldiers*. New York: Oxford University Press.

Sledge, E. B. (2007). *With the old breed: at Peleliu and Okinawa*. New York: Presidio Press.

Steinberg, M. (2004). Systematic assessment of post-traumatic dissociation. *Assessing psychological trauma and PTSD*. J. P. Wilson & T. M. Keane, Eds. New York: The Guilford Press, Ch. 5.

Sullivan, S. D. (1988). *Psychological activity in Homer: a study of phren*. Montreal: McGill University Queen's Press.

Tick, E. (2005). *War and the soul: healing our nation's veterans from post-traumatic stress disorder*. Wheaton, IL: Quest Books.

———. (2014). *Warrior's return: restoring the soul after war*. Louisville, CO: Sounds True Publishers.

van der Kolk, B. A. (2002). The assessment and treatment of complex PTSD. *Treating trauma survivors with PTSD*. R. Yehuda, Ed.Washington, DC: American Psychiatric Publishing, Inc, Ch. 7.

Wilcox, V. (2000). Burnout in military personnel. *Military psychiatry*. R. Zajtchuk & R. F. Bellamy, Eds. Washington, DC: Department of Defense, Ch. 3.

Wizelman, L. (Ed. 2011). *When the war never ends: the voices of military members with PTSD and their families*. Lanham, MD: Rowman and Littlefield.

Wood, D. (2016). *What have we done: the moral injury of our longest wars*. Boston, MA: Little, Brown & Co.

Index